HUMAN LIFE

MATTERS

Dedication

From one to the one.
For the unborn children.
Dedicated to she who hears the weeping world.
For Gill, who follows in her footsteps.
For Florence, who taught me dignity.
For Colleen, for still hoping.
But most of all,

For my sons,

Ryan and Nathan.

INDEX

Book Outline and Raison D'Etre

The aim of this book is to nurture and encourage wider conversation about the nature of injustice and its relevance to human development. It is hoped that, at this particular historical time, deep comprehension of the human proclivity to revert to dominance and control when in positions of comfort or power, will rouse us, and assist us to form effective defiances so that we may transform the vast global imbalances we face. Profound understanding may also clarify the urgency for, and relative simplicity of, the many resistances and viable solutions available to us. People of goodwill need to be united in effective alliance if dominance tactics are to be halted and humanity is to survive. The meditative understanding of why human dignity is central to suffering and happiness needs once more to be at the forefront of human consciousness. 'We hold these truths to be self evident...'

Secondly, this book attempts to explain why the next revolution must be waged on behalf of the defenceless and the voiceless by those who have much to lose. It seeks to clarify the limitations of human revolution based on power and control and the insidiousness of greed clothed as a conservative. In doing so, it must explore the danger of the uneducated conservative, crystallize realities of 'No heart – no soul,' and highlight the threat the idiot tyrant poses to human continuance.

The second part of the book aims to seek commitment from the reader and includes some basic ideas about what is required, who is required and how they are required. It seeks to provide explanation of what the average person can do. The assertion made is that we have now reached a position in the global slide where hero/ineism is required in the advocacy for, and insubordinate insistence upon, human dignity as the foundation for all global, national, local and individual decision making. Decisions based on human dignity will have to defy, resist and transform the established order and, therefore, must expect resistance. Caring alliance, effective resistance, radical thought and transformative behaviour will each be essential if we are to overturn the oligarchy of oppressive human control.

One of the desired outcomes of this text is that those of goodwill might more clearly understand the centrality and absolute necessity of their active, vocal, and visible solidarity. Some steps forward are suggested and some hopes and dreams provided. The book concludes with a focus on possibility and openness and on the critical need for revolutionary dialogue. My personal stance is to disagree with the widespread delusion that violent socialization is a functional or an inevitable part of human societies. I particularly want to challenge the brutalization of youth and children currently occurring under the umbrella of socialization and the misnomer of care in western culture. Arguably, such brutalization occurs across many cultures but merciless, calloused disregard for children seems to increase in 'developing' countries as they industrialize. This book is written particularly for the youth who haven't yet had their chance and for the children who haven't yet been harmed. It asks the core question: Why should we accept misery as the core of human existence?

In the 21st century, only full effort will provide us with full victory. Throughout human history there have been tyrants, aristocrats and oppressive classes and in the end they have always, always, fallen. Therefore, the human record enables us to move forward in joyful uncertainty because we are assured by fact, by statistics, by research, and by experience, that whatever we face, human tyranny is not the route that will bring our species to its future.

We are guilty
Of many errors and many faults,
But our worst crime
Is abandoning the children,
Neglecting the fountain of life.
Many of the things we need can wait.
The child cannot.
Right now is the time
Bones are being formed,
Blood is being made,
Senses are being developed.
To the child we cannot answer 'Tomorrow.'
The child's name is 'Today.'

Gabriela Mistral (Chilean Nobel Laureate Poet), 'The Child's Name is Today.'

INTRODUCTION

It became patently clear during the last two decades of the twentieth century, that we were experiencing devolution, spawned by the values of greed and self-interest, and nurtured by the mythology of the moral superiority of the wealthy. This led to the rise of a concentrated form of barbarism. It is the nature, workings and consequences of this barbarism that are the subject of this tome.

Unfettered and unbridled aggression – whether in the name of the market, economics, religion or race – cannot be permitted in civilized human societies. It certainly cannot be lauded or glorified if human civilization is to advance and if many of the planet's living species are to continue to exist. The central premise of this treatise is that, unless we reverse the empowerment of those who value aggressive competitive behaviours, (for the purpose of this text named 'barbarians') and ensure that those in power have human wellbeing as their core concern and guiding principle for decisions – the human species will not survive. Human greed and aggression are like fire, they know no natural limit and burn until all fuel is gone. Unfortunately, in the case of greed, human life and the environment is the tinder.

If we wish to maintain and develop increasingly civilized societies we cannot afford to allow the insentient and the barbaric strong to rule. By insentient I mean those who do not see, hear, or care about, the suffering of others. Man's aggression has always had to be controlled in order for society to advance. We can no longer afford practices, systems and periods of time, where; not only does this control lapse, but aggression is actively fostered and rewarded in societies, cultures, nations or individuals. The best way for us to halt barbaric tenure is to become clear about the signs, nature, and consequences of barbarism and how to prevent its ascendance.

The re-emergence of the rule of barbaric savagery since the 1980s in the name of 'the market' - whereby unfettered aggression against people, the environment and the ecology have been actively encouraged in order to foster the profit of an elite few - has been disastrous. It has accelerated man's destruction of the planet, and of himself as a species, by an unconscionable rate. If we are to halt the damage being perpetrated by humans in the environmental ecology then we must address the damaged human ecology. Injured and pillaged humans, societies and cultures wreak further devastation on themselves and on the environments in which they subsist. Addressing human ecology damage is the most effective route to environmental repair and must occur concurrently with such repair if we wish to prevent future, and ongoing, environmental harm.

Unfortunately, greed, because of its insatiable nature, remains blind, deaf and dumb until it hits a wall. Exploitation and greed are non-recursive cycles which do not allow feedback from the world from which resources are being taken. They are unstable and dangerous bases for any interactions with living systems: be they human, animal or environmental. An additional risk of greed is that both the senses and the will to hear can be numbed by surfeit. On the other hand, the capacity to exploit others is facilitated and strengthened by the numbness of surfeit, as well as by the capacity that privilege gives to distance from the consequences of ones' actions on others' lives.

Even though the capacity to distance from the suffering and decimation wrought by exploitative and greedy acts usually has a time limit; it is one that may not expire until after the lifespan of the perpetrator. Thus, he or she may personally experience few, if any, of the negative consequences of his or her actions. Even in the 21st Century, where it may no longer be possible to evade all of the effects of ecological exploitation in one's lifetime, the insulation of privilege still serves to ensure that those who exploit the resources of many may directly experience few, if any, of the adverse consequences of their behaviours.

Lack of incentive for positive personal change has ballooned in recent decades, fed and engorged by the new social acceptability of greed, of boundless personal accumulation, and of exhibitionistic displays of individual wealth. Fostered by the dearth of adequate laws, inter and intra-national restraints at a global level that could prevent or even slow the exploitation of nations, peoples and natural resources, a new, powerful economic elite has emerged – nourished to life by the pillaging of private and public domains. Thus, we have witnessed, within a few short decades, the re-creation of the aristocracies of old – a new economic elite - buffered by obscene amounts of personal wealth and reified by the so-called 'rule of the market.' An overthrow of liberte', egalite' and fraternite', the revolution paid for with commoner's blood, after centuries of struggle and sacrifice was perpetrated in virtual silence. A stealth bomb successfully detonated in the heart of democracy.

The re-concentration of national and international decision making and control of resources into the hands of a few has resulted in social decay and devolution at community, national and global levels. An insidious form of cross-cultural colonization has begun as wealthy people are now able to colonize the resources not just of one nation, but of many nations across the globe. As the new market aristocracy establish wider and wider bases of unrestrained privilege they increasingly retreat into walled estates which separate them from the social, cultural and global by-products of the reification of the market. Thus, we see the castles of old reconstructed in the walled and well guarded suburbs of elites, with their focus as the personal security of elite members and buffering them from the external realities of social and environmental decay.

At this juncture I wish to identify myself as one of the elite, as are the vast majority of citizens living in first world societies. Elite privilege does not define one's morality, intention or goodness; it is simply a marker of access to an unequal proportion of resources in comparison to the average human...the rest of the global family. While there is some crossover between the categories of wealth and barbarism, and while there are some reasons that increased privilege increases the tendency for humans to embrace barbarism; one category does not define the other. There are people who are anti-barbarism yet have great privilege. There are also people who have few resources but who think and behave barbarically. The critical difference is that the actions and behaviours of a lower power member are constrained by lack of power and therefore impact on fewer people. A high power person with unequal access to resources who believes in barbarism poses significant threat to all, simply because high power enables catastrophic damage to be inflicted on the lives of many, and the effects reach far beyond walled worlds of privilege.

Concentrated power in the hands of a privileged few in developed and developing nations is a problem alongside the inequilibrium of power between nations. The essential idea is not that individual elites deserve to be persecuted but that there are predictable deleterious consequences when the gap in privilege between the 'haves' and the 'have nots' is widened. This is a conundrum we need to address as a species. It is important that we come to grips with the fact that the immediate natural, environmental and social consequences of exploitative behaviours provide little incentive for individuals to curb their personal greed. Vulnerable humans, resources and environments must therefore be protected from exploitation by forces of equal power to the resources of the powerful - by social norms and enforceable laws to which all; including the powerful, the wealthy and the cruel, are held accountable. Such laws must be of sufficient power to be able to effectively respond to the reality that not all those who hold power are fair; that powerful barbarians are violent when challenged; and that they are often prepared to use merciless force against anyone they perceive as a threat to their power base.

FUNDAMENTALS OF INJUSTICE

Clear Sight

As a balancing disclaimer and a clarifying statement for this text, it must be said that there is certainly a great deal of good in the world. There are people who act ethically, who put the welfare of humans as their highest priority, people who love and care in their relationships and who nurture their children, and others, with a strong sense of their human responsibility for the creation of the human world. Furthermore, in the 21st century there are large numbers of people engaged in all sorts of humanitarian activisms: anti-war, anti-poverty, anti-racism, anti-slavery, anti-sexism; prevention of child abuse, prevention of violence against women, children and the vulnerable; people involved in advocacy for human rights, for effective disaster response and in advocacy for ethical trade, business, law & policies, at local, national and global levels. There is certainly much good in the world.

The problem being addressed in this book is that, in the 21st century, such good is still not the ruling force.

Cultural Slices

The fact remains that, even in economically prosperous cultures like the US and Australia, vast numbers of people suffer terribly. Most of this suffering comes from human choices made about systems, not from the inevitable realities of human life. Such human suffering is therefore preventable and points us to flaws in the systems that we have created and that we can change. Australia and America are both societies that verbally advocate for human freedom; therefore, our example matters, and we can do better.

Those who have little systemic power - the poor, the marginalised, children, elderly, disabled people - are increasingly denied access, not only to material wealth, but to the human riches of dignity, community, belonging, safety and possibility. Those who wish to obtain these rights in western systems must now overwork and sacrifice their family and individual lives to the wealth bargain, or forever accept an inferior and uncertain status in cultures increasingly shaped for an elite few.

This book is a treatise on the need for cultural transformation in global systems. It suggests that what needs to be addressed is the dominant rule of the financially and physically strong over the lives of the majority; the increased centrality of raw, competitive greed in cultural life; and the imposition of dominance and aggression onto most human interactions. Increase in barbarism has been implicated in the fostering of unnecessary wars in the last 60 years and the ecological destruction of the planet, which is leading to global warming, but is also needs to be implicated in the unnecessary violence, suffering, and deprivation which it foists on those who cannot, or will not, compete or dominate. It is this tight fisted aspect of current systems which must be challenged and changed. There are vast possibilities for human systems and cultures which should be expanded, not contracted, by technological advance. Cultural transformation is not only possible, it is eminently advisable, and should be our most serious and focused endeavour.

In a healthy culture the care of children is one of the highest priorities of the system. By extension, caregiving is valued and rewarded financially, and with social status. Cultural systems that encourage people to enter caring professions on the basis of pay rates, vacation time, and low university entrance score will inevitably attract not only people with good interpersonal skills, but also those who are narcissistic or who enjoy domination and control over others. Children need to be protected from these personality types and from being placed in a position of subjection to such people in their critical formative years. One sure way to reduce antisocial psychopathology in the population is to reduce children's exposures to cruel, narcissistic, or calloused, people in their early years when they are too small to defend themselves. This is the time they are developing critical patterns for future behaviour by internalising adult models. People desiring to enter professions such as teaching or child care where they have huge impact on children's development and lifelong intellectual, and emotional, wellbeing need to be carefully screened for narcissism, domineering tendency, lack of empathy, cruelty and low social or emotional intelligence. Testing should also identify if the prospective candidate genuinely likes children. People who don't like children should be barred from working with them. Advanced human cultural development requires careful attention to the people children are subjected to, and controlled by, when they are small.

'What Is' vs. 'What Could Be.'

The deluded and harsh adult conceptualisation of toughening children up for the 'real world' is based on erroneous confounding of what 'is' with what 'could be'. The fact that there is a lot of brutality in our cultures and systems at this current time does not mean that it is inevitable. Suggesting that it is, and then brutalising children in a procrustean move to fit them to the current system, guarantees its continuance. The next brutalised generation will also believe that how it 'is' is the only way it 'can be' and their early conditioning will make it a difficult experience for them to think outside of this box.

One of the main reasons we are facing cultural decay in systems such as the US and Australia, is that people are not taught the difference between what is and what could be. Routinely, Westerners are trained to see future cultural systems as extrapolations of the present. From science to popular culture, future life is portrayed as a narrow extrapolation of the industrialised model. Politicians, decision makers, architects, and town planners, are not exempt from believing the mythology that the future has to be an extension of the present. They then perpetuate the myth through their decisions to create structures based on a limited, polluting, industrialised template. Thus, our visual reality is repopulated by homogenized icons of the 19th and 20th centuries.

The caregiving of children is linked intrinsically to possibility and to the capacity for change and for accelerated human development. Ever since the Industrial Revolution caregiving; and particularly the caregiving of children; has been trivialised, disregarded, dismissed as unimportant, and socially devalued. The feminist revolution of the 60s was used by bureaucrats and neoliberals to further devalue and disregard the caregiving of children and the role of mothering. The agitation for civil rights for women was exploited by powerholders to gain cheap labour and used to force poor women into uncompensated menial work that fed the life of the economy, but not of the child or the culture. The sacrifice of the cultural strength that comes from consistent caregiving of young children is yet to be felt in its full effect, but even the ripple tremors of drug and alcohol abuse, mental health and social problems we are already experiencing; are bringing us to our knees.

In Australia, conservative regimes erased almost 200 years of human rights struggles with sweeping changes to industrial legislation, the welfare system, and family law. While the changes to industrial law received much attention and organised resistance, the changes to the status of women and welfare recipients received almost no public or media attention. Laws were changed without public debate or scrutiny, in what amounted to behind the door, hand-shake moves between the then Prime Minister and the economically powerful. These changes have effected the greatest impact, now and for the future, on Australian cultural life, since the 1905 act gave white authorities the right to remove Aboriginal children from their families. Australia's willingness to disrespect the work of caring for children at their most vulnerable is a reflection of increased barbarism. Even Spartans waited until children were out of the critical early development period before separating them from their primary caregiver. The Spartans wanted warriors who were emotionally, as well as physically whole. They understood the importance of early constancy and nurturing to develop adults who could be disciplined and focused. Any culture based on the denial of dignity or rights of any of its members cannot develop transformatively. We must understand the critical importance of caring for, and protecting, children if we are to survive and advance as a species.

Power and Control

At this historical time, people who value competition, greed and dominance have had several decades of accumulating vast reserves and resources at local, national and international levels and increasing their power exponentially. This amplified and unfettered decisional power has had, and continues to have, powerful negative effects. In the US the top one percent of households hold over 42% of the entire wealth. During the so called 'economic boom' of the 90s and early 2000s, this top one percent of incomes also took two thirds of the income gains with the result that US income inequality is now greater than that of the Great 1930s Depression. In 2010 the US faces ten percent unemployment with over fifteen million individuals and their families suffering greatly as a direct result of massive increase in profits for the very few. Profiteers will largely escape any of the pain caused by the one-sided gains made since the 80s. These gains so increased inequity that powerful barbaric raiders created global laws and policies which have legalised and enshrined their capacity to profit for the foreseeable future. Therefore, even during recession, the privileged continue to be able to exploit resources, irrespective of the consequences of past profiteering. While it is difficult to face this reality, such understanding provides us with a rational explanation for much of the unnecessary human suffering we face in the 21st century. It also gives us critical understanding of what the next steps can be if we are to enact powerful change.

Even with recent positive leadership change in some of the large industrialised countries such as the United States and Australia, it is a mammoth task for new leaders to redress the damage done during this thirty year barbaric era. Simply rectifying the damage will not be enough. We must go beyond repealing barbaric legislation to take norms back to pre-barbarian levels and move further to effect global cultural transformation that can ensure there are no more barbaric insurgencies. Human sustainability is under such threat--ecologically, technologically and numerically -- that we cannot afford another barbaric coup if species survival is to be ensured. It is critical that we use this present cycle of change to go beyond mending the damage wrought by barbarism to acting to fundamentally changing systems, structures and beliefs so that barbarians can no longer infiltrate, and annex, national and cultural systems. As we examine the human face of self interest behind many of the decisions marketed as 'inevitable' in the past decades it becomes patently clear that, not only is positive change possible and sustainable, but that it may be far less problematic than we have been told.

The Barbaric Norm

In many places, including Australia, barbarism was the philosophy of choice for the last decades of the 20th century and into the 21st. Indeed, barbaric behaviour has now become such an acceptable social norm that many have spoken openly and proudly about their aggressive social, personal and business behaviours. During this time, the social normalisation of aggression and greed enabled powerholders who venerate aggression to block much needed protective legislation, policy, and social change, that could have increased wellbeing and opportunity for vulnerable and low power groups. Even the dissemination of information about social and legislative alternatives which could promote the welfare of people was frequently blocked by individuals who could marshal vast financial reserves to protect their own self-interest.

Elite control of, and access to, media rose to unprecedented levels enabling self-interested elite viewpoints to be peddled as 'scientific', 'rational' or 'inevitable.' Simultaneously, elites were able to block the dissemination of information about the best interests of the average citizen, and to veto information detailing how lower power people might be harmed by elite plans. Market and media manipulation were of critical importance during this time because economic, environmental and human resources were being pillaged at unprecedented levels. The quantity of propaganda spawned in these decades created enormous public confusion about why social devolution was occurring.

One of the primary media manipulation techniques used by elites was to describe the damage occurring to public domains as 'being wrought by market forces' – language which obscured what was really happening. Anthropomorphizing the market is a popular strategy because it distracts public awareness from the shifts of vast amounts of public resources to the coffers of living, breathing individuals. The gambit of reification of the 'market,' as though it were an entity which acts independently, veils the human faces of those who profit from resource shifting. Peddling the mythology that 'the market' and 'the economy' possess life and independent consciousness, rather than being human constructions constantly directed and shaped by human decisions, enables individual elites to siphon vast quantities of resources from the public purse without being held personally accountable.

In a double assault, the public purse has had to be drained a second time by federal stimulus schemes to replace the massive blood loss caused by decades of private vampiric draining of financial veins in public bodies such as banks, hospitals and schools. Monies earned by the average citizen and the poor must now pay for the damage done to public social and financial institutions by private exploitation as we try to repair the 'recession.' In effect, the poor are paying twice to facilitate the excesses of the rich, thus further increasing the gap between the rich and the poor and, in fact, consolidating and reifying the divide.

Historically, language distortion and obfuscation of issues such as the aforementioned example of the market have always been central to increasing the divide between the rich and the poor. This is because the process of gap widening would be immobilized if a critical mass of people became aware of, and were enabled to focus on, the possibility of different ways of being. While disparities in resource access will always exist in human societies, the size of the disproportion has profound impacts on the quality of life for all citizens. This impact is so real that even the health and lifespan of individuals within a country can be predicted by the size of the rich-poor gap. While differences in wealth are not inherently bad in and of themselves, the size of the difference is problematic. A widening gap is not in the best interests of a citizen's life expectancy or the national budget because it causes haemorrhaging of vital veins of cultural, family and community health.

When the proportion of elite advantage and unearned access to resources is increased, there is often a concurrent decrease in elite understanding of the real difficulties and barriers faced by those living in the lower echelons of a culture, and of the globe. This is because the daily lived experiences of rich and poor become so vastly different that the percentage of shared life experience decreases. As the lives of the wealthy become insulated by privilege, the decreased overlap of their daily life with the average citizen suffocates elite understanding of life realities at any level except their own. Distance is its own disadvantage; and physical and emotional distance from people who are suffering dilutes individual political, and personal, motivation. Decreased understanding of the very real obstacles and barriers faced by disadvantaged people decreases compassion for, and sense of shared humanity with, those who suffer. The willingness to understand or support social change to relieve the suffering of others is thereby diminished and the urgent imperative of social justice is obscured.

Each human has responsibility for the wider social outside of their own personal lives and the level of social responsibility accrued should increase with advantage. Instead, insulated elite living tends to decrease the willingness to accept the social responsibility that comes with privilege. The fact that the privileged have greater decision making power and social control than other groups of people makes insulated, privileged decision making particularly problematic for the development of human civilization. It must be stated that social responsibility is not social control. The two concepts are vastly different. In fact, elite tendency to confound these two constructs and lack of understanding about the differences between responsibility and control is, in itself, a huge social problem. The social distancing that occurs when there is a large gap between rich and poor means that elite solutions to social problems may be ignorant, unrealistic, and therefore ineffective. At worst, they become inhumane and oppressive.

Vast differences in resource distribution generate the fundamental democratic predicament of how to maintain meaningful and effective checks and balances on individuals' use of power. Increased concentration of power in elite groups gives increased capacity for influence over, and therefore control over, the lives of those who are less well resourced – a process which itself limits and undermines democratic process. While the historical evidence of great, humanitarian leaders demonstrates that it is actually possible to manage power differentials in ways that can be beneficial; we must be realistic and acknowledge that few people are great, humanitarian, leaders and that having wealth or power does not guarantee these character traits.

In fact, vast resource differentials, in and of themselves, create powerful psychological land mines and challenges which many individuals are unable or unwilling to master. [These landmines are discussed in the section on the effects of power differentials.] When individuals who believe in barbarism gain greatly increased resource control, the human rights of the rest of the population, and democracy itself, is placed at grave risk. When barbarism is the ruling philosophy the quality of life of the average citizen will certainly be eroded and the most powerless will find their lives ravaged and pillaged.

Thus, one of the few advantages of the past two decades of reversion to barbaric philosophy is that it gives us, in the early 21st century, insight into the mechanisms of barbarism; the damage it wreaks when it achieves unilateral control or decision making capacity; and the techniques with which barbaric zealots defend and advance their territory. This recent resurgence of barbarism is a unique opportunity for us to become clear about what barbaric philosophy is, where it is prevalent and where it has infiltrated, or dictated, the construction of the axiomatic social order. This places us in an advantageous historical position for effecting powerful systemic change.

If we so choose, we can redeem the damage wrought by barbarism by using this most recent re-emergence of barbarism to identify the crevasses, foundations and spaces where barbaric philosophy has provided the underpinnings for our societies and cultures. Examination of barbaric philosophy can enable us to see where it has become part of our personal worldview as well as where it has been embedded into our community and government systems in ways to which we have become inured or that we have blindly accepted. Understanding the mechanisms of barbarism is critical if we want to take a more active position towards developing human civilization and halting the global slide. Examining our cultural and systemic assumptions for evidence of barbaric philosophy and addressing barbaric infiltration can enable quantum, transformative human change.

Consciousness

In order to challenge blind devotion to any belief system it is first necessary to increase conscious awareness of that belief system – its presence, mechanisms and effects. Clear understanding is needed to halt unthinking compliance to ideologies and practices which deplete the capacity for humans to advance. In order to challenge our uncritical devotion to, and acceptance of, barbaric philosophy, we must first become much more conscious about what it is and become very clear about how it operates in our daily life and worldview. The manipulation of language and organized promotion of information that was used to advance barbaric interests during the barbaric insurgency has left many confused about the real causes of social crises, including those we now face. It is only when we are clear about the effects of barbarism that we can actively consider alternatives and develop the mass awareness necessary for change and, if we so choose, for ideological transformation.

In uncovering barbarism at its roots it is important to concurrently highlight the existence of the innumerable ways of being from which humans can select. Many of these are far more amenable to human and global advancement than barbarism, as well as infinitely more pleasurable.

SECTION I

DEFINITIONS AND PARAMETERS

CHAPTER 1: DEFINING BARBARISM

In this book the words barbarian, barbarism and barbarous are used to describe a cluster of beliefs and behaviours that were dominant in the 20th century and remain dominant in the 21st century. Originally the word Barbarian was a term used for the Vikings and Goths who colonized and raided Europe; the Goths at the end of the Roman Empire in the 3rd and 4th centuries and the Vikings in the 8th to 11th century. Barbaric raids were, in fact, considered the significant force in the initiation of the Dark Ages (476-1000AD) – a period of time in which human development and learning were repressed and violent control permeated peoples' everyday lives. Wherever barbarians have ruled it has resulted in historical periods where human social progress has been cauterized and cultural, legal and artistic output stunted, hence the utility of the term. In addition, barbarism has always resulted in untold suffering for those peoples unfortunate enough to be subjugated to barbarian rule.

Historians have argued that colonization of cultures by barbarians resulted in societies terrorized by an elite few aristocrats, soldiers or clergy, who had almost unlimited power over the lives and fates of people under their rule. Access to disproportionate amounts of power by an elite few who are distanced from those whose lives they control has, throughout human history, been demonstrated to be problematic. When imbalance in power and control is married with barbarism, human atrocities inevitably occur. The significance of the alliance between faith (belief systems) and militaristic control should be noted as significant.

The etymology and historical usage of the words barbarous, barbaric and barbarian are less central to the premises of this text than the current meanings of barbarian. Today, the word barbarian is generally used in two ways. The first is to refer to someone who is considered to be uncouth or to have an inferior level of culture or civilization to one's own, as in the ancient Greek meaning of the word barbaros to signify any person who was not Greek, and therefore considered inferior. The second definition of barbarian means someone who is merciless, brutal, ruthless, savage, harsh, vicious, unfeeling, remorseless, heartless or cruel. It is this second meaning of the words barbaric and barbarian to which this text primarily refers. Of course, the first meaning of barbarism is also correct in that barbarism is, in fact, an inferior level of human civilization when compared to other possible forms.

Barbarism can include, but is not limited to, tendencies of lacking pity or compassion for others; being prepared to act with great force or intensity in a merciless manner; being disposed to inflict pain; finding satisfaction in the suffering of others; being predisposed to inflict hardship on others and being willing to criticize savagely. Thesaurus references often include 'inhuman' as one of the synonyms for barbarism. 'Barbarians' are defined as people who value and enact warlike, savage insensitivity towards other human beings and towards life sustaining systems. Synonyms include calloused, sadistic, brutish, soulless, hardhearted, obdurate, cold, indifferent, insensitive or lacking in compassion.

This text is not primarily derogation of individual barbarians but rather of the cult and philosophy of barbarism. Barbarism is a way of thinking which translates into barbaric decisions, actions and behaviours. If an individual believes in barbarism passionately enough, as an ideology and therefore as a mantra for their conduct, then their barbarism translates into a way of being that endangers other people. The rigid adherence to, and increased belief in, barbarism as an acceptable way to live and to conduct oneself, is currently wreaking havoc with our family systems, life systems and ecological systems. The acceptance of barbaric philosophy, and the unholy wedlock of barbarism with religious, legal and cultural systems resulted in human suffering and atrocities in the past, and it continues to place human survival at grave risk today.

High Priest, Rich Man, Poor Man, Beggar Man, Thief...

Like any belief system barbarism has different grades of adherence with a hierarchy of levels of ecclesiasticism and loyalty. Barbaric ideology has a power core of high priests, leaders and gurus, trained clergy, disciples and passionate devotees, as well as ranks of more casual members who use the philosophy superficially and who falter when the system advocates extremes of savagery. The spectrum of followers ranges from total, blind devotees who believe any tactic acceptable to ensuring the maintenance of barbaric rule, to those who simply see barbarism as a generally effective philosophy and who use it for daily decision making without much thought. Both levels are dangerous to life systems.

Barbarism is synonymous with a belief in the superiority of some people and a willingness to use cruel or vicious behaviours towards those who are considered inferior or undeserving in any way. It is considered acceptable within barbaric philosophy to exert power and control over those who are classed by barbaric philosophy as less powerful or 'unworthy' and to use whatever tactics are most effective to maintain control over said humans, including tactics which are inhumane or cruel.

This writing is primarily concerned with, and aims to address, the deification of barbarism that has swept the globe alongside the phenomena of market reification, globalism and neo-liberalism. The glorification of barbarism has left in its wake increased levels of antisocial norms, mass naivete' about power and about the effects of different uses of power, and widespread social acceptance of inhumane behaviours and of ineffective responses to halting human atrocities. In turn, this level of social acceptance of barbarism creates ideal hothouse conditions for maintaining barbarian rule, for indoctrinating the next generation of barbarians and for perpetuating barbarism as immutable culture. This cannot be allowed to occur.

It is patently obvious that barbaric behaviour was financially advantageous in the late 20th and early 21st century global market. 'Cut-throat' tactics and 'hostile takeovers' not only enabled profiteering but were lauded as model conduct. Under the powerful benefaction of the reified market; ruthless, brutal and even savage behaviours towards other human beings gained immunity from social stigma. Calloused indifference towards the suffering of individuals, families, communities and nations exploited in the name of profit, not only became de rigueur, but progressed in social acceptability to socially normal and finally, to the position of being cited as a prototype for success.

Individuals who acted ruthlessly for 'market gain', without concern for the misery this caused others, even to the point of lacking human sensibility, were no longer castigated or considered moral outcasts. Within supposedly democratic societies, tyranny and despotism became socially acceptable to the extent that even imperium was seen as an acceptable outcome - as long as the tactics resulted in 'market gain' or increased profit. Indeed, the widespread willingness of privileged first world people to turn a 'blind eye' when pitiless exploitation or savagery occurred to the most vulnerable in our own countries, and to the poor in developing nations, is to our historical shame and part of our own barbaric legacy which must now be addressed.

The sub-prime mortgage crisis in the United States is just one small example of how the dilution of pro-social norms allowed barbaric raiders to profit, causing suffering mainly for lower power, underprivileged and minority groups. Under the barbaric creed [defined in the next section], the manipulation of others' ignorance, suffering, or their desire for a better future, is considered 'fair' if the manipulation results in dominance or profit. When social approval of market-barbarism increased in the eighties it concurrently increased general social acceptance of ruthless, cruel and uncaring conduct, and this enabled barbaric philosophy to more deeply penetrate the domains of social, community and family life. Once barbarism infiltrated the social realm and became accepted as normal within our cultures we began rapid cultural devolution.

Widespread propagation of barbaric philosophy shifted general public perception of harsh, brutal and sadistic actions from being 'abhorrent and disgraceful' to being considered as falling within the range of acceptable social behaviour. As barbarism became increasingly accepted as a social norm, violence became the rule rather than the exception. Interpersonal violence and bullying in workplaces, schools, homes and cyberspace increased exponentially. Naturally, as with any imposition of the barbaric creed, this had greater consequences for those of lower layers of privilege – according to such markers as race, ethnicity, gender, socio-economic status, sexual preference, age or disability – than for those who had enough resources to resist acts of hostility or to counterattack.

Inverting Ab-normal Norms

Reversing the slide towards communal tolerance and approbation of merciless, brutal, remorseless, heartless or cruel interpersonal behaviour, is possibly the most important step we can take towards the advancement of human civilization in the 21st Century. We must go beyond reversing norms to pre-barbarian levels of social tolerance to set new levels of pro-social norms for behaviour. Humans cannot afford to have barbaric behaviours tolerated, let alone acclaimed or respected, if we are to survive as a species.

An initial step will be addressing and reversing the processes by which barbaric behaviour came to be seen as normal and falling within the fundamental values of our societies. Willingness to inflict pain on others or to act brutally and without mercy can not be seen as collectively or culturally acceptable if we are to survive and advance the human race. Humans can't afford to praise, adulate, or honour, any behaviour which is an expression of hostility towards the species. Individuals who express willingness to inflict pain, or to act with great force in a merciless manner towards others, must be responded to as the very real threat to humane, civilized society, and to cultural advancement, that they pose. The predisposition to inflict hardship on others without human compassion cannot be sanctioned in advanced societies. Barbarism is anti-social, inhumane and, therefore, a threat to species survival.

The marketing of barbarism as a ubiquitous human trait has been a manipulative ploy that has allowed base behaviour to infiltrate democratic systems. In fact, the advancement of civilization, science and culture, has always depended on humans resisting, limiting and curtailing barbaric behaviour and insisting on pro-social individual and collective behaviour and norms. It is in the best interests of the collective if individuals who find satisfaction in the suffering of others are not rewarded with power, fame or affirmation. Social functionality requires that barbaric behaviour be seen as reprehensible, unattractive, socially stigmatic and, as rendering individuals outside of the acceptable standard for social inclusion, esteem, and advancement. The willingness to criticize savagely and to inflict suffering on those with few defenses or resources cannot be applauded. In fact, human civilization advances most rapidly when behavioural standards and norms are set at a level that protects the most vulnerable of the species.

Species advancement requires that members who value and enact warlike, savage insensitivities not be considered sane, reasonable or well adjusted – but that they experience the containment, social recoil, and disgrace that brutish behaviour elicits in healthy systems. Sadistic, unfeeling and insensitive responses towards the suffering inflicted on others by one's actions needs to result in the social censure which marks behaviour as anti-social. It is important that individuals not be ranked as well adjusted and lucid when they behave inhumanely. If we are to address the massive challenges we face in the 21st century we cannot afford to have inhuman, callous behaviours considered as standard. Current levels of social acceptance of barbarism must be reversed for democracy to survive and evolve. Barbarism must be addressed and a counter-offensive must be mounted to reverse the process by which barbarism came to be accepted as a social more'. The somnambulance and apathy created by years of barbaric propaganda must be replaced by the appropriate urgency our social and environmental damage, and crises, suggest. Public confusion can be replaced by crystal lucidity about the depth and scope of change required. Calm, widespread, and rational commitment to this change can be fostered.

From the Tsunami, not the Pulpit

Countering and censuring the 21st century levels of barbarism must emerge from a wider framework than the limited base of moral do-gooding and religious preaching. It is critical that an anti-barbarism movement does not increase religious control. The acceptance of some tenets of barbarism within most religious cultures means that religion cannot contain, and therefore can not direct, the anti-barbarian movement. While anti-barbarism is obviously consonant with the true bases of all religious faiths, religions will have their work cut out for them if they are to address the barbarism which has infiltrated, and in some cases founded, their ranks. Pure religion, untouched by cultural and barbaric mythology, is naturally anti-barbaric because it opposes cruelty to human beings. Unfortunately, dogma and cultural pollution may place religious organizations, hierarchy, dogma and practice, far from the purity of their founding philosophy.

An anti-barbaric movement needs to be able to accurately identify barbaric infiltration and corruption of religious philosophy and have the discriminatory capacity to separate such infiltrations from pure religion. Many religious fundamentalist positions are basically and inherently barbaric in that they seek to subjugate others. This aim, combined with willingness to condemn and inflict suffering on humans who do not fit an idiosyncratic religious requirement for conformity, is part of what separates religious barbarism from the pure centre of religious theologies. An anti-barbaric movement needs to be able to clearly and accurately discriminate between humanitarian theology and barbaric religious organizations and cultures.

Simultaneously, a successful reversal of the barbaric tide needs to happen without activating, utilizing, or increasing, global levels of religious control, fundamentalism and militancy. The task of engaging religious faiths in an anti-barbarism movement would be a delicate and difficult procedure. Ultimately, tackling barbarism from a position outside of all religious faiths, but inclusive of all anti-barbaric religious people, would be a great achievement. The partnership of religious leaders willing to address barbarism and blind prejudice within their own ranks would be an invaluable and powerful catalytic aid to anti-barbaric movements.

Even though most religions began as humanitarian revolutions in their own time, once they are infiltrated by barbarism, they tend to anesthetize rather than foster their members' urges towards social justice. Religious dogma and superstition can cloud rather than clarify peoples' vision and enthusiasm for autonomous, humanitarian living. Not all religious sects would profit from human evolution and empowerment. Aggressive fundamentalist religious groups are barbaric at the core and share the same philosophy as capital market barbarians in their goal of totalitarian reign.

Counting the Cost

As part of the recovery from the rise of barbarism it is critical that the real costs, not just of the sub-prime crisis, but of countless counts of barbarism against average citizens, minority groups and developing cultures be exposed and examined so that we fully understand the human cost of allowing barbaric ascendancy. Unless we calculate and face the real and full effects of barbarism, it will be difficult for us to garner the motivation and determination necessary to put in place the changes needed to reverse the tide of barbaric infiltration, and to create transformative change. Effective global and national legislation, pushed by the demands of many people from many cultures, will be needed to address the effects of the past two decades of barbaric dominance and to prevent the rise and recurrence of barbarism in the future. The following section aims to clarify some of the core tenets of barbaric philosophy and how these tenets foster harsh, aggressive human behaviours.

The Barbaric Creed: Barbaros Ultimus

Barbarism can be identified by behaviours, beliefs and effects of the creed. Barbaric advancement is characterised by, and served through, adherence to these tenets. Devoted barbarians can be identified by their almost fanatical attachment and fidelity to these concepts.

THE BARBARIAN CODE

   I. **Destruction of Life Systems.**

  II. **Survival of the Fittest.**

 III. **Inherent Barbaric Superiority.**

  IV. **Rigid Filtering of Information.**

   V. **Low Complexity Planning.**

  VI. **Aggressive Competitive Dominance.**

 VII. **Eradicating & Suppressing Human Vulnerability.**

VIII. **Self-Sufficiency.**

  IX. **Pillaging the Resources of the Future.**

   X. **Blaming the Victim.**

These categories do not exist in isolation but feed each other in a symbiotic fashion to create a coherent barbaric ideology and worldview. The following section explains the networked hybrid of barbaric creed and conduct that coalesce to form barbarism.

I. Destruction of Life Systems

Barbarism is primarily a parasitic system not a revivifying or a creative one. Barbarians tend not to create living systems but rather to destroy and feed off existing systems. Typically those who adhere to the barbaric creed destroy existing life and relational systems in order to build artificial structures over which they can have more personal control. These structures must invariably restrict human living in ways that impinge on lifestyles and individual freedoms because barbaric constructions cannot survive without the coerced or manipulated extraction of labour and resources from others. The energy and resources of existing life systems are the primary vehicle used to perpetuate individual power and barbaric rule.

Barbaric social orders are not self-sufficient living systems and are not sustainable or self-revivifying. Similar to other dead edifices, barbarism, in order to maintain its artificial continuance, must exploit the resources of self-replenishing systems such as intrapsychic, familial, ecological and community life. In order to increase barbaric control, living relational systems – of individuals, families and cultures - must often be destroyed or, at the very least, put in service to barbaric systems. Barbarians erect lifeless forms which extract human energy and resources, often against the will of those who are subjugated, in order to feed their own Frankenstein. This is why barbaric systems are threatened by self-sustaining, living systems which are able to exist external to barbaric control. It is also why barbarism opposes and undermines movements promoting human rights, autonomy, dignity and freedom.

Extracting resources from less powerful others not only increases the resources of the elite but serves a second function of simultaneously depleting the energies of those who have been subjugated. This lowers the likelihood of effective or organized resistance and prevents challenges to barbaric dominance. Exploiting the self-revivifying properties of creative intrapsychic, individual, interpersonal and community life, ensures that this vital energy cannot be used to marshal resistance against barbarism, or to create viable alternatives. Exploitation of the energy of others is critical for the perpetuance of barbaric rule. Exploitation and coercion of other human beings also enables barbarians to maintain the dual illusions of personal superiority and the omnipotence of barbaric philosophy.

These truths are illustrated beautifully in the allegorical tale of good and evil, 'The Dark Crystal' produced by Frank Oz and the talented muppets creator Jim Henson. In this movie a race called Skectics maintain their youth and vitality by draining the youth and life essence of prisoners. For this to occur the captive is forced to cycle on a stationary bicycle and to stare at a brilliant light while hooked up to tubes which drain their life energy into vials. The combination of enslavement, mesmerisation, and enforced movement, ages the unfortunate hostage as years of their vitality is taken from them. The prisoners' life energy is then consumed by the ruling class, almost in the way one would enjoy a boutique wine. Skectics' energy and youthfulness is perpetually restored at the cost of years of the captives' lives. The aged, debilitated and weakened slaves remain in bondage to the masters for the rest of their hapless existence while Skectic masters are constantly rejuvenated by the life energy of slaves. The critical point made by this allegory is that it is not inherent barbarian superiority; but their access to, and constant consumption of, the resources of others' vital lives that perpetuates their dominion. The drained bodies and diminished lives of workers around the world attest to the truth of this allegory, from the factories and forced prison labourers of China; to child labour sweatshops; to the 'work for welfare,' and 'nickled and dimed,' labour markets of the US and Australia.

Lifeless systems have always had to control humans, block creativity and prevent species advancement, in order to ensure their own continuance. Because barbaric edifices are not living systems they are not self-sustaining. In order to be perpetuated they need human life to be subjugated in unyielding and, preferably unquestioning, service so that the energy of the many can be directed to the lives of the few. In part, this is why the converging forces of mass marketing, the cult of consumerism, and the reification of the market in the eighties were so critical to fostering the re-emergence of barbarism. Individuals trapped in low paid labour and inhumane work conditions are fixated on the bright light of lifestyles of the elite, not on barbaric system flaws.

In summary, a dead system of social laws and controls is distinguished from a healthy, sustainable system by the following qualities: Dead system replenishment occurs in a non-synergistic and non-sustainable manner. Because it relies on the unequal coercive extraction of resources from less powerful groups, a dead system must constantly regulate and control the lives of others. A dead structure survives on the basis of living human and ecological resources but does not feed vital, autonomous, creative human life or return an equal or greater amount of energy to the living systems from which resources are extracted (ecologies, individuals, families, relationships, communities and cultures).

Because dead systems rely on coercive control they are invariably pitted against independent, self-reliant, passion-filled human living. By very nature, barbaric systems must curtail human creative life and freedoms in order to be able to control, and then tap, the human energy required for the continuance of their own dead, inanimate structure. In order for barbarism to maintain the rule and restraint necessary to be able to continually plunder individual lives and resources, any resistance must be suppressed and defiance must be brutally punished. The concepts of revolution or human transformative capacity must be marketed as an historical relic or, even better, to the realm of children's faerie tale.

Ancient mythology, science fiction and even modern media, coalesce in their mirroring of this truth. The Matrix trilogy shows a vision of the future where human life has become fodder for unthinking, unfeeling systems. The machines regard all human life as mere 'batteries' – energy packs for the continuance of a mechanistic system which does not have its own energy and which relies on human life for survival and continuance. Liberated human life is seen as a threat to the survival of inanimate existence, and therefore is actively hunted down and destroyed. Responsive and uncontrolled human life has been forced underground where existence and survival are a constant struggle performed in the context of ongoing war against masters who possess no inherent life energy of their own. The machines are exanimate masters, without mercy or pity for the suffering caused to humans by extracting their life energy. The machines, similar to the bureaucrats legalising inhumane work conditions, are concerned only with survival of their mechanistic system.

The Orcs in Tolkien's 'Lord of the Ring' trilogy also represent barbaric human consciousness enslaving and destroying living systems in unthinking compliance to aggression, self-interest and the quest for dominance. Orcs are ignorant of the value of living systems – be they human, animal or plant. They see life matter only as fodder for the making of war implements. Orcs fit the definition of barbarians: merciless, savage, brutal and inhuman. They force human life into slavery, again 'below ground,' in conditions of temperature and toil, and consider all human life as valueless and expendable. Concepts of quality of life, sustainability, relationship or caring, are incomprehensible to them. They only understand fear, brutality and control.

Orcs, as manufactured life-forms, cannot grasp the long-term consequences of their destruction of the living environment and thus their destructiveness is without rational or moral boundary. They have no compunction about vicious, war-like behaviour and no capacity for long-term thought. Orcian constructions, like the dark, smoke-filled landscape and factories around the Eye of Sauron, are metaphors for, and examples of, barbaric production. They cannot be called creations in the true sense of the word because they destroy land and living systems and use human and other life forms as fodder. More recently the movie Avatar focussed on the willingness of human resource 'cor-pirates' to destroy living planetary, species, community and family systems, to feed personal wealth. All barbaric constructions are ultimately unsustainable because they destroy the very life they require to continue in existence.

Destruction of life systems is a core marker of barbaric modus operandi and rule.

II. Survival of the Fittest

This core organizing principle of barbaric thought is built upon an incomplete fragment of Darwin's theory of natural selection. Darwin defined natural selection as a process occurring in nature whereby the best genetically adapted organisms for an environment are more likely to survive than those which are less well genetically adapted. His theory was formulated to describe a process he personally observed occurring in the physical environment. It is important to note that he was observing natural processes different not only in function, but in essence, from human devised systems and organizations which are influenced heavily by human choice as well as by the capacity for humans to plan, change their minds, and make active decisions. It is also important to note that Darwin was opposed to genetic determinism.

Darwin's domain of study is entirely dissimilar to, and incongruent with, studies of systems and behaviours created by human intent. Barbarians conveniently ignore the fact that the domain of Darwin's theory was the physical environment and naturally occurring selective processes and that he was concerned with the continuance of physical, not psychological, characteristics. Barbarians erroneously use Darwin's theory of natural selection to explain behaviours where there is little environmental influence and a high degree of choice based on the human capacities for conceptualization, planning and conscious decision.

Darwin's theory is popular with barbarians because they can distort his intent and use fragmented, decontextualised pieces of his work to justify personal acts of violence and unprovoked aggression against other, typically less powerful, people. Barbarians cite 'natural selection' when justifying personal behaviours where they have attacked and pillaged other people's resources – particularly those people who are most defenceless. Darwin would be outraged.

In particular, barbarians misconstrue Darwin's words 'survival of the fittest' to justify acts of violence they have perpetrated and loosely quote theory to claim that barbaric acts are not only normal but 'necessary' to the advancement of the species. Those who oppose barbarism are accused of standing in the way of 'human progress.' In reality, initiating hostilities; being aggressive towards those who resist force; stealing the resources of vulnerable humans; intimidating and being brutal to others; are all anti-social behaviours. These, in fact, retard human development and divert human resources away from humane progress and human advancement.

Adherents to barbaric philosophy rely heavily on literal interpretation of the taxonomic classification of humans into the animal kingdom. Ignoring the etymology of animalia, 'possessing soul', barbarians insist that humans are animals in order to emphasize animal instinct as the organizing influence for human behaviour. Citing animal instinct as the rationale for human behaviour disregards the overwhelming majority of human faculties. To maintain the position that human behaviours are primarily driven by animal instinct one would have to exclude from consideration the human abilities of conscious choice, language, intention, motivation and will. In addition, the weight of evidence to the contrary has to be denied. This includes, but is not limited to, all current and historic human creativity, quantum theoretical and social change, conscious decisions and transformational practice. Narrow, dogmatic emphasis on animal instinct as an exonerating rationale for human

13

behaviour is, however, expedient if you want to excuse animalistic, cruel and savage behaviours. Generally, barbarians cite animal instinct in areas in which the status quo gives them personal advantage and in which they have no intention of effecting change. The claim that humans are animals, accompanied by a shoulder shrug is barbarian for, 'No. I hold the power. Things will stay as they are.' This is often communicated simply as the unilateral, authoritarian, 'No.'

Propaganda and Ploys

Barbarians also misuse Darwin's theory of the survival of the fittest as part of a tautological argument they use to justify their own unequal possession of resources. Barbaric ideology touts the mythology that variations in access to resources are simply the outcome of fair competition between equal competitors. Barbarian philosophy does not acknowledge that variations in resource allocation can result from competitions conducted where one party has unfair advantage or where one party uses tactics of violence, exploitation, coercion, thievery, trickery or manipulation. Strategically, barbaric mythology usually remains silent about such realities unless the propaganda machine has failed and the imperative to repair public image overrides the strategic use of silence (a favoured barbaric tactical manoeuvre).

When justifying exploitation, barbarians will not only ignore the issue of power differentials between people but will use forceful interpersonal aggression if the issue is raised. This use of aggression to block discussion and prevent rumination or exploration of the issue is commonly via the route of argumentum ad hominem. Barbarians defend the illusion of equal power between people because, without recognition of power differentials and acknowledgment that power differences do exist and that they increase the capacity of powerholders to manipulate or coerce less powerful people, exploitative behaviours cannot be named. If they cannot be named, they cannot be prevented, halted or penalized. Therefore, refusing to acknowledge the existence of real power differentials between people is a handy tool to employ if you wish to maintain unequal privilege as a barbarian raider.

Instead, barbarians will insist that all people have equal chance for, and access to, resources. They will also steadfastly maintain core barbarian mythology that all competition is 'fair' competition, conducted in a mutually agreed upon manner between 'equals.' Incidentally, this is one of the very few times that barbarians will agree that all humans are equal; and only in order to protect their own unequal access to resources.

Barbaric tactics of force and coercion are most effective when the other party has less power and therefore is less able to resist and can be more easily manipulated by misinformation. This tactic works best when coercion is conducted away from public view or scrutiny. When parties have more power parity, the manipulation and exploitation of others' resources becomes much more difficult and requires the investment of more barbarian resources of time and energy. This is why lower power and vulnerable people are the most appetizing to the barbaric palate. The more helpless, innocent and undefended the victim, the greater the salivation of barbaric raiders. Typically, barbarians will blame the victim for their defencelessness as though this absolves barbarians from pillaging, raping and looting the victim's resources.

The mythology of the level playing field is central to the maintenance of barbaric control because, when married with the Darwinian theory of 'survival of the fittest', it is a convenient tool that can be used as justification for acts of violence against others, for propagation of barbaric theory, and for the maintenance of barbarian power.

III. Inherent Barbaric Superiority

In a tautological argument linked closely with the previous point, barbarians purport that their own access to unequal amounts of resources proves their superiority as 'the fittest.' Barbarians see themselves as inherently, genetically or personally, superior and of more value than, non-barbaric human beings. Barbarians claim that their personal wealth or privilege is a result of this superiority rather than of unearned advantage or the use of exploitation or aggression.

Barbarians have categorical systems which place different value on different human lives, and, barbarians inevitably categorize themselves in the category of the human life with the most value. When the Spaniards colonized South America they were labelled Godo which came from the local slang term for arrogance. In turn, this phrase came from local's previous experience of barbarians because 'haciéndose los godos' meant literally, 'to be making yourself behave like the Goths.' In other words, barbarism is an inherently arrogant and self-aggrandizing philosophy.

This conceited aspect of barbaric philosophy is a case of deluded self-inflation. It is curiously mismatched with other realities of barbaric culture reflected in the word's meaning including the characteristics of being uncivilized, savagely cruel, lacking culture and being coarse. Barbarian self interest is, of course, served by beliefs of inherent superiority to other human beings who are either of less station or of less fortune. Using the mythology of being inherently or genetically superior to other people enables Barbarians to make the claim that their dominance over others is 'serving the species.' Barbarians commonly use this delusion, along with an incompatible meld of theories of evolution, equality and competition, to maintain self-interest.

The delusion of barbaric superiority also enables rationalization of the 'need' for exploitation of supposedly 'inferior people' as a necessary 'sacrifice' for maintaining 'humanity's best interests' ie: a tautological argument made by barbaric dominants that advancing barbaric dominance is the best avenue for advancing the species.

IV. Rigid Filtering of Information

Barbarians are non-responsive to any external feedback, culture or idea which does not foster barbaric interest. Barbaric communication systems are insulated loops which have filtering devices to ensure that only feedback in consonance with barbaric philosophy is able to pass and that other information is blocked.

Historically, barbarians were considered distinct from savages in that they were perceived as being willfully ignorant, choosing to preserve their way of life despite contact with more civilized societies which presented them with alternative ways of being. The rigidity of this stance continues to the current day. The definition of barbarian includes concepts such as uneducated, boorish, ignorant and uninformed. These definitions, in part, reflect the outcomes of an insulated information system penetrated only by feedback which supports and affirms narrow barbaric ideology.

The restricted nature of barbaric information sourcing is also the reason barbaric rulers are often ill-informed about the real living conditions of those subjugated under their rule, and often extremely ignorant of the fundamentals of social sustainability. Marie Antoinette's famous frustration with the 'idiocy' of the masses who would not eat cake when they lacked bread, reflects the type of limited understanding that occurs when there is an insulated, restricted, closed information access system.

Barbarian worldview includes the belief that there is no real human altruism and that all acts of human caring are simply manipulation to establish dominance over others. Freud would call this a projection. Because barbarians are unlikely to believe in human caring, they reject evidence to the contrary and project their own barbaric motivations onto altruism (ie: citing them to be acts of ego, self-advancement, desire for control or for manipulation of other people). Hard bitten cynicism about human good is a strong feature of barbarian belief. Portraying all people as inherently barbaric at core (and as aggressively self-interested) is essential to core barbaric belief that aggression is inevitable. It also fosters belief that aggression is the most effective way to interact with other human beings which is then used to justify pre-emptive and unprovoked attacks on others ie: 'Get them before they get you.'

While barbaric information systems do not typically focus on the existence of truly altruistic behaviours the exception is when they wish to identify a group which might be more easily exploited ie: carers. People who are caring, naïve, co-operative, or non-aggressive, are a favourite target for barbaric raiders. Except for data sourced when searching for the easy prey of such 'soft' groups, any evidence of great humanitarian and caring acts which enter barbaric knowledge systems are viewed as 'aberrations', as inconsequential data, and are quickly dismissed. In other words, barbarian information systems are designed only to include data which defend barbarian philosophy and which rationalize self-interest, and aggressive and hostile behaviour. Ultimately, this not only supports barbaric philosophy but also leads to ignorance and to limited capacity in decision making processes.

V. Low Complexity Planning

A direct result of having an insulated information system with restricted exposure to feedback data is that barbarian potentates often have mediocre or only superficial understanding of the domains they are subjugating or using. When this level of ignorance of the conditions outside elite domains is combined with inadequate information it results in naïve, facile, and oversimplified planning processes. Often barbarians have not thought about, do not adequately understand, or have not counted the full human, social, and environmental costs of what they are doing. They are often acting in wilful ignorance. The tendency for barbarians to access only pro-barbarian information sources means there is more risk of them using oversimplified planning based on short term vision and narrow cost assessment.

When this restricted information access is combined with the barbaric tendency to act primarily on base instinct, their ignorance of the domains they are controlling and lack of understanding of the full cost of what they are doing, can be disastrous. Even when barbarians exercise full unilateral control over environments, peoples' lives and lifestyles, they may be naïve, dumb, or completely ignorant about the lived realities within those spheres. With the exception of costs that affect their immediate self-interest, barbarians typically put insufficient time into understanding the complex human, social and environmental consequences which may flow from their decisions. The shallow, superficial, and simplistic planning that emerges from this poor understanding, usually results in inferior and inadequate system responses which may have disastrous or even genocidal effects, for peoples or territories under subjugation.

For the original barbarians this was not a big problem. Roman usage of the term for Teutonic barbarians held the dual meaning of both 'illiterate' and 'wanderer' which referred to barbaric willingness to plunder resources and destroy environments with the attitude that they could always move on to a new resource pool. Remnants of this attitude are still evident in the barbaric 21st Century attitude to the environment even though the certainty of a new resource pool no longer exists.

VI. Aggressive, Competitive Dominance

Brutality is highly valued within the barbarian system. Ferocious assault of the most vulnerable is particularly prized. Humiliating, taunting and deriding those who cannot defend themselves is a favourite sport. Barbarians particularly enjoy using the domain of the social to manipulate human conformity to get a group ridiculing or attacking a lone, defenceless victim. This behaviour is distinct from the more casual social teasing that occurs between equals, because the barbarian uses an inequity in power base; drawn from power of the group or power of their personal privilege; to tear into another person's dignity, to destroy their social standing, and thus render them more vulnerable to future group attack. Mocking and attacking those who can't defend themselves is a savagery in which barbarians take great delight.

Within barbaric domains cruel, derogatory epithets hurled towards others, particularly the vanquished, is also applauded. From the workplace to the sports field to reality television, increasingly vicious, inhumane savaging of other human beings has become inculcated into international consciousness during this recent barbaric era. On popular reality TV shows contestants may be savaged by judges who justify their personal use of unmitigated viciousness on the basis of wider savagery in the social domain. One instance of savagery does not excuse another. The mythology used in game shows such as Idol that the judges are savage because critics are savage, lowers the emotional and cultural intelligence of those who accept it. Crude and violent wounding of another human being, through derogation and public humiliation, cannot be seen as an acceptable public sport. The rise of barbarism in the colosseum has always signalled a culture's demise.

Unnecessary aggression, even under the guise of 'helpful' (which it is not) criticism still speaks volumes about the quality of the person who is inflicting the pain. Vicious aggression and public shaming of an individual harms them. We cannot afford the confusion of barbaric propaganda which peddles the myth that public savaging is productive. People who are willing to publicly savage and shame other human beings need to experience social censure so that their behaviour does not become idolised as a social norm. Those who advocate vicious criticism, derogation, and wounding of, other human beings need to be confined in their influence.

The Mythology of the Level Playing Field

Within barbaric mythology unequal resource distribution is conceptualised only as an outcome of competition and never as a precursor which might affect competition outcome. This is a convenient part of barbaric philosophy because a major barbaric strategy is to choose competition with those who have less power and resources in order to guarantee victory. Barbarians will either select 'opponents' who have less strength than they do (so that they have a very good chance of winning), or over whom they have some sort of tactical power advantage. Because barbarians believe that victory is part of what marks them as superior they place great emphasis on being victorious and have no compunction about using coercive and unfair tactics. The easiest way for a barbarian to achieve victory is to choose a less powerful adversary or a defenceless adversary with whom to 'compete'.

Barbarians invariably advocate competition as the way to determine resource allocation amongst people. This penchant for competition, and particularly aggressive competition, is the primary tactic enabling them to profit for self-interest and to establish control over others. Barbarians are often shrewd and calculating. They know full well that behaving as though relations between people were 'equal' and requiring the lower power body to compete or to negotiate as though they had equal power ensures easy barbaric victory. Barbarians are only too well aware of this axiom:

'SO CALLED EQUAL RELATIONS BETWEEN UNEQUALS REINFORCES INEQUITY.'

The consequences of the mythology of the so-called 'level playing field' for any but the privileged and the elite, are disastrous. In effect it means that a social order is constructed that addresses the needs and the reality of only the top few percent of a population. Hence, while the global population scrabbled to 'compete' in the so-called economic 'boom', only the top few percent actually had access to its profits. So-called 'global competition' for resources was actually the exploitation of lower power countries, and populations, by high power individuals. When one side is so hobbled the 'race' is a cruel farce. When all of the rules for competing within a society are tailored to those with the most resources then the rest of the population can't successfully compete. The few whose lives have been particularly fortunate (the young heirs and heiresses of the barbaric aristocracy) are iconized and the rest of the population ends up accepting barbaric mythology that this is because they didn't 'try' hard enough or are 'inferior' in some way. This may give people a way to psychologically rationalize their inability to be 'on the top' but it is wrong and such fallacious mythology damages not only the individual but also cultural capacity, and global motivation, for achievable change.

Competitive dominance is a dangerous mythology because it focuses the attention of the entire population on a few individuals rather than on the value of each human life in the remaining 99% of the population. Barbarism devalues most human lives. As a competitive elite system, barbarism is more likely to create structures, programs, laws and rules that reinforce, buttress, and protect, barbarian power bases. Such rules serve the few rather than the many. They certainly don't serve the underprivileged or the average citizen.

Competition and the Reification of Privilege

As mentioned previously, the barbaric belief in competition as the superior way to determine resource distribution coupled with the barbaric philosophy that the outcome of said competition (unequal resource distribution), determines the worth of human beings is a circular argument which will always lead to barbarians classing themselves as superior. Aggressive competition is therefore a vehicle that reinforces barbaric privilege and perpetuates barbaric rule.

The categorization of people into 'victors' or 'vanquished' which is encouraged by the philosophy of competition is dangerous, particularly when it is used as justification for ignoring or diminishing the human rights of some human beings. Such discrimination may be classed as 'fair' by barbarians when people are seen to be 'vanquished' on the mythological 'level playing field.' Aggressive, competitive dominance is a philosophy that only serves barbaric self interest and cannot serve the needs of human social, cultural, and species, advancement.

VII. Eradicating and Suppressing Human Vulnerability

Barbarians see human advancement as occurring primarily through the eradication of human vulnerability and they will often act under the full-blown, almost obsessive, delusion that this is even possible. Such a delusion ignores the reality that human life has unavoidable stages of vulnerability embedded within it across the lifespan. Humans are vulnerable when they are born, when pregnant, when birthing, while they are infants, when they are sick, when they are injured, when they are old, when they are dying, and in a myriad of other circumstances. All humans are extremely vulnerable during birth and infancy. Childhood is a time of vulnerability; being ill or having a disability is vulnerability; being female is vulnerability. Children have less power and strength than adults; illness weakens and limits humans; and human females have less muscle mass pound for pound than males – just ask any rape or domestic violence victim. These qualities are an inherent part of the species condition. Phases of vulnerability across the lifespan are a part of every human's life. Because barbarism does not adequately consider the whole lifespan, it cannot effectively respond to human need. It is therefore an inadequate system for the species.

In an aggressive system, even the social vulnerability which is inflicted by human prejudice is seen as an excuse to attack people by virtue of race, ethnicity, gender, sexual preference or whatever ignorance is the current fad. Being black or any colour other than white is a vulnerability in barbaric western systems; being of an ethnic minority or of same-sex preference, being under the age of 12 are all vulnerabilities. Any system or philosophy which attacks human vulnerability, attacks the very conditions of our human existence. Any philosophy which attacks the human vulnerability of any singular human attacks us all. Barbarism is a flawed and inadequate system for advancement of our species.

In western democracies you are handicapped in the so-called 'fair competition' realm if you were abused as a child, if you are disabled, not white, have any physical appearance 'deficit', are very old or very young or get sick.... The list is endless. Rather than accepting the barbarian solution of eradicating or oppressing the vulnerable, it is important to remember that barbarian mythology is based on flawed and limited thinking. In fact, protection of human vulnerability might be just the focus we need in order to construct healthy, robust human societies which can foster human creative, transformative potential of all of its members. Any society that can respond to vulnerability in positive, empowering and strengthening ways holds the key to human transformation process. This is illustrated beautifully by the Somali proverb, 'God hides his secret in the weak.'

Barbarians conceptualize human compassion and vulnerability as unnecessary, or as weaknesses to be eradicated in the species. Under barbaric rule, necessary caring activities must be under barbaric control and not granted the rights and autonomy afforded to other workers. Much caring work is unpaid, undervalued and exploited in barbaric systems. Barbarians typically conceptualize caring as foolish and even as damaging to the capacity for human advancement because they see it as ineffective in achieving dominance in the 'real world.' This ignores the reality that the social world is constructed by human choice and therefore that we always have a myriad of real worlds we can construct. What barbarians mean is that caring does not ensure dominance within an aggressive, competitive, barbaric system.

This derogation of caring also ignores the reality that all human life subsists and is nurtured to self-sufficiency through human care and that there are phases across the lifespan where all of us are in need of care. Studies of infants left in orphanages with their basic physical needs met but given no additional care or touch have found that they fail to thrive, usually suffer irreversible brain and developmental damage, and often die. Nonetheless, barbarians have been relentless in their attacks on the economic and subsistence rights of carers in the past two decades, in many cases forcing carers to abandon infants and other dependents so that the low-pay labour market (a lifeless system) could be fed.

Barbaric philosophy would fail human quality assurance analysis because it is unable to respond to the full spectrum of human needs across the lifespan. It is an incompetent, unsatisfactory, and inadequate system for the sustenance of human life and of people. It is patently unequal to the advanced task of fostering human social evolution.

VIII. Barbaric Self-Sufficiency

The primary reason that barbarians devalue carers and caring work is because of the illusion of barbaric self-sufficiency. Barbarian philosophy operates under the fundamentally flawed assumption that barbaric dominance results primarily and entirely, from individual effort; with neither privilege nor fortune contributing to barbaric dominion. Because barbarians do not acknowledge the fundamental interdependence of all human life, they also do not recognize the contributions of other people and resources to their ascendance. Where possible, anti-barbarians must learn how to rescind complicity to barbarian rule and to withdraw their own personal energy, skill and talent from the feeding of barbaric privilege and therefore from sustaining this delusion.

This illusion of self-sufficiency is part of why barbarians are unwilling to accept social responsibility. The barbaric mythology of the rugged, superior, self-sufficient individual contributes to one of the most brutal aspects of barbaric philosophy, the belief in the disposability of others.

If, as barbarians suppose, all human success is the end result of the senior labour, superior skill, and higher intelligence of elite members of the species (barbarians), then the promotion of individual barbarians is the highest possible goal for humanity. The flipside of this skewed philosophy is the erroneous belief that no price is too great if it results in barbaric advancement; including the loss or sacrifice of other members of the species who, within the barbarian paradigm, are defined as being of less value. It is this bizarre aspect of barbaric mythology that leads, at one extreme, to the horrors of ethnic cleansing and genocide and; at the other, to the advocacy of inhumane work conditions and low pay for so-called inferior members of the species.

If, as barbarians suppose, some members of the species are more disposable than others, then the death of so-called lesser individuals is a relatively unproblematic event as long as barbarian interests are served. Death is not always by the more horrifying processes of concentration camps or genocide but is sometimes in the less visible lethal processes of polluting people's living environments; working people beyond sustainable levels; or manipulating media to propagate ideas and norms which are injurious and lead to early death; particularly for the poor.

Some historians link barbarian willingness to see individuals as disposable to the beliefs of the original Goths who dwelt in such a war-based manner that willingness to face inevitable death was crucial to cultural coherence and continuance. The original Goths saw death merely as a transition to Valhalla - paradise where all your earthly needs would be met if you had been brave and ferocious in battle. Unfortunately, the truth behind modern barbaric willingness to see humans as disposable is far less romantic. Barbarian willingness to see individual people, cultures, and communities, as expendable is based on illusions of superiority and self-sufficiency. More ominously, it is a direct result of the emotional hardening and dumbing down that occurs to humans when they engage in vicious behaviours towards other members of the species.

The Calloused Heart

One of the many deleterious psychological effects of ongoing expressions of brutality and cruelty towards other people, is desensitization. Desensitization is the process whereby a person is made emotionally insensitive or where a continually repeated behaviour no longer elicits an emotional response. Repetitious cruelty and vicious behaviours enacted towards other people cause a person to lose his or her capacity for compassion, to begin to devalue human life, and to become emotionally calloused. This emotional hardening further fuels his or her willingness to inflict hardship on others, thus beginning a very dangerous cycle. The devaluation of other people dehumanizes both the barbarian and their victim, but results in barbarians sliding closer to the definition of inhuman. Visceral understanding of this reality was expressed by a survivor of a Nazi concentration camp who described sadistic soldiers and guards as: '...not from Germany. Cowards have no country of their own. Those demons were from hell.' (as recounted by Social Activist Dr. Clarissa Pinkola Este's). Albert Camus' tale of the Plague illustrated that human cruelty, like a virus, can infect any healthy human body if we bring it into our life system by living it.

One of the reasons barbarians are at risk of this emotional slide towards animalistic and inhumane behaviour is because they do not believe in the interdependence of all life. The illusion of barbaric self-sufficiency results in a flippant and careless attitude towards other living beings to whom barbarians are connected and in which their own life is embedded. From the contributions received from trees and clear water; to the unpaid care given by significant others; to the work of people who man their factories and clean their homes; barbarians routinely underestimate the contributions from others that sustain their own viability. They may be completely oblivious to the way their lives are woven together by complex interconnections, and multifaceted gifts, from other living beings. The brutal, callous and savage behaviours enacted by barbarians towards other people both lead to, and are reinforced by, the barbaric delusion that they are self-sufficient and can survive alone.

25

IX: Pillaging Resources of the Future & the Many

All of the afore-mentioned characteristics lead to the barbarian propensity for short-sighted, narrow-minded, lifestyles and behaviour. Barbarians take the Latin admonition 'Carpe diem' beyond its zenith into hedonistic pursuit of self gratification that knows no rational bounds. Barbaric predisposition for living for the moment, without any sense of social responsibility, enables unconscionable and often blind and wasteful consumption. The global damage to old growth forests in the past two decades is just one example of the many irreplaceable resources that took centuries to develop; decimated by barbarians in less than one lifetime. It is this type of damage, which destroys resources, not just for one, or two generations, but for many generations to come, that is the hallmark of careless barbarian dominion.

The loss of thousands of species through thoughtless, cash driven, profiteering in the name of development is another example of the irreparable damage that can be inflicted during barbarian insurgency. The fact that, during periods of barbaric rule, vast amounts of resources can be pillaged and rapaciously consumed within a very short period of time is one of the many reasons humanity cannot afford another era of incursion. It is one of the signs of barbaric ascendancy that, as soon as they gain power, barbarians sign contracts and rush to change legislation so that, not only those under their rule, but future generations and leaders, are contractually bound to projects that exploit public, environmental, and human resources.

As one example, here in Australia, within days of winning a State election barbaric elites gave permission for the mining of uranium, a highly contentious and dangerous environmental act with consequences for countless generations to come. This had been vetoed by the previous administration because of a long campaign of public protest, as well as expressions of concern from environmental scientists about the complexities of the half life of uranium, and toxic environmental damage. This example graphically illustrates why the capacity for a few self-interested individuals to make decisions that negatively impact on future generations must be removed if our societies and democratic systems are to survive. Present generations must be held accountable for their impact on the resources of as yet unborn children. The rights of the voiceless must be protected from the greed of the self-interested few.

Blood-letting: Pillaging the Potential of Children

Perhaps even more troubling than the pillaging of natural resources, is the wastage of youth that is so common in the barbaric coliseum. Barbaric puncturing of the life vein of the future occurs in a myriad of ways. From the domains of prenatal health to housing, education and welfare, the few resources left to moisten the parched lives of the most impoverished are soaked up by insatiable barbaric raiders. The separation of caregivers from their children for the purposes of enforced factory or low pay labour directly depletes the well-being, emotional resources and capacities, of the adults of the future. There are a myriad of ways that the time, care, attention, and resources, that rightfully belong to the next generation are diverted by barbarians to irrigate the vast paddies of personal profit margins. Fastidiously and meticulously absorbing all available resource pools, even those reserved for small children, is typical barbaric behaviour. Obsessive draining of every drop, from even the toddler's tiny wading pool, advantages barbarians by creating exclusive resource control. In turn, this fosters deprivation and gives greater coercive control over the labour, and remaining resources, of other members of the species.

The future of poor and lower middle-class children is obviously most seriously affected by barbarian reign, because the removal of even a few resources leaves them in desperate need; often without even the basics needed to ensure their healthy, normal development and sometimes impairing their capacities for life. The pillaging of children: their energy, the potential, their vision, their hopes and dreams, their emotional wellbeing, their family life, their educational opportunities, and the physical environment of their future, is symptomatic of the pillaging that occurs across all resource domains during barbaric rule. In fact, the past two decades of exploitation of resources, has so widened the gap between the rich and the poor, that it is no longer possible for a single generation to breach it with a lifetime of hard labour. With the current disparities, it cannot be breached in two, three, or even four lifetimes. Hence, we have firmly recreated the aristocracy of past centuries. In so doing we have pillaged the democratic possibilities that belonged to the next three to four generations of humans. In effect, we have pillaged the future of all children, except those of the elite.

Weaponry against Welfare

One of the definitions of barbarian is one who is willing to inflict pain and suffering on others pitilessly. The obsession with which even the scant resources available to those on welfare or disability are tracked during barbaric rule, down to the last dollar and cent, and the militancy with which punishments are imposed onto low power people who might have taken a single dollar or cent too many, are evidence of this willingness to inflict pain. Recently, in Western Australia, there was a disturbing and scandalous example of this type of unnecessarily punitive cruelty when police laid a criminal charge against a 12 year old boy who had accepted a stolen 50 cent chocolate frog from another child. In addition to the charge the adult police physically removed the child at 8am on a school day and imprisoned him for several hours in their station cell. One can only imagine the terror experienced by this young boy. The hard hearted nature of barbarism can be seen in this unnecessary traumatisation of a child and in the small outcry this act generated.

It appears that the US is not immune to this type of punitive barbaric simple mindedness. A 12 year old girl was arrested, handcuffed, and police escorted out of her New York school for writing, 'I love my friends Abby and Faith...' in marker on her desk. The barbarian double standard (protection for those with systemic power and increased accountability for the undefended) is also reflected in the fact that, in the US, there are no national tracking statistics to document how often minors are arrested by police for nonviolent crimes in schools. Given the huge impact of, not only the traumatisation of arrest, but of a criminal record on a young person's life and possibilities, it would seem that surveillance of adult actions should be a bare minimum. General acceptance of these types of unnecessary brutality towards children, and towards other low power populations, is a sign of cultural contagion and strong barbaric norms. Tom Sawyer would be a fingerprinted juvenile in such a system.

The ruthless, hard-hearted, and relentless, barbaric approach was also evident during the Howard regime in Australia in the harsh penalties instituted against people who were defined as 'non compliant' with barbaric demands for labour or who voluntarily left any employment. Penalties of eight weeks were imposed, even if people had been subjected to inhumane or exploitative employment conditions, or been harassed or bullied at work. The fact that penalties were imposed irrespective of the conditions under which people were working and whether or not they had dependents highlights the militant, merciless absolutism of barbarian rule. The calloused barbarian attitude of taking all resources for elites is intransigent, even when there is harm for children and other vulnerable groups. The suffering of children was considered a tolerable price to pay by barbarian decision makers when the focus was total subjugation of the labour force.

During a barbaric era, the threat, menace and harsh penalties instituted in welfare, employment and education systems; are all targeted towards the least powerful and most vulnerable, while power holders are often immune to prosecution even for massive acts of profiteering and exploitation. The message that is forcefully communicated to the general population is that, during barbaric reign, there will be no mercy for the most vulnerable. The underlying subtext of the propaganda is that absolute conformity to barbaric rule is the 'only safe space.' Such a message, along with the harshness of penalties imposed for nonconformity to barbaric rules, drove Australians to working the longest hours in the OECD in the last decade; often submitting to exploitative work, poor conditions and many hours of unpaid labour. Driven by fear, Australians in 2009, with a working population of less than 11 million, work over 2 billion hours of unpaid labour per annum, [an average of 90 minutes of free labour per day] and have over 123 million days of leave owed ($33 billion worth).

The second important message given to the populous when merciless penalties are imposed is that; under barbaric reign, savagery in the social realm committed by power holders will go unchecked and unpunished. Under barbarism only those who are barbaric rulers, or who have sufficient personal resources to protect themselves from aggression, are safe from savagery. Nonconformity to barbaric interests and demands is met with the full force of barbaric viciousness, amplified by their huge resource backing. The force and viciousness are designed to eradicate any opposition and to intimidate. Bureaucrats and officials who are harsh, vicious, and unsparing, in their use of power and the law, have no penalty to fear for their anti-social behaviour; not even public reprobation or social ostracism. The menace and meaning of unchecked barbaric power is understood by most people even if they do not consciously register the warning. As the majority of the population subjugate themselves to barbaric demand– those who actually should be the focus of restraint - powerful corporate raiders and other profiteers, are enabled to run amok pillaging the resources of the culture, and the future, free from fear of rebuke or penalty.

This familiar quote, attributed to the Native Americans, sums up the effects of the barbaric propensity to pillage the future through insatiable present-day consumption, 'Only when the last tree is cut, the last river poisoned, and the last fish is dead will the white man discover he can't eat money.' Hopefully, Indigenous consciousness will permeate our thick white skulls early enough that we will obviate this dire prophecy. Otherwise, we are all dead men walking to a very dry last meal.

X. Blaming the Victim

Even though examples of blaming the victim have been mentioned in each of the previous categories, this is such a significant aspect of barbarian ideology that it merits separate consideration. Barbaric illusions of superiority, self-sufficiency, and invulnerability, combine to create judgmental, arrogant and cruel responses to the misery of others. The calloused and merciless attitude that barbarians take towards the suffering of other people is a core feature of the barbarian creed and is the aspect which, during barbaric rule, results in a flurry of inhumane laws, policies and penalties mainly designed to target the less fortunate.

In stark contrast to compassionate belief systems illustrated in phrases such as, 'But for the grace of God there go I,' 'Before you judge a man walk a mile in his mocassins', 'Inshallah' and similar philosophical positions, barbarians take the experience of their good fortune as a sign of personal superiority and use it to condemn and oppress those with fewer resources than themselves. It is this arrogance which leads to barbarian decision makers creating systems which are oppressive and heartless towards the poor and the less privileged. The merciless nature of these systems generates panic in the overall population. The average person becomes willing to work harder, longer, and even without pay as they frantically scrabble to avoid falling into misfortune which could place them within range of the extra abuse barbarians reserve especially for the poor.

This is much of the reason for the mania and overwork spawned in the Howard and Bush eras. It was this overwork, much of it unpaid, which increased profit margins for the wealthy and artificially and unsustainably inflated economic output while simultaneously draining individual, community, family and social resources. In contrast; a more humane system allows people to work for a good living without evoking a pervasive atmosphere of abject terror or mania. Perhaps even more than poverty, humans fear the social exclusion, cruelty, humiliation, and unnecessary brutality which barbarians inflict on the poor.

The Ignorance of Privilege

Barbarian decision makers and rulers are often so financially privileged and have such a huge buffer of accumulated resources that they will never in their lifetimes experience the deprivation of the lower classes. Hence, barbarians often arrogantly complain about the apathy or low motivation of lower classes without being able to conceptualize the countless numbers of hardships the poor face, deal with, and often transcend, daily. Entrenched ignorance about the lived constraints of poverty is evident in all of those nations where the aristocracy has been recreated where a very small echelon (5-20%) of the population now own more than half or two thirds of all of the available wealth (For statistics google wealth inequality or income distribution for Australia, the United States, global etc.).

Whether or not the hardships, barriers, prejudice and ignominy faced daily by the poor could be withstood by the wealthy themselves for a year, a month, or a week would be an interesting social experiment. Nonetheless, barbaric elites have no compunction about increasing the burdens of the poor; adding unnecessary bureaucratic restrictions, requirements and penalties, onto lives already filled with real limits and difficulties. These needless, humanly imposed, hardships usually have no evidence base of positive social effect. Whether or not they are effective is irrelevant to barbaric rulers who are driven to impose their philosophical creed, irrespective of value or merit. Using the barbaric creed recreates its negative effects, thereby spawning spurious 'validation' of barbaric mythology.

Ironically, increasing hardship for the disadvantaged prevents social mobility and locks new generations of the poor into poverty. Recursively, this is what provides so-called 'hard evidence' of the barbaric delusion that the poor are innately inferior. Examples of artificial barbarian hardships imposed on the poor are changes in law which criminalize forms of poverty such as homelessness; the aforementioned increases in surveillance, bureaucracy and 'non-compliance' penalties; increased restrictions in welfare and resource access; and increased incarceration and social penalties for those who cannot comply with barbaric edicts or meet elite requirements.

Complex Knowledge

Privileged barbarians don't have to seriously consider the mulitiplicity and complexity of oppressive conditions in homes, communities, laws, cultural attitudes, the schooling and penal systems, which coalesce to produce the seemingly intractable problems of the poor. Elites do not have to consider the numerous hurdles faced by the disadvantaged in the completion of even routine tasks. The impact of overcrowded environments with little access to resources means people have limited power to advocate for maintenance or better conditions. Travel is one small example where low power translates into time and energy disadvantage for the poor. Parents using public transport to travel to work, to get small children to and from reliable childcare or to school, have additional transport hours, difficulties and rigid timetabling not faced by the privileged. This is without considering the difficulty of getting groceries home for a family or providing children with extracurricular activities using public rides. The differences in travel privilege can sap several hours each day from the poor. This loss of 8 to 10 'free' hours per week may create insuperable hurdles to what elites see as 'simple' tasks for career and economic advancement.

Travel is one slice of the wedge of disadvantages that the poor manage while completing paid labour. The elite do not factor in, and often are unable to conceptualise, the impact of dealing with numerous negative events, environments and hardships on a daily basis, year after year. Complex knowledge is needed to understand that it is the year in, and year out, experience of multiple hardships of poverty and inequity which finally overwhelm the formidable psychological resources of the marginalised. It is the multiplicity of disadvantages that inculcate the hard lesson that all their hard work and personal efforts will not enable them to cross the gap of inequity between themselves and the privileged. Artificial barriers imposed by simple thinking, uncaring elites are the most dispiriting for the poor. They are often keenly aware that they face many unnecessary additional hardships and barriers because of the ignorance, arrogance, and lack of care, of many people in many layers above them. Intransigence of the poor in the face of this may be functional.

In contrast, the philosophy of blaming the victim allows barbarian elites to lay the entire social and personal responsibility for the problems and hopelessness faced by those born into poverty back on the shoulders of those with the least power. Elites can then retreat into the comfortable philosophical position of blaming mass social problems on individual people making 'poor choices' or lacking motivation. This is simply untrue. Blaming individuals for their misfortune, as well as for social inequity, is simply another form of oppression inflicted by those with many resources onto those already experiencing the suffering of having few.

Taking Pause

The unnecessary cruelty and increased hardship visited on the poor during barbaric insurgency is rarely considered as a possible contributing factor to their fate. The statistics on homelessness in the United States are one example that should give us pause. Even though up to a quarter of homeless people are women with small children, attitudes of heartlessness and pitiless judgment have abounded in the last two decades towards the homeless. Simplistic platitudes about people 'helping themselves' and 'taking personal responsibility' also proliferated while the vulnerability and realities of the homeless mother, the preschool child and the grandmother were not considered. When people read statistics about the highest rates of assaults, rapes and murders being experienced by the homeless, they rarely see the faces of mothers, babies and grandmothers in their mental pictures.

Barbarism encourages the general populace to accept violence towards those who are the most unprotected, as an extra burden the poor 'should' bear along with their poverty, as part of their 'punishment' for their 'poor choices.' In reality, because of the relative powerlessness of children and their status as citizens, their fate and protection is actually the responsibility of the wider social and of those with power. If many Scandinavian countries can have little forced homelessness, despite accepting floods of refugees, then much of what we accept as inevitable is simply an ideological and cultural choice and needs to be faced as such.

The Two Faces of Responsibility: The Social and the Personal

Blaming the victim is a convenient way to reify barbarian rule and simultaneously absolve people from any social responsibility towards their fellow man. Heartlessness and cold judgmentalism towards those who are the most hopeless and the most powerless inflicts pain; compounds suffering; and rubs salt in the ever present psychic wounds of the unfortunate. The fact that barbarism and violent behaviour may also have infiltrated the environments and social norms of the poor does not absolve powerholders from the increased social responsibility that accrues with power, or from their personal heartless responses to others.

Barbaric double standard comes to the fore when elites communicate with people who live in conditions they couldn't countenance for five minutes let alone a lifetime. When facing people whose lives are inured in hardship barbarians are likely to throw out the adage that if people just had a 'more positive attitude' and were willing to 'work harder' the real social barriers and blocks they face would evaporate. This type of wishful thinking should be confined to the movie making arena. New age philosophy was never intended as a means of philosophising away real inequity, but barbarians have leapt upon the popularity of the new-age mantra of 'Be Positive' as a weapon that can be brandished over the heads of the least fortunate and used to further condemn them for their suffering. While telling people to be positive may be a slick manoeuvre to avoid tackling the real issues of deprivation, it is a cheap trick.

Barbarians go one step further than this, using the 'Be Positive' mantra to require low power people to take personal responsibility for conditions that are out of their control (ie: accept personal blame for social inequity), and, even more oppressively, to wear a mask of happiness while they bear the brunt of social inequity in their own lives. The requirement for the poor to wear a mask of happiness in the face of a deprivation is simply another sacrifice demanded from the most vulnerable. The enforced 'happy mask' ensures that the comfortable world of elites is not sullied by having to bear witness to the suffering outside the palace walls. Denial of the suffering of the poor is oppression enough, but requiring them to be happy and express a positive attitude while you savage and exploit them, particularly as low paid labour, is simply sadistic.

SUMMARY

When barbarians rule is incumbent all, or most, of these characteristics sweep through social norms in a manner akin to a fashion craze or Beatles mania. Over time, as barbaric norms become dominant in the culture, the ongoing brutalisation of vulnerable citizens and declining quality of life for the average citizen comes to be marketed as, and believed to be, inevitable. Those who envision change are labelled unrealistic, and those who advocate change are publicly chastised as fools, or even prosecuted as dangerous dissidents. A core barbarian technique is to advocate that the barbaric creed is an inevitable and immutable part of human existence, notwithstanding the significant historical record that humans have to the contrary. Barbaric dogmatism, combined with powerful media manipulation, has meant that many have come to see barbarism as inevitable. This myth needs to be challenged so that the majority can see the propaganda that is feeding elite advantage.

As a culture slides into devolution the relentless barbarian propaganda machine ensures that this slide is not seen as a direct result of the enactment of barbarian ideology, but rather as an 'unchangeable facet' of human existence. The fact that other more humane alternatives have been subjugated, or ignored, in order to enact barbaric worldview is information that gets screened from public awareness. Barbarism is a game tactic of aggression, power, domination, and exploitation. Enormous investment is made in media and social and cultural diversions that can distract the majority of the populace from focusing on the fact that barbarian insurgency has resulted in a society that is fear driven, manic, less humane and much more plastic. The fact that it also results in far less human, orgasmic, and everyday pleasure is seldom noted.

CHAPTER 2: THE EFFECTS OF POWER

One of the reasons that barbaric rise has been so endemic throughout human history is because of the metamorphic effects that power has on human beings. The following section describes the research and psychological findings in regards to these effects, why humans must be vigilant to the problem of barbarism, and why transformative cultural change is essential to rooting out barbarism from our future.

The Psychological Problem of Privilege

There is an inherent psychological risk which is created by large inequities of power. An eminent research psychologist by the name of David Kipnis found that having more power than others caused humans to develop a range of thought distortions which he called the 'Metamorphic Effects of Power.' Basically, 'Metamorphic Effects' is a term used to describe the cognitive and perceptual distortions and human tendencies which arise when people are given power over others.

Kipnis successfully demonstrated that having more power than others causes a cognitive distortion whereby people become less able to accurately perceive the extent to which successful outcomes are the result of their own effort and to which extent they are the result of others' efforts. In other words, power causes thought distortion. This tendency must be actively resisted if we wish to behave equitably and humanely. Specifically, Kipnis found that when there is a power differential, high power people misperceive and overestimate the extent to which their effort contributes to an outcome and underestimate the contribution of lower power members. His studies clearly demonstrated that having power can cause perceptual distortions that cause us to think we are doing more, and better, than we actually are. The metamorphic effects of power are illustrated beautifully in the following little ditty a comedian sang about money:

'It makes you feel happy and it makes you want to fight,
It makes you think you're the only one that's right,
It makes you think you're the best that there is...
For no good reason at all!'

The comedian then announced he would now sing a song about religion…and sang the same song; then about alcohol, and sang the same song. He was emphasizing the range of tools humans use to get delusions of individual superiority over others. Power is one of them.

We don't know why power causes thought distortion. It may occur partially as a result of the adrenaline rush which comes from power, command, and control over others. Kipnis felt that it might result from a basic calculation error power holders make when receiving flattery. Ingratiation from lower power members can be mistaken as adulation when it is just the main influence tool available to subordinates. Compliant, servile, or fawning behaviour are some of the limited range of tools the poor and the oppressed have at their disposal to try to influence the more powerful. They don't always signify admiration or respect.

A classic textbook example of elites discounting the real effects of power differential and misinterpreting the enforced compliance of subordinates is found in the black mammy stereotype perpetrated by whites during slavery and into the 20th century. In this stereotype the African American nurse was conceptualised by white 'owners' as 'naturally' preferring to raise and nurse a white baby rather than to attend to the needs of her own children. Such an assumption is a classic demonstration of the distorted thinking, and subsequent idiocy, and arrogance that power can foster.

Kipnis designed a range of ingenious studies to measure the effects of power. Through the random assignation of people into groups with high or low power he was able to demonstrate that simply having more power than others typically increases the human tendency to use domination and control. Specifically, when people are given a lot more power than others they tend to increase their coercive behaviours and to decrease their use of collaborative behaviours. In other words, simply having power makes us more likely to use it to intimidate other people to do what we want. It becomes easier for us to ignore and override the dignity of another person. Rather than working respectfully and collaboratively, we are more likely to use force. In his experiments, Kipnis discovered that simply having more power than others typically causes people to increase their attempts to manipulate and control other people of lower power.

Dominance and Control

There were other interesting things Kipnis noted in his studies of power differences. For example, when there was a wide power differential between groups, the most commonly used influence tactics used were control and coercion. In contrast, when power differences were smaller, power holders were more likely to try to influence using reason. When people were given unilateral (total) control over others, they were far less likely to give people choices and autonomy and rather, were more likely to increase surveillance and control of others.

In other words, the more control we have over others the greater will be our tendency to deprive others of their human freedom and human dignity. Kipnis surmised that this happens because power holders can decrease the autonomy of others without any consequences for themselves personally. That is, if people have more power than others and they can get away with it they are likely to be coercive and controlling. Hence the core problematic of large power differentials between people.

If, as Kipnis has found, this is a species tendency, then we must have legislation, norms and social controls in place to protect those who have little power and few resources. It is also of critical import that humans who lack compassion for those with lower power; who have only shallow understanding of the problems of human inequity; who have no commitment to resisting the tendency to use coercion; or who are philosophically committed to merciless and obdurate approaches towards others, be actively blocked from access to great power.

This tendency - whereby having access to more power causes an increase in the likelihood that we will use coercive control tactics over others - should be of grave concern to those interested in human progress and the development of civilized societies. At this point in time, preventive measures must be taken to pre-empt the likelihood of those who actively nurture the thought distortion of inherent superiority from attaining large resource quantities and decisional power.

Self-Regard

Kipnis found that having more resources causes people to try to create social and psychological distance between themselves and those of lesser power. Power often leads to the construction of a boundary around ones' sense of moral community, an imaginary impenetrable wall between the haves and have nots, a limit beyond which one's own compassion, supposedly, does not need to be extended. A human compassion 'quarantine zone' if you will.

This imaginary emotional boundary is important because it spares high power people from experiencing discomfort when instructing lower power people to do unpalatable tasks. It also spares powerholders from having to weigh the human social responsibilities which accrue with privilege. The illusion of a moral divide between high and low power people detaches power holders from any suffering that their directives inflict on others. Unfortunately, this mythology of some sort of divide also creates a level of emotional detachment which can facilitate cruel or brutal behaviours towards subordinates. Within this delusion human beings fall into one of two categories: those within the fictitious circle of 'eligibility' for human compassion and duty of care, and those outside of it.

While people may construct mental illusions about the justification and criteria used to create a moral boundary, in real-life, the delineation is usually based on wealth and power. The impenetrable wall of moral care and compassion tends to be raised most fixedly between the lives of the haves and the lives of the have nots. In other words, this illusory boundary operates not only to short circuit the need for taking one's social responsibility for all human life seriously but also; and significantly, to protect one's personal resource pile.

It is the privileged who most need a fictitious moral boundary to separate them from the suffering of others and from wider human responsibility. Unfortunately, the emotional distance created by an illusion of a limited moral community is a dangerous block to the development of healthy human societies, because it fosters the delusion that those who have less power are less skilled, less talented, less deserving, or qualitatively different, in some way to powerholders. It fosters the notion of intrinsic human difference. It also fosters the delusion that humans can be separated into different categories of compassion-worthiness, and that power holders can be morally distanced from the consequences of their behaviours for lower power members.

In a closely linked finding, Kipnis discovered that power holding also causes thought distortion whereby self regard increases in a manner unrelated to actual skill or ability. Kipnis hypothesized that having the type of power fostered by having more resources or unilateral control over the lives of others creates this inflated sense of self regard. To put it bluntly, humans are social animals, and one of the side-effects of having more power than others is that it leads us down the path of believing that we are inherently superior to those who have less than we do. Where there are wide disparities in access to resources, those humans with more resources are at grave risk of having a distorted and overinflated perception of their capacity, skill and value.

Hence, we westerners, as relatively powerful global citizens, have difficulty ratifying decisions that will cause us minimal discomfort compared to the suffering of hunger, starvation or death, caused to other global citizens if we do not. While a mere reduction of 5% in our living standards could ensure the survival of all other members of the global family, we are reluctant to accede. We have bought into the hypertrophic delusion that our luxury is more important than the survival of other humans. Of course there are fears of global barbaric exploitation, and predatory behaviours, towards nations that demonstrate compassion, but these can be addressed. We need to acknowledge that the thought distortion of inflated self valuation that occurs for the powerful is also a major factor in such decisions.

The Social Problem of Large Gaps between the Rich and the Poor

Obviously then, huge inequities in power are a social problem because the metamorphic effects of power impede the development of emotional links between people, which in turn discourages social consciousness and impedes social responsibility. Power inequity fosters circular reasoning that can justify and reinforce power differences and preserve the chimera of curtailed human moral community. Subsequently, the constructed illusion of a circumscribed moral community facilitates inhumane behaviour and impedes the development of just social systems.

There is abundant historical evidence of humans in the grip of negative metamorphic effects of power and their subsequent willingness to perpetrate atrocities on other people. Whether we are examining the massacres of American Indian people by whites; of Indigenous people in the Latin Americas; the atrocities in Sudan, the Congo, Sierra Leone or Uganda; or simply the enslavement of the poor in the mines and factories of wealthy industrialists; the metamorphic effects of power have served throughout history to buffer powerholders from the realities of their barbarism. The barbaric creed, beliefs in the inherent superiority of the powerful, and moral distancing rationalizations, have always come to the fore when there have been wide or widening gaps between rich and poor.

In the last century alone, the belief in barbaric superiority and inherent difference from other humans was endemic during the excesses of the roaring twenties when eugenics was used to explain class difference; during the fifties when intelligence testing became the vogue; and, in the nineties when bio-genetics came to the fore. So-called 'scientific' tests 'proving' barbaric superiority come into vogue during periods of large social inequity to justify the status quo, consolidate elite privilege, and justify inequitable resource access, by supposedly 'proving' that higher power people are somehow inherently superior to other people. Such philosophies are the result of people refusing to consider that wealth differences between groups of people might mainly be the result of resource inequities, which themselves might have resulted from the perpetuation of historical power differentials, and which may be little related to individual merit or effort.

It would be impossible to comprehensively list all of the historical examples where metamorphic power effects have fostered the barbaric behaviour of one group of humans towards another. In the nineteenth century Australians attempted systematic genocide towards the original inhabitants of this land and; that having failed, moved in the twentieth century to tear mixed-caste Indigenous children away from their mothers and families so that Aboriginality could be 'bred out' over time. The destruction and decimation caused by just this one example of barbarism is incalculable. On a lesser scale, but still under the barbaric creed, the recent era in Australia has seen higher education fees introduced by those who did not pay for their own education; welfare cuts made by those who have never been, and never will be, dependent on welfare; cuts to public health made by those who have access to private health care and so on. As people come to see themselves as differentiated from lower power members, not by power but by some fanciful and imagined superiority, they dumb down emotionally and are more likely to damage or exploit the lives and resources of lower power human beings.

Groupthink and Conformity: More Perils for the Pie

When you combine the psychological effects of power differentials with the human propensity for groupthink and conformity you double the recipe for human disaster and for barbaric ascendancy. Psychological studies have found that, although people – particularly westerners - prefer to think of themselves as independent free thinkers, in reality situation can have a powerful effect on how we act.

After World War II, many Westerners arrogantly underestimated the effects of situation, deprivation, conformity and groupthink and believed that the atrocities perpetrated by Fascists were national and not human possibilities. Two separate psychological studies discredited this notion and graphically demonstrated some of the human influences contributing to barbaric behaviours such as genocide. The first was a series of obedience studies conducted by Stanley Milgram at Yale University in 1961 and 1962. Milgram informed participants that he had designed an experiment about learning. In his experiment, 'Scientists' in lab coats asked participants (ordinary citizens who were randomly selected from the community), to administer painful electric shocks to other people when they made 'errors' in learning. Milgram hypothesised that most average citizens would resist this command and that people would refuse to continue once they heard screams from 'learners' (paid actors). As the so called 'learning errors' continued participants were asked to increase the voltage, and hence the pain, they were administering to 'learners.'

Milgram hypothesised that people would refuse to shock other people; would become more resistant when asked to increase the voltage; and that none of the participants would be prepared to administer the maximum shock voltage of 450 volts. Milgram clearly labelled the level of 450 volts dangerous and possibly lethal. Actors hired to pretend to be the unfortunate learners, screamed with pain when the 'punishment' was administered and begged for mercy and release. Citizens involved in administering the 'shocks' thought that both the voltage and subsequent screams of pain were real.

To Milgram's horror a full 65% of the ordinary citizens who took part in the study were willing to administer potentially lethal shocks when asked to do so. While some people questioned the so-called experts (those in lab coats) they were prepared to continue when directed confidently by an authority. This experiment made it perfectly obvious to what extent blind conformity to authority (power over) is a human risk factor in the perpetration of human atrocities.

The second study was conducted by Phillip Zimbardo at Stanford University in 1971. Zimbardo designed an experiment in which students were randomly assigned to the roles of prison guard or inmate and asked to live in a makeshift prison which was constructed in a campus dormitory. Even though the students knew this was an experiment; that they were being paid for participation and that they were physically safe; conditions quickly deteriorated to become starkly similar in tone and content to the real-life examples of Auschwitz and other prison settings. The sense of shared moral community between prisoner and guard (student peers) disappeared almost immediately upon assignation of roles. The subsequent cruel and brutal behaviour of the student 'guards' dramatically illustrated the human tendency to revert to barbaric and coercive behaviours when given unilateral control over others. These 'guard' behaviours, combined with the deteriorating mental health of the student 'prisoners' meant the experiment had to be halted after days.

Both of these experiments demonstrate not only the power of conformity; but also the danger of having barbaric cultural norms. They demonstrate that the human tendencies towards Groupthink and blind conformity to authority are catastrophic when combined with the illusion of limited moral community and acceptance of the barbaric creed. It is obvious that barbarism is a human tendency which can be resisted. Unfortunately, the profit making raison d'etre for modern societies which fosters exploitation and coercion as social practice, has supported barbaric brutality rather than encouraging resistance.

Increased Risk

In his book on technology and power Kipnis warned that increasing advanced technology was dangerous to species survival until we developed the intrapsychic, social, legal, and cultural, mechanisms which could adequately address this species issue of the metamorphic effects of power. He accurately foresaw that, as technology increased, the capacity for powerholders to have more control over; and therefore to increase the exploitation of, many people was a huge risk. The past two decades have validated his concerns. As individuals gained access to technology which increased their personal power to new levels, havoc was wrought on social, cultural and individual resources. Unfortunately, access to technological power was given without concomitant requirement for social accountability and without necessary protective checks and balances.

As a result, we now have graphic evidence of the amount and type of human and environmental damage that can be sustained, even in a relatively short period of time, when barbarism is married with the power of advanced technology. In the workplace we moved from the limited surveillance capacity done by human supervisors to mechanised surveillance of every aspect of employee behaviour from the number of typing movements performed per minute for the employer to the number of minutes 'wasted' to use the bathroom. Big Brother has not been used for the benefit of the least powerful or to enhance employee welfare.

From these and other similar experiences of advanced technology, whether it is the example of increased elite control over media, over labour or over the capacity to exploit the natural environment we see the following formula in effect:

Aggression + Advanced Technology + Power = Increased Control and Coercion

This is the perfect formula for human, social and ecological damage.

The realm of media manipulation is one small domain in which the impact of the increased power of technology is clearly demonstrated. The proliferation of technology in the past two decades, with a virtual explosion in the number and type of mobile communication devices which people keep on their person at all times; has increased access to, and capacity for control over, what individual people regularly think about. The individual sphere of private thought is now constantly deluged by influence mediums, many with the sole aim of increasing elite profit through manipulation of individual self perception. The private social realms of everyday life can now be penetrated constantly by images of what elites are buying, wearing and doing, along with messages about the imperative to self-monitor and mold ones' own behaviour similarly. This is a Molotov cocktail for social control. Beyond the problematic of increasing social conformity to superficial images, the distraction of peoples' consciousness and attention away from their own lives, and creative consciousness, damages species evolutionary capacity.

The possibilities for influencing people's thoughts and emotions and actions are now in hourly, minute-by-minute and even second-by-second bytes. Siphoning off private thinking time into the superficial and the mundane is disastrous for the species' intelligence and problem solving capacities. Great creative geniuses such as Einstein, Mozart and Emerson all attested that fostering human creativity and lateral thought processes required substantial periods of time without external intrusion. Humans' last bastion of uncolonized space; the space of uninterrupted thought, has been squandered for ready cash. Entrepreneurs, with or without social conscience, have leapt upon the gravy train of conditioning by repetitively interrupting human muse to develop ingrained habits which can be manipulated for financial profit.

Increase in technology has not been used to market the type of changes which would advance human rights or create pro-social change. It has primarily been used to foster obsession with; and willingness to conform to; increasingly narrow images of social acceptability. With few alternatives offered, individuals have been subjected to a flood of marketing to shape their sense of self value by brand, and by the perception consumerism is the sole raison d'etre' for human existence.

The constant bombardment of youth consciousness makes them more vulnerable to the marketing of products, behaviours and choices that serve the market. Concurrently, and with greater harm, this bombardment of attention, draws the focus and energy of young people away from their own lives and diminishes their sense of the value of their own life, their own thoughts and contributions, as well as eroding their capacity to creatively mold the future. From this vantage point, the resurgence of 50s style girly-culture modelled by Brittney Spears and Paris Hilton types, takes on a more sinister tone. The risk is that these 'pre-molded' and overly controlled generations will simply reproduce the lifestyle and tastes of the generation before them, forfeiting their capacity to make their own mark, and placing humankind in a perpetual stasis of twentieth century thought.

Subsequently, we see those most vulnerable to media manipulation, the very young; emerging as a generation who may accumulate crippling consumer debt before they even enter adulthood. In effect, not only their adolescence, but often their education and early adult life, have been consumed by market peddling that will only benefit and fortify the

46

resources of their parents' generation, while condemning their generation to decades of repetitious labour and penury. By the time a young person realizes this, they are often so far into debt that many years of their life are already indentured to the low pay labour market. More importantly, they may then be condemned to poverty for life because their own career and educational development has been forfeited to early consumer debt.

While barbarians will quickly revert to the elite high ground of 'responsibility for individual choice' in the face of an epidemic of Gen Y debt; the flooding of youth consciousness with products; in an era where consumerism is equated with maturity and status, is exploitative behaviour. The fact that the young were not flooded with a similar level of messages giving alternative ways of obtaining power and legitimacy and explaining possible future consequences of purchases is a failure of the older generation's duty of care to the next generation. It is mainly the baby boomers who have profited from this period of market barbarism. Exploitation of the young and vulnerable is an acceptable tenet within the barbaric creed.

Consequences

In the 21st Century the reality of resource limits has come to the fore. It is critical that we use our resources to prepare and deal with real threats, not imagined ones. We need some new habits, some new norms, and new ways of being, to transform our living and conceptualisation of life options. Barbarism is a philosophical system which caters only for the elite and the privileged; not for all human beings nor for all phases across a single lifespan. The fragmented ideology of the 'survival of the fittest' is not an adequate system to enable species development or even survival. Barbarism is not able to sustain the living world and the living systems in which humans are able to live. It certainly is not capable of developing systems in which people can flourish and where human potential can be nurtured.

The findings on power, conformity and obedience demonstrate how easy it is to slide into barbarism. We all behave barbarically at times but it is the rabid and fervent belief in; and acceptance of; barbaric behaviour that has created the mass habits and norms of barbarism that are crippling advancement in the 21st century. Kipnis' work demonstrated that the closer humans are to a power base the higher the risk that barbarian beliefs serve their self-interest and the more humans want to rationalize barbaric aggression against other, less powerful others.

Achieving dominance cannot be a main aim of human interaction because aggressive dominance damages human relationships – the webs within which human passion and capacity are cradled and nurtured to life. Individual lives matter. Humans are a social species and the quality and type of our interactions feeds our capacity for progress.

The extensive harm rendered to individual lives, and to individuals' intimate and community relationships in the recent barbarian insurgency has had catastrophic cultural and global consequences. Cultural interpenetration by market marauders and, predominantly western but also eastern, pirates, has led to increased global acceptance of aggression. In turn this acceptance has encouraged pillaging and exploitative acts which have decimated indigenous and non-homogenized cultural life. As a consequence, the prima materia of species life – caring for others and social norms of pro-social conduct – has been overrun by barbarian codes of greed and competitive dominance.

It is when the barbarian creed is fervently believed and rabidly proselytised throughout the globe, as it has been in the recent era that it pillages cultures, dehumanizes norms, and decimates human rights. We then enter a period of human devolution and species' survival risk. Because barbarism is circular and self-reinforcing and does not allow feedback from the systems in which it is interacting, or exploiting, damage can occur without check and great violence can be done.

Penetration of the Intimate: The Realm of Human Relationship

The marketplace is only one domain which was raided by barbarians in search of plunder. Barbaric incursion into the sphere of the human relational world has wrought incalculable decimation and suffering. Rapacious pillaging of peoples' intimate, relational and cultural lives has led untold numbers of people to depression, anxiety, social isolation and alienation. By impaling human relational life on the narrow stake of profiteering, barbarism has wrought havoc on relationships, families, communities and cultures.

The infiltration of the intimate spheres of couple, family and friendship relationships with barbaric norms of hostility, greed, interpersonal force and manipulation has damaged much of the web of care which we have traditionally taken for granted. This invisible web, spun by countless acts of kindness and human compassion, is the foundation of human evolutionary development. It is this web of behaviours that keeps the majority of people in a society psychologically intact and healthy and that enables the society to function. When people, and especially vulnerable people such as those in the lower socio-economic strata of a society (the poor), are exposed daily and regularly to acts of hostility, aggression and injustice, the very fabric of society becomes eroded.

Because the poor have few material resources and live in adverse material conditions, the web which is woven by acts of care between, among, and towards, them is essential to sustaining their lives. The imposition of additional external burdens destroys the small patch from which the poor eke strands of time and energy to weave home and family life. When only work life remains sustainable for the poor we have, in effect, reconstituted slavery.

This is of no consequence to profiteers. Large corporations benefit from being able to force the poor to work on weekends and in shift work without penalty rates, but the cost to vulnerable children and families from the disruption this type of labour causes to relational life may be more than their small system of care can sustain. The resultant costs, particularly for children, can be irreparable in the long term. Violation of interpersonal norms of care, through the dual mechanisms firstly, of barbaric promotion of exploitative behaviour, and secondly; of promoting and advocating abandonment, and detachment towards other human beings, has wrought as much havoc on the unseen landscape of the psyche as it has created visible damage in the ecological world.

The increased pressure on individuals, couples, families and communities, generated by a greedy, insatiable corporate world has led to increased stress and suffering at the level of the average person's daily emotional life. Ballooning corporate profits in the past two decades were directly fed by the private resources of individuals' lives, families, children, health, happiness, and personal time and energy. Divorce, violence and suffering, catalysed by lowered living and work standards are rarely attributed to those same standards – to unrecompensed weekend and overtime work; to inhumane work lives. Glutted barbaric focus on production, consumption, and overwork, has drained our interpersonal, psychological and emotional systems of essential nutrients.

It is irrelevant whether these acts are perpetrated by individuals, corporations or government policies; it is the number and repetitious nature of the daily stresses which are heaped upon individuals that can deplete and overwhelm their life energy and coping capacities. Quality, complex human relationships, mediated through psychological, emotional and social nurturing; determine much of the species capacity for beneficial progress. The realms of the psyche and emotional wellbeing are core to human development. Channelling such a vast proportion of the available human life resources into the neoliberal dam of 'profit uber alles' has all but exhausted the small resource ponds left for human relationships, nurturing, care and genius. Directing the majority of human life resources into profiteering, mindless production, and needless consumption; has depleted the resource pond of complex human capacity and the intangibles that foster human species advancement. In particular, barbaric profiteering and exploitation of the labour market in the past two decades removed critical resources from the daily lives of children that were vital to their healthy, normal development.

Pillaging the Future
The future of any society rests in its children and more specifically in its treatment of its children. Barbaric pillaging has caused enormous suffering for children and created norms and structures that will continue to cause suffering for the forseeable future. Whereas Indigenous groups encouraged adults to assume providership, guardianship, and social responsibility, for seven generations to follow their own, the emotional malnutrition spawned by barbaric greed may deprive a similar number of future generations of essential nutrients unless we act decisively.

In the so called 'economic boom' of the Howard and Bush era, corporate profit, coming from cheap labour and work for welfare laws fattened itself on the resources critical to the mental health and wellbeing of children – a voiceless, voteless population who could not resist. The loss of appropriate care for children in the home through forcing their parent or parents into the low pay labour market or 'welfare-to-work' schemes can literally result in brain and emotional damage for poor children in the vulnerable first five years of their lives. This will affect their lifelong capacity as adults and all of their experiences. While the brain capacities

50

are obviously inestimably precious for species' development, more importantly, such damage hurts the smallest, most vulnerable members of our societies.

Care of the next generation is one of the marks of any species that is going to survive.

Compassionate humans respond to misery and distress in small children by providing soothing, care and protection. Compassion and care are hallmarks of healthy relationship and, as humans are social creatures, relational capacity is critical to our advancement as a species. In contrast, the depths of deprivation fostered by barbaric profiteering and calloused disregard of those too powerless to 'resist' (including children) has created incalculable damage which will show itself in the decades to come and will produce social cost which everyone, not primarily the wealthy, will bear. If we could visually witness the scarring perpetrated on the brains of poor children during this 'economic boom' we would recoil in horror. It is this index, not the Dow, the ASX or the NYSE, that should be monitored to gauge progress. Spiralling increases in school failure, employment difficulty, psychopathology, depression, drug and alcohol abuse and criminal statistics will eventually make the invisible damage rendered to young children during this era visible. By then the time lapse will serve to perpetrate barbaric mythology that all personal privilege is deserved profit and that profiteers bear no personal responsibility for the deluge of problems in the public realm.

Aggression as Damaged Interpersonal Capacity

The willingness to use aggression against another person is a sign of damaged interpersonal capacity. It is also a sign of some level of adherence to, and belief in, barbaric philosophy. Humans use aggression to try to force others to do what they want, or to control the behaviours and choices of others through intimidation. This definition of aggression needs to be clearly distinguished from the similar level of force which must be used by humans who are trying to block an aggressive attack initiated against them. Resistance to barbaric incursion is not a barbaric act, even though it may be forceful. In contrast, the act of initiating hostilities towards another is always barbaric.

In this era, even those who are non-barbaric must deal with aggression because of the interpenetration of barbaric behaviour into not only the spheres of work life but also into social and intimate relational life. Cases of unprovoked acts of aggression against non-barbaric adherents and communities have become so common that they have come to be accepted as 'normal.' Here again, 'normal' represents behaviours that have become socially prevalent, not those that are socially desirable.

Because barbaric disciples interpret submission as invitation to further pillaging; individuals, families and communities have to be prepared to stand firm against barbaric attack. Such resistance often consumes vast quantities of individuals' personal, limited resource pile, particularly when they stand against a powerful corporation or someone with much greater power. Those without resource power cannot resist attack and are easily overrun. Those who have a few resources may be able to resist the first attack but such resistance may leave them with depleted survival resources and none to resist a second assault. Individuals should not be forced by corporate aggression to use their personal resources in resistance against power brokers with massive resource piles. An uneven fight is, of course, a barbaric favourite, but such sport unfairly depletes the personal lives of the less powerful.

Response to a barbaric attack requires actions and a level of willingness and commitment to the protection of one's self, family, and assets, that is at an equal level to the aggression initiated. This is why the widespread lack of clarity about barbarism, fostered and supported by mass marketing, has been so dangerous. The illusion created by marketing was of a false sense of security which eroded peoples' clarity and therefore their individual and collective preparation and capacity to resist barbaric incursion into their personal and social resources.

Initiating hostilities, being aggressive towards those who resist force; stealing the resources of vulnerable others; intimidating and being brutal to others; are all anti-social behaviours that do not advance the species and which retard human development. They deplete and pillage the social and human resources that should be devoted to advancing human progress. Whether the aggression is in the form of a hostile corporate takeover; gang bullies in the schoolyard, the pub or the boardroom; aggressive 'Work for Welfare' or Industrial Relations laws; social practices of hazing freshmen; domestic or physical violence - all aggressive behaviour fosters barbaric penetration of the culture. In fact, the disproportionate amounts of energy that individuals, families and communities have had to use in recent times to resist ongoing barbaric attempts to gain control over and to hoard all available resources, has placed human survival at risk. The precious and limited human time and energy that should be devoted to meeting the care needs of children; to mending the damage that has been sustained in the relational world; and to seriously dealing with the serious human sustainability issues we face, has all too often been siphoned off into cheap production labour

If we are to halt the planetary and social destructions which are the hallmark of the threats we face in the 21st century, then the dominance of barbaric philosophy must be challenged, defiantly resisted and overturned. We must become recalcitrant. It is the premise of this text that clearer identification of, and resistance to, barbarism at every level; including that of our own consciousness, of our intimate relationships, interpersonal lives, our clubs, groups, societies and nations; is central to the transformation of human civilization. Barbarism is a deeply relational issue which has been rapidly eroding the global social fabric and human quality of life. Humans now face profound social, environmental and economic consequences which must be addressed. When we understand that barbarism is a dangerous philosophy which poses real threat to human survival, and that its penetration into civilized life can be resisted, we can more marshal our resources for effective response.

Further Consideration

The following sections are an examination of the mechanisms, effect and consequences of barbarism, and its infiltration into our systems, cultural assumptions, and norms, in relation to the domains of: The physical environment, the built environment, worklife, family life, intimate relationships, child development, internal intrapsychic life, personal and cultural quality of life. These are all domains which have been invaded and which must be reclaimed if the 21st Century is to be a period of human transformation. It moves beyond generalities to specifics of how barbarism is enacted in human life and the direct consequences of this enactment. It begins with an examination of the damage perpetrated on the physical world but is focused greatly on examination of the intrapsychic realm and childhood. It is the branding of fledgling humans with the hot iron of barbarism that curdles our species' future.

SECTION II

IDENTIFYING BARBARIC INCURSION

Generalities to Specifics: From Everywhere to Somewhere

CHAPTER 3: THE ENVIRONMENT

The Environment and Barbaric Manoeuvres

In 1962 a well-published biologist, Rachael Carson, released 'Silent Spring,' a record of scientific findings in which she meticulously detailed the environmental destruction being wrought by industrial production and the unchecked use of pesticides. In this text she presented evidence that what was being done to the environment in the name of 'industry, progress and profit' was destructive – not just at the major level of ugliness and destroying quality of life for local people – but also at the level of global ecology and of threatening the long-term viability of human life on earth.

Ms. Carson drew from reliable biological findings in the four and a half years she spent writing the text. In spite of this, upon its release she was publicly ridiculed by scientists and industry magnates as a 'fruitcake' – a kind of modern day Nostradamus – and her ideas as being as ludicrous as the wild-eyed ravings of a mad-woman. The chemical industry used a spokesman, Dr. Robert White-Stevens, to discredit her work:

> 'The major claims of Miss Rachel Carson's book, 'Silent Spring,' are gross distortions of the actual facts, completely unsupported by scientific, experimental evidence, and general practical experience in the field.'

Many scientists and powerful people asserted that her writing was not grounded in either scientific fact or plausibility. Government officials and industry tycoons alike leapt on the tar wagon, scorning her findings and labelling her a modern Carrie Nation. Ms. Nation was a mentally unbalanced member of the temperance movement, who would enter saloons with an axe and destroy the bar, claiming to have visions from

God and to be acting on the basis of hearing God's voice. Such a derogatory comparison was clearly to discredit Ms. Carson and to cause the public to doubt her mental faculties. Unfortunately, then, as now, cultural conditioning is such that the public often has difficulty differentiating fact from a smear campaign which meant that the general populace were swayed by the offensive against her.

Today, Rachel Carson's book is recognized as a seminal work in environmental health and is used by experts around the globe. She is considered a founder of the modern environmental movement. 'Silent Spring' is now acknowledged as an accurate and scientific observation of the damage to the environment caused by unchecked industry and development. If, as was happening routinely in the 50s, a community was now to be sprayed with DDT, they would be up in arms because, thanks to Ms. Carson, they now have ready access to the facts of DDT's toxicity. Ms. Carson died the following year of breast cancer. With the impact of stress on the immune system and cancer growth one wonders about the smear campaign's effect on her longevity.

Unfortunately, the assertions of industrialists that Ms. Carson's claims were absurd, and the subsequent media tarring of her professionalism, diluted the public impact of her message, effectively defusing the maelstrom of urgency that her facts were arousing. Further disinformation and dissemination of deceit by industry racketeers effectively slowed industry regulation and the development of the environmental protection movement. The dilution of public urgency, fed by mendacious slander of Ms. Carson and purposeful dissemination of falsehood; meant that a generation and a half passed where limited progress was made on the environmental front. Consequently the damage being wrought by industry, environmental destruction and varieties of pollution, is still on a scale that threatens human viability.

While industry manipulation can be understood on the basis of self-interest we might ask why Ms. Carson's scientifically sound work was also lampooned by scientists and government officials. At the time of their attacks, the people who claimed that Ms. Carson was unqualified (argumentum ad hominem) and that her assertions were far fetched seemed to be people of authority and integrity, or people carrying the supposed objectivity of science. In hindsight it is easy to see that the people who ridiculed and lambasted Ms. Carson either had an agenda of their own personal profit and little sense of their social responsibility as human beings, (responsibility extending beyond self-interest to include the wellbeing of other members of the human race) or, were vastly ignorant. Using the definitions of this text we can see that these attackers were adherents to many tenets of the barbaric creed: Dependence on the destruction of life systems for profit, rigid filtering of information, low complexity planning, aggressive competitive dominance and pillaging the resources of the future.

Forward Thinking and Delay Tactics

In hindsight we realize the past fifty years of delay tactics were critical ones for our species to have made massive reductions in industrial and modern pollution. They were decades in which developed nations needed to alter core aspects of the modus operandi of industrialization and to assist developing nations towards sustainable growth. This was a period of husbandry, where changed practices in developed nations and effective support of the large populations in developing nations, was essential to human viability. The global target needed to be sustainable human progress, with a moratorium on any activity that did not improve species viability. Such an imperative; as the basis for decision making within developed and developing nations, could have halted the inexorable momentum of global warming. Instead, corporate piracy and multinational aggression and exploitation reached unprecedented levels during this period; effectively branding developing nations with the notion that barbarism is synonymous with development. The delay to appropriate regulatory responses has already cost many human lives and, unless we move with more commitment than we have to date, may still cost human survival on earth.

The delay tactics utilized by profiteers and those who hold to the barbaric creed is no small thing. Ms. Carson's visionary book was one of the first times the general public was given access to information about the long term unsustainability of our style of industrialization. The impact of scientists, politicians and industry tycoons ridiculing her work was to create confusion; defuse the sense of urgency that her findings suggested, and to prevent the effective mobilization of the public. Once the media machine kicked in, the resultant public confusion and false sense of security generated by those who discredited Ms. Carson allowed almost another half century of poorly regulated pollution and environmental damage.

Barbaric tactical combinations of ridiculing the truth, confusing the public and downplaying real threat, defuse public urgency which delays the public momentum that pushes critical legislation for monitoring and the implementation of more stringent pollution limits.

There has been almost an additional half century where corporate bodies and wealthy industrialists have evaded both financial costs and social responsibility for environmental damage created by the same production from which they have drawn considerable personal wealth. Industrialists and entrepreneurs should reap not only personal profit from production but also a fair bill for all public resources utilized and any harm caused to public supplies. While this would render some avenues of self-interest no longer economically lucrative it would effectively halt plundering of public resources simply for the making of personal wealth.

In hindsight, the tactic of a smear campaign and spreading misinformation can be clearly seen as subterfuge for protecting the profits and financial gain of an elite few. These individuals clearly believed in Barbaric Creed tenets II & III: Inherent barbaric superiority and survival of the fittest. Pillaging the environment is inevitably rationalized using the ideas of 'democratic freedom' and 'first in, first served,' as though the natural world was a salad bar or a party prize. Such a claim relies on the person's belief in, and adherence to, Barbaric Creed tenets: II, III. IX & X.

The smear campaign against Rachel Carson gave industry magnates additional decades to loot the physical world and to build individual personal wealth without accruing any of the associated costs of using, ransacking or despoiling the physical environment in which all humanity must now live. The smear campaign against Carson is therefore a case of racketeering and obstruction of justice for the purpose of financial gain.

Making money is not in and of itself problematic. It is when making money happens on the basis of looting, pilfering, stripping or sacking public resources for personal gain and without appropriate social reparation that it becomes racketeering. Any money making system whose viability depends on pillaging and damaging the life systems in which it is embedded and from which it draws the capacity to operate is inherently unsustainable and untenable. Any system that strains and tears the global social and ecological fabric of the human race simply for the financial profit of a few species members is unviable. Irrespective of the power of the entrepreneur, unsustainable environmental practices must be illegal. In the case of destroying the environment the analogy of defecating in one's own bath water becomes inadequate and the analogy of a bird setting fire to its own feathers becomes more appropriate.

Rachel Carson was labelled an 'alarmist' by many in the chemical industry yet her 'alarm' could have woken us a generation earlier and helped us avoid some of the massive environmental challenges we now face. The confusion generated by the smear campaign against Ms. Carson delayed the formation of popular support for the generation of viable, sustainable alternatives and enabled environmental racketeering for at least four more decades. Ms. Carson was in possession of clear scientific fact which did not, until recent times, escape the media vetting of those with vested interests. For example in the months before her death she did a series for CBS entitled, 'The Silent Spring' and stated,

> 'Water, which is probably our most important natural resource, is now used and re-used with incredible recklessness......Now, I truly believe, that we in this generation, must come to terms with nature, and I think we're challenged as mankind has never been challenged before to prove our maturity and our mastery, not of nature, but of ourselves.'

While her position on water was ridiculed in the 60s, its accuracy seems almost prescient with the data we have available 50 years later. In fact she was not using prescience but knowledge she gathered from data that was readily available in the 1950s! How much more data is available today and how much of it is lampooned and dismissed by industry magnates? We need to be smart enough to understand that the manipulation of media to foster public ignorance and inaction is a ploy used by those who believe steadfastly in the barbaric code. We need to be rooted strongly enough in sane principles to not be suckered.

Facing Propaganda: Separating Fact from Fiction

Those who attempt to illuminate the role of human predatory, or uncaring, decisions in the creation of many human problems often find themselves labelled as dangerous by corporate barbarians. Business magnates, with vast marketing and media resources at their disposal, have no compunction (and face little legislative threat) when they use those resources to publicize whatever messages serve the interests of their personal profit (or of profiteering). Researchers and others who illuminate the realities of the harm that result from greedy, profit-based, or aggressive human choices may find, similar to Rachel Carson, themselves publicly labelled as 'destructive pessimists,' and worse.

In fact, when people gather facts in order to determine the nature and size of a problem they are neither pessimistic nor optimistic to do so, just following an essential first step. If you are an ostrich, having your head in the sand does not protect your backside from hyenas. When humans want to respond effectively to a problem they must first accurately identify the nature and the size of the challenge; plan effectively and then draw upon skills, resources and human capacity to choose.

The general population is the critical force in maintaining current culture and norms. Adherents to the barbaric code are well aware of this. The accumulation of daily decisions made by the general populace is vital to sustaining the status quo. An uneducated public fed a constant stream of propaganda will make and support choices directed by that propaganda. On a daily basis these decisions and behaviours actively construct and maintain economies and societies. What the public are being fed is of central significance to the seeming intransigence of our social problems and to the funnelling of human energy into channels that benefit only a few.

Feeding the public misinformation, falsehoods and mendacious slander is considered acceptable within the barbaric code because Barbaric Tenet VI purports that: 'Aggressive and underhanded tactics are acceptable if they increase individual barbaric profit and competitive advantage'. For example, it is common in the modern world for popular media to anthropomorphize the market. When a citizenry is fed daily media rhetoric such as: 'The indexes had spent much of 2010 searching for direction;' 'Global markets are getting more and more mature;' 'Markets around the world are looking to us and saying...' (Googled 'Economy' 3/3/10) then people begin to forget that a 'market' is a human construction which cannot exist without ongoing human input, support, decisions and energy. Markets cannot search, mature or 'look' – these are human activities. Such language dulls public awareness of the choices being made by specific people who drive the effects (negative and positive) the general population then experience in their personal lives. There is no magic involved. Constant verbal allusions to the market as a living 'body' work like voodoo to create the illusion of a cognizant creature. This has a similar effect to voodoo because the public begins to respond to the market 'entity' with fear and obeisance.

It is interesting to note similar tactics used by Barbaric insurgents wanting to control public energy during the Inquisitions. The 1578 handbook for inquisitors spelled out the purpose of inquisitorial penalties, a purpose strikingly similar to the purpose of modern day smear campaigns and the intimidation of the public in the domain of money making and profiteering,

> '... for punishment does not take place primarily and per se for the correction and good of the person punished, but for the public good in order that others may become terrified and weaned away from the evils they would commit.' Directorium Inquisitorum, edition of 1578, Book 3, page 137, column 1. Online in the Cornell University Witchcraft Collection. Retrieved: 2008-05-16.

The word 'evil' was then, as it is now, a subjective term often used simply to frighten and alarm. Thus, there is distinct benefit for racketeers to be gained from peddling the mythology that the market is a living thing. When newsreaders talk about the 'heart' of the economy and the 'health' of the economy and so forth such language obfuscates the reality that there are people conditioned to feed the 'health' of the market through labour on a daily basis (often through sacrifice of their own wellbeing) and fewer people who benefit in an unequal way from this stream of unquestioning human energy and focus. Developing an elite populace in this manner leads to concentration of decision making power which erodes benefits for all and the survival prospects of a democracy.

Propaganda which feeds the misperception of the market as a live decision making entity encourages people to continue to invest their hopes and energy into an inanimate construction without having them agitate for concomitant influence over its design and outcomes. We are encouraged to 'feed' market energy before our children and our own lives. Without the committed energy of a public trained to anxiously and obsessively 'feed the market' the inanimate economic system of a culture is affected because economics relies on the conformity of many. Economics are simply human decisions made about money.

It is critical to note that democracy is not the central tenet of the 21st century market system. Rather; racketeering, exploitation, profiteering, and adherence to all tenets of the barbaric creed, currently serve as its spinal column and major muscular system. Democracy is increasingly limited in naïve western industrialized cultures where the human propensities for greed, arrogance and aggression have not been fully factored into legal and governmental processes. Presenting the market as a living, autonomous, decision making entity distracts public focus from the realities of how 'market' decisions occur. Decisions are not made by ephemeral market, economic or policy 'forces' but by human people. If decisions are made by those who believe the barbaric creed, then the decisions will be made on the basis of limited self-interest. Capitalist market economies have, due to lack of adequate legislative protection, been largely directed by elite barbarians and therefore they serve the self-interest of this group more than that of the general population. On the positive side, this means that much more sustainable societies, work lives, and environmental effects, are possible within capitalist market economies than we are currently experiencing.

Because the economy is a humanly constructed, inanimate system, not a living thing, it has neither ears nor eyes to perceive neither human suffering nor the heart to respond. Therefore using the 'economy' or 'economic growth' as a default decision maker for a society is like flying in a plane without an automatic pilot and then blithely leaving the helm to go watch a movie. The delusion of safety will not avoid the inevitable crash. Similarly, pretending the economy is anything other than a system we have constructed and then relying on it for 'direction' is a reckless position which leads to practices which are unsustainable, harmful, or destructive for human beings. Humans need to consciously and fully weigh the costs of any constructed system and to actively choose to support continuance in its current form or to reshape.

On the positive side this means that social change may be much easier than we have been led to believe. Humans have built the current system and therefore it can be reshaped in ways to better serve the human race.

Balanced Realism Enables Effective Response.

Personalized attacks of social critics, such as those levelled at Rachel Carson, detract public focus from the reality that because much human suffering is man-made it is therefore unnecessary and preventable. Without clear understanding, alternative possibilities are neither considered nor acted upon and those who profit from dominance and from oppressive ways of interacting with other human beings remain unchallenged. The purpose of the critics is achieved when the status-quo is re-asserted as immutable and the critical mass is lulled back into somnambulance.

Propaganda is a primary and effective tool in the barbarian's aggressive arsenal. It is deployed whenever barbaric self interest is felt to be threatened. Distracting from a focus on the costs of the current system supports the delusion that positive, humanitarian societies are unattainable. When the public has been conditioned to avoid looking at the costs of current systems then significant change becomes unlikely. Therefore, whenever the current system exhibits flaws or breaks down, as in the sub-prime crisis, the 2009 recession or the woeful government response to Hurricane Katrina hitting New Orleans, the public is sent back to sleep with the lullaby that the current systemic problems do not come from human decisions but from inexorable 'natural' market forces that are as unpredictable 'as a hurricane'. When there is a crisis which highlights or exposes flaws in the current system a confused public is, in essence, told to look the other way if they value human wellbeing.

The public is not encouraged to examine the costs of current decisions, to evaluate all available alternatives, and create new ones themselves. The fact that our current systems have been designed with heavy weighting to reward aggression and profiteering is quickly re-concealed. Human generative activity is thereby disembowelled before its first movement.

Propaganda Two: Naïve change?

Researchers and others who critique exploitative and aggressive corporate, political and social behaviours are often belittled as being 'naïve' and lacking in understanding about the complexities of 21st century reality and the 'difficulties' of achieving significant human change. Such an attack implies that it is more constructive to pretend that what we have now is based on the best of human intentions rather than face the real consequences of current social structures, and global decisions, based primarily on ethics of aggression, self-interest and greed. Attacking any social evaluation of current decision making processes implies that good decision making can occur without full understanding of the range of choices available. Attacking the critic (argumentum ad hominum) focuses the public fearfully on personal costs of questioning the status quo and away from the lived consequences; across the population, of adherence and conformity to the barbaric creed.

The new age movement has re-focussed western human societies on positive thinking as foundational for achieving change. While this philosophy has usefulness, the popularity and familiarity of new age rhetoric has given dominant power-holders a new tool to silence those who dare speak about the critical necessity of significant social change. Those who attempt to highlight the suffering and real impacts of current systems for the lived experiences of vulnerable people are dismissed with the platitude, 'You are just being negative – focus on the positive.' Those who agitate for change and who talk about the very human, individual profit motives behind decisions which cause much human suffering, may find themselves vilified for 'creating negativity' rather than recognized for exposing it. Researchers may have their findings dismissed because they do not focus on the positive, the ethical and the caring human acts which are also an integral part of human societies.

However, if we wish to create change we need to understand that there are humans behind the destructive corporate, personal and policy choices which cause much so-called 'intractable' human suffering and that this means there are other possible human choices. When the messenger highlighting the costs of current choices is vilified the reality that there are other viable choices which could have been made is obscured.

There is a grain of truth in the need for optimism when tackling the problems of human social systems. It is when and how optimism is utilized that is the issue. The general population is affected by the widely disseminated propaganda that current human difficulties are inevitable and insuperable. Such propaganda breeds fear and reluctance to acknowledge the unworkable and negative aspects of current systems. Optimism and a strong sense of hope are required if we are not to be overwhelmed by despair when we come to understand the consequences of our current decisions and the real effects; sometimes horrific, on the lives of the vulnerable and those who are the most powerless and voiceless in the human race.

Serious Matters

A third and final point relates to the obfuscation which occurs when issues are simplistically categorized into negative or positive rather than considered complexly as trivial or weighty human matters. Confusion occurs when the issue of priorities is confounded with that of optimism. The issue of priorities is the one that is most apposite to 21st century progress. We live in a historical period where humans have been 'dumbed down' by such a flood of media emphasizing the trivial that many humans have great difficulty identifying which issues are truly important and needful of attention. When we don't know how to discriminate between the urgent and the trivial we can prioritize the unimportant and fritter our energy and choices away.

Adherence to the barbaric creed with its emphasis on nugatory achievements such as superiority, dominance or individual fame; has led to the development of superficial societies where we reflexively shy away from issues requiring mature, adult attention. When the brand of toothpaste we use is accorded more media time than halting global warming we are firmly in the realm of the Mad Hatter. We are fed the falsehood that human difficulties are insuperable when the issue is actually wastage of human energy. Human focus and attention make the critical difference. In reality, our human capacities are such that we are well able to resolve those problems to which we give our focussed attention, adult consideration, resources and combined effort.

Barbarism is an immature, unfledged philosophy which neither draws upon our most evolved capacities nor positions our species for advancement. The Barbaric Creed is constructed on overly simplistic notions which are inadequate for the serious matters of sustaining and crafting human life. It is an antiquated system which feeds on simple mindedness and cannot deal with complexity. Hence human energy is easily siphoned off into the trivial ie: funding for a new football stadium instead of child welfare or maternal health. When humans wonder why social problems seem intransigent barbaric adherents have at hand a ready mixed infant pap of irrational, sentimental trivia to dull our senses and soothe us back to sleep. An insentient majority, overfed on rubbish, is a pliable majority.

The weighty matters of human evolutionary progress require wakefulness and vigilance in the domains of attention, compassion, intelligent choice, and resolute action. An adolescent society can easily be seduced into prioritizing the silly, the inane and the unimportant. We must acknowledge that the primary barbaric use of scientific advances in psychology has been the construction and marketing of gaudy baubles which effectively keep the general populace in the role of children. Corrupt marketing of insignificant trifles as urgencies must be recognized as mendacious. An advanced society has structures, systems and funding to ensure that serious matters are prioritized as well as citizen education that ensures the populace are able to discriminate between matters of import to the species and taradiddle.

In the 21st century we must hone our discriminatory capacity to know what must be taken seriously and refuse to be distracted by shallow categorization into simplistic poles of negativity/positivity. All of the positive thinking in the world won't cure the thousands of 12 and 13 year old HIV positive female children in sub-Saharan Africa who have been infected against their will in societies where men use physical and social power with impunity. This is a weighty matter which requires prioritization. We must tackle weighty, serious human matters with urgency, energy and committed resources, and resolutely refuse to fritter precious resources on trivia.

Skullduggery in the House

The perpetration of fraud to enable profiteering is lightly dismissed under a barbarian regime. Those who fabricate, misrepresent, or mislead the public for financial profit are rarely held to account for deceit or for subsequent environmental damage. In societies where social responsibility is set at the levels of the barbaric creed individuals are rarely required to make restitution for the damage to the public good perpetrated by their personal actions. This could be changed. The Senators who dismissed scientific data and publicly attacked Al Gore as 'possibly perpetrating the biggest hoax on the American people in recorded history' could be held to account for irresponsible use of public power. They could retract duplicitous statements and remedy the swindle with financial restitution and do public service time disseminating climate facts. Al Gore's succinct statement about the environment could be broadened to encompass acts of mendacity perpetrated to hoodwink the public, 'The era of procrastination is over. We are now in the era of consequences.'

The realities of humanly caused environmental damage are readily available to all who have access to Information Technology. The International Union for the Conservation of Nature estimates that species loss is happening at 100-1,000 times the rate suggested by fossil records before humans. This puts us in a species loss situation comparable only to the five previous 'mass extinctions' in earth's history

– the last of which wiped out the dinosaurs. Ironically, our species, drawing on the decaying matter from the dinosaur's extinction, fossil fuel, risks the next mass wipeout. Perhaps excavating and then combusting extinguished matter is not such a great idea.

The World Health Organization has warned that the global ecosystem is being used so unsustainably that most of the elements essential to life on earth: stable climate, fresh air, clean water, are already degraded, with significantly worse effects expected in the next 50 years. Again we need to realize that the delay caused by ridiculing Ms. Carson and discrediting her work may have prevented the public response that could have averted the levels of global warming and environmental destruction we face in the 21st century. During that time period the Arctic icecap diminished by 40%. In a similar block of time scientists predict the icecap will no longer exist in summer: removing the sustainable habitat for species such as the polar bear as well as the giant ice mirror which currently reflects heat and moderates earth temperature. Forty percent of the world's population get their drinking water from fast disappearing glaciers. Damage to the global ecosystem will lead to rises in diseases such as cholera and malaria and increased risk of global pandemics. Pundits who have taken the public resources of the environment for granted in so-called economic growth schemes will find profiteering more difficult in a damaged ecosystem, although so called 'market adaptation' (profiteering focus) will probably see them selling potable water at prices affordable only for elites.

Ocean ecosystems are perishing under the onslaught of uncontrolled fishing and pollution. In 38 years, a decade less than time elapsed since Carson's book was released, our oceans may be completely fished out. Already, over 90% of our big fish are gone and at the current rate of global warming and ocean, all coral reefs will be destroyed by pollution in 100 years. Our species is having no small impact. In the face of these facts the UK government moved to create a marine protected area in the Indian Ocean around the worlds largest coral atoll; the 55 islands of Chagos. In ominous tones reminiscent of Rachel Carson, fishing magnates moved to ridicule, block and oppose this move through lobbying but ultimately public opinion pushed the decision for protection through.

In an Australian example of corruption and industry influencing government a chlorine bleach pulp mill (Gunn's) was pushed through parliament. There had been vehement public protest as the mill plans did not meet environmental standards of the independent sustainability assessment panel yet approval for the mill was given with a parliamentary caveat which removed the public's right to appeal. Significantly, the Chief Technical Advisor for the independent evaluation, Dr. Raverty, had resigned, citing political corruption. Those funded by the mill, had seven times the income to invest on public persuasion as those who opposed the mill on the basis of environmental damage. Media touted the mill with headings such as, 'Gunns Back in the Money!' One Tasmanian, making a statement on a site for public feedback stated, 'I feel sickened by the proposed pulp mill. I have always been an easygoing person but I find myself filled with hate and anger. I love Tasmania but feel I have lost my home.' Such social and human losses are not recompensed or assessed when the focus is narrowly on 'economic growth.' Conservative estimations of the damage this mill will cause, cite comparability to an additional 2.3 million cars on the road each year. It is not true that destruction of the environment for economic profit automatically brings human benefit.

Climate science is clear, but world leaders face determined and powerful industrialists, who can invest obscene amounts in advertising propaganda in order to remove what; from the barbaric viewpoint, are simply obstructions between themselves and their next billion dollars. Obviously Exxon marketing representatives cannot provide an unbiased view on environmental sustainability because their very existence depends on the continued use of fossil fuels. Irrespective of this obvious conflict of interest only one of their UK ads claiming climate-friendliness was taken off the air last year for deception. Obviously our evaluation standards need greater depth and intelligence.

The obstruction to environmental sustainability posed by powerholders in the fossil fuel lobby can be seen in the fact that; facing increased opposition in the west, they have simply shifted bases for profiteering. Consequently, in the last six months of 2009, the rate of global warming increased rather than decreased due primarily to increased coal emissions in China. It appears that barbarians, lost in the arousal of power and new profiteering options, only focus blindly on increasing thrust and speed. Increased speed is not a benefit when the underpinning model is that of the Lemmings.

Getting Smart

Once public agitation over climate change reached a point where it could no longer be lulled back into insentience by the dissemination of spurious facts; barbarians shifted the game to gaining control over how the global warming issue would be addressed so racketeering could continue. The preferred method was carbon trading which basically says, 'Yes, you can continue to pollute the atmosphere and to warm the planet to a certain point and just pay a fine for 'extra' environmental damage. If you reduce the amount that you are warming the globe you can make a profit from that by trading your unused carbon credits.' The problem with this approach is that profiteering has once again been made the epicentre of the motivation and decision making process. Carbon trading can be manipulated to increase costs for the public while increasing personal profit for a few. This is exactly the scenario which led to unsustainable environmental practice in the first place. Carbon trading may become yet another example of how having profiteers control decision making perpetuates the current system of short-sighted barbaric exploitation. In Copenhagen the fossil fuel, industrial lobbies, and associated barbaric interests; had enough of a power base to exert coercive aggression and to block much needed global emissions agreements and regulations.

It is not true that destruction of the environment for economic profit automatically brings human benefit. If powerholders are vehemently attacking a campaign and investing large amounts of money to do so then you can bet your bottom dollar their personal financial interests are involved. Inequity in power means that magnates have no need to defend their power core unless a public message will disrupt a profiteering base. The renewable energy and environmental sector is outnumbered 8 to 1 in number of industrial lobbyists. This means that the public must become adept at checking the messenger behind the message. The public must also become more adept at identifying markers of the public good, and language of compassion in advertising, as distinct from the imperative anthropomorphism and economic bias of barbarism, ie: 'The market must be maintained.' The barbarian has not changed his game. We need to change our anticipation, our offense and our defence.

Even when shifting the focus from environmental destruction to that of degradation – where we can visibly observe the damage to the living world of manufacturing and industrial pollutants - barbarians adhere rigidly to the Barbaric Code. As vast swathes of the Amazon disappear on a daily basis barbarians simply avert their gaze and ignore resultant global conditions. In a peculiarly dogmatic manner, rather than consider the limitations of the barbaric creed, barbarians will inflexibly advocate the continuance of unsustainable use of the environment for profiteering.

For example, barbarians will promote wild-eyed, truly baseless schemes such as man-made, material systems – bubbles, domes, walled cities – as the penultimate solution to environmental pollution and degradation. Because they have privileged access to an unequal share of resources barbarians can afford to invest in the creation of insular sub-environments which might preserve their personal living conditions. Such a position derives from the Creed's underpinning tenets of survival of the fittest (Tenet II) and inherent barbarian superiority (Tenet III).

When challenged to face the limitations of this approach barbarians spout fantastical alternatives to the sane option of taking care of the world. In barbaric adherence to the precepts of limited information access and lack of complex planning, environmental plunderers try to hawk the untenable solution of relocating the entire human race to another planet. Such a notion preserves the outdated barbarian perspective that there are always new habitats to exploit and dominate; but such a view has no basis in rationality.

We have abundant data that we have the capacity to maintain the habitability of this planet. In contrast, we have no evidence that there are other habitable planets within our reach, even after space probes have travelled for many years. Irrespective, the bizarre notion of planetary relocation is proffered as though it were equal in merit to the scientifically backed, eminently achievable, strategy of switching to sustainable environmental practices. Without any of the statistical rigour they require of scientists, barbarians are willing to sell the public the ignis fatuus, unworkable con of moving earth's population into outer space! One must wonder if the transport of a billion Indians and a billion Chinese has been included in these imaginary conjugations. The Mad Hatter reappears and we are all invited to tea.

Issues of human transportation and the myriad complex issues raised by the notion of relocating billions of humans to a new planet are dismissed with an airy wave of the barbarian paw whose disregard for the destruction of living systems (Creed Tenet I), limited willingness to engage with all the available information (Tenet IV,) and low capacity for complex planning, all lead to schemes which cannot be executed. The real issue is that the world in which all other human beings must live is not a big concern for those living by the barbaric creed (Tenet VIII: Self Sufficiency, Tenet IX: Pillaging the Resources of the Future). Considerations of the scope of environmental destruction do not consume the waking hours of the barbaric industrial potentate. The barbaric creed does not facilitate thought at a level to enable serious consideration and response to issues as complex and sensitive as ecological survival.

We need to rehumanize industrialists and bring them back to right size. When the globe heats up or we face the real effects of irreparable environmental damage industrialists will be as frightened as everybody else and looking desperately for someone who can 'fix it.' We can learn from the manner in which most magnates and business leaders distanced themselves from the 2008-2009 financial melt down. The fact that, in the face of the sub-prime crisis, the collapse of the banking system and the Wall Street slide; many financial 'leaders' claimed helplessness, even though the crisis was clearly driven by their collective decisions for unsustainable profiteering; should serve as a good slap in the collective face. If we reflect on the reality that these people quickly claimed they had 'no power' and, rather; that the public would have to pay for, and bail out, the very system from which they draw immense personal wealth, then we have a ready antidote to administer whenever we are tempted to be swayed by their public spin. The way in which financiers, entrepreneurs, and industry representatives, simply washed their hands of responsibility and took a detached position towards the suffering of the many, should remind us of the real costs to the average person of having a system tailored to the wellbeing of an elite few.

It should also remind us of the humanity of these individuals and evoke compassionate wisdom. People with money are not gods. We can remember that, just as the poor are simply humans without money, the rich are just humans with money. The last few decades have taught us that people with money can behave very badly, and the power behind their decisions can cause disastrous effects for all. We can draw on the research into the metamorphic effects of power and remember that, while having money and making good decisions are not mutually exclusive, the effects of power in a barbaric, profiteering system mean it is unlikely there will be much overlap. Economic growth is an inadequate target or growth criteria for the development of human societies because self interest is such a powerful aphrodisiac. The long term mature planning focus we need is exemplified in the quote from Trueblood, 'A man has made at least a start on discovering the meaning of human life when he plants shade trees under which he knows full well he will never sit.'

The Fictitious Necessity of Uglification

Although it is not usually accorded much attention, an issue linked to environmental sustainability that has great impact on human evolutionary progress, is the unwarranted uglification of the human world. A great deal of built development creates unnecessary misery for the human animal by despoiling his or her living space and making it unpleasant. Pundits who quibble over global warming and environmental sustainability sidestep an issue of almost equal import – the damage done to unspoiled living worlds and environments by hideous constructions. The so-called industrial revolution conditioned us to accept disfigurement of our visual and lived environment as an inevitable part of progress. This is simply not so.

There is no need for the entrepreneur to uglify people's lives by cluttering their world with distasteful, obnoxious constructions. The natural world is filled with unquestionable beauty and splendour – soothing to the eye, the ear, the nose and all human senses. Uglification increases human stress, limits human sense of possibility, and is a violation of the rights of those who must then live in disfigured environments. Manufacturers polluting the environment with emissions and unsightly constructions, are befouling the spaces in which people must birth their babies, raise their children, and live their entire existences. The designs, not only of factories, but also of urban centres and of cities is planned, chosen, and often greatly driven by profiteers who have limited vision (Tenets V & IX), or who may be uncaring about human living conditions in domains they do not frequent. These modifications to the natural and physical world are planned and selected from amongst a myriad of other possibilities.

72

Industrialists want us to believe that the uglification of our built environment is an essential part of 'progress' but this is untrue. We have progressed little from the unrefined, rudimentary and coarse planning of Victorian industrialists with their offensive, polluting, dank constructions. In most global cities the common person's access to the skyline is increasingly limited. This is an avoidable sin. The repugnancy of the crass skyscraper and boorish eyesores of huge retail complexes, cheaply constructed accommodation; begrimed, dilapidated freeways and unwieldy multi-level parking structures; are all results of adherence to the antiquated map of early industrialists. Ugly edifices that disfigure the human world are a human choice. The crude efforts of fledgling, ignorant industrialists do not need to be the map for our future.

Across the globe, the average person is experiencing increasingly limited access to public resources such as the ocean, trees and natural spaces along with increased encroachment of unpalatable, unwanted constructions into their living areas. There is no need for built environments to be crammed cheek to jowl with monstrosities. Eyesores for the general population are often so constructed because of adherence to the barbaric creed and overemphasis on profit. The planning and erection of ugly, offensive retail, apartment and manufacturing structures for the purposes of entrepreneurial profit is an unnecessary despoiling of human environments. Planning which prioritizes human welfare could render the sprawling modern city with its grey lines and crammed unsightly corridors an anachronism.

The environment can be redecorated, nurtured and festooned by human progress; despoiling it is simply a human choice. Human cities could just as easily be designed on the matrix of Hundterwasser or Rivendell as on the model of Los Angeles, Mexico City, Shanghai or Mumbai. As an example, we can go to the structures created by Hundterwasser whose work was based on ecological planning and belief in the inherent dignity of the human animal, the need for beauty in human living, and the unlimited possibilities of vermicular and alternative construction. His combination of ecology, art and landscape design is just one demonstration of the multitude of structural possibilities available when planning is not based on the barbaric creed. All of Hundterwasser's structures, from his thermal power plant to his treed energy recycling homes; his childcare complex to the Kawakawa public toilets; inspire and enervate. He actively disproved the barbaric mantra that the living environment must be degraded to create the built environment. Hundterwasser's constructions proved that it was possible to construct while simultaneously conserving public resources of beauty, fresh air and visual soothing. His work demonstrates clearly that the living space of the human animal can reflect the inherent beauty of that animal.

When uglifying people's communities and living spaces for the purpose of profit we must consider the impact of unsightly structures and repulsive environments on children. Children are sensory creatures who are soothed, shaped, and far more dependent upon, and responsive to, the external environment than adults. Children reared in linear, gray industrial spaces, or vile environments of squalor, have their sensory learning conditioned by degradation. We should not then wonder at their inability to respond to possibility. By denying vast numbers of the human population the capacity to be nurtured by beauty and possibility in their environment, we seriously hobble human transformative evolutionary possibility.

In the main, the natural environment has been sacked, damaged and made unfit for human evolutionary progress through development which has a narrow and primary focus on financial profit. In many cities the uncluttered skyline is now only accessible to the elite few of the penthouse population. Uglifying the environment causes human unhappiness and this, in itself, is cause enough for it to be halted. Limiting human access to the beautiful, the calm and the soothing, by destroying the natural environment which is the birthright of all people; and then allowing only the few to have access to the beauty of nature's resources, is an unjustifiable co-optation of the resources of the many.

'We do not inherit the earth from our ancestors, we borrow it from our children.' Native American proverb

As the excesses of wealth generated in the past few decades have demonstrated, the wealthy can of accumulate obscene amounts of money, and still be unsatisfied. It is time that people stood up and demanded accountability for the visual, olfactory and auditory pollution to which they are subjected on a daily basis simply to line the pockets of the wealthy. Profit-making must include responsibility to ensure the lived environments of fellow man remain intact and unpolluted.

`

'If you don't care for it, you can't have it.'

In terms of consumerism: goods need to cost enough that we value the earth resources used to make them, that we can only afford a sustainable range and number, and are therefore motivated to take care of them. Non-biodegradable products must be made to last, for generations if possible; with sustainable systems set up to reclaim and recycle materials. It is hard for the average person not to leave a large ecological footprint at the moment because we do not have systems, patterns of living, norms of community life; or models for home, town, and city construction that foster the ability of the average citizen to live sustainably. There must be social and systemic support if individual actions are going to be fully effective. We can't push the poor to pay for environmental degradation when that removes essential survival resources from already pillaged home and family lives. If we are all safe, in non-competitive non-aggressive, environments then extra goods, houses and 'things' may no longer be seen as so desirable. In a world where 'stuff' is the measure of your worth; clutter is a psychologically reassuring buffer from external derogatory evaluation.

Summary

The full spectrum of human life isn't considered under the barbaric philosophy and therefore barbarians have difficulty understanding that the lived environment is an inseparable part of human life. Disfigurement and damage to the environment harms human living, human dignity, and the possibilities for joy. Under a philosophy in which all members of the life world are valued, the environment and the built world can be nurtured, tended, embellished, and beautified, by human development. Those who hold the dog-eat-dog, 'survival of the fittest' philosophy have been simplistically conditioned to focus on preserving intraspecies competition in which their personal stockpile of resources ensures they are never the one eaten. This is no protection, even for the ignorant barbarian, in the face of the true outcomes of foolhardy development and barbaric global competition. The philosophy behind continual agglomeration of resources for the few has terrifying implications for human survival. While the 'war on terror' was conducted outside of many nations, barbarism slid under the radar to infiltrate most cultures; and to continue quietly and inexorably to its target of human extinction. It is this destruction, in all of the forms in which it manifests, that comprises the real domain of terror.

CHAPTER 4: BARBARISM & INTRAPSYCHIC LIFE

Mutilating Psyche

Let us now consider an annihilation occurring throughout human history which has accelerated in momentum and ferocity in the 21st Century: The mutilation of the human psyche. Unseen except to the mind's eye and usually occurring early in childhood, the wounding and dismemberment of the human psyche has incalculable effect. Barbaric dismemberment in childhood is serious, not only because it compounds social problems and destroys resources needed for survival, but because it involves the torture of the smallest, most vulnerable and defenceless members of our species. Similar wounding can occur later in life if people experience extreme atrocities and great injustice, but is rarer in comparison to the widespread maim which is routinely perpetrated on children.

Human Somnambulance

Humans have difficulty acknowledging and responding effectively to destruction that can be visibly seen – such as industrial pollution or deforestation – and infinitely greater difficulty acknowledging and responding to havoc being wrought in the unseen realm of the psyche. Even when external damage effects are patently visible to the human eye such as with deforestation or chemical spills; people can still be swayed by a glib tongue that asserts that external destruction is 'not so bad' or is 'an inevitable part of progress.' Persuading the general public to doubt their experience of reality is a core weapon in the barbaric arsenal. Seduction and mass delusion are others. It is only when these stealth weapons have failed that coercion is utilized. Given this context; the global evidence we have of forceful coercion in indigenous, local and national communities wrought in the interests of 'economics,' cause us to wonder how much hustle we have already consumed through media manipulation. Local people who protest the destruction of their homes, their quality of life or their environment may be lampooned or dismissed as 'diehards' or as 'uneducated hicks', 'hoons' or 'natives' who don't understand 'progress.'(Argumentum ad hominum or ad populum)

Even when visual destruction is shockingly perpetuated against the human body; such as when children's arms and legs were hacked off in Sierra Leone or when whole communities were raped and slaughtered in the Congo and Rwanda; the human community rouses itself slowly from its slumber, and not with the swift eye and razored intent which can halt atrocity. It often takes months or years for humans to acknowledge atrocity is occurring, and even longer to rouse the strength of will to stop its continuance. In the case of genocide we routinely take years, even decades, to establish international justice tribunals, and usually allow so much time to elapse that we are unable to bring even a handful of the perpetrators to account. It is no wonder that victims of these types of atrocities often flounder in despair or go mad in the face of the apathy of their fellow man.

If humans have this much difficulty responding to clearly visible material destruction occurring in the outside world; how much more difficult is it for human beings to come to terms with, and formulate appropriate responses to, damage perpetrated in the unseen landscape of self and the psyche?

Unseen Landscapes

Damage inflicted on the human psyche during childhood has kept human development at Paleolithic levels throughout much of recorded history. It is unclear what types of societies, environments and achievements might have been possible if the psyche was left unmutilated. The domain of intact, and appropriately nurtured, human possibility is still largely uncharted territory although the impairment effects of deforming the psyche are well documented. If we conceptualize the damage wrought in the material world – in the environment and in the physical and emotional violence humans perpetrate on one another – as having a template first written on the human psyche we begin to have some understanding of the extent of destruction which many people carry as their internal (and therefore major) reality. We can no longer afford the high price of early mutilation of the human psyche. This is our greatest resource for the species as well as the site from which human caring, consciousness, energy, relationship and creativity are generated.

The mutilation of the psyche of children currently occurs at a phenomenal rate even within wealthy industrialized societies such as Australia and America. The destruction it wreaks cannot be fully calculated because a culture cannot apprehend or measure full loss when what is destroyed is latent capacity. The damage effects of psyche mutilation can be compared to the practices of Female Genital Mutilation in Africa or the old Chinese practice of foot binding where the damage was routinely inflicted, culturally normalized, and widely iconized as healthy cultural practice. The cost of destroying latent capacity is difficult when most members of the culture are routinely dismembered. The individual victim has no way of experiencing his or her excised capacity and no external cultural reference for comparison. Hence, mutilation is most effective when practiced on the majority of a population, because normalization renders the loss less noticeable and perceptible, and thus, more easily concealed.

As an illustrative instance let us consider the common cultural process in many African countries of cutting out the sensitive genitals of female children. In Africa 6,000 girls are at risk of this procedure every day with some countries boasting 90% excision rate. Deep wounding done to such tender regions of the body is, in itself a violent crime against a child. The girl's psyche suffers parallel maim in its experiential capacity for pleasure. If we consider an individual woman whose genitals were cut out when she was four or five years of age we have an example of the difficulty of calculating loss when there is early dismemberment. The excision and discard of her sexual viscera as a child means that, as an adult woman, she does not have the organs and nerve endings for sensations of sexual pleasure, arousal and orgasm. Consequently she has no way of fully understanding the pleasure she could have experienced if her genitals had not been hacked off. When the sensory organs which enable female sexual pleasure are removed so is the woman's reference point for understanding her lost sensing capacity. You then have a pliable adult population unable, or unwilling, to come to terms with their own loss; and willing to support the castration of their own children.

The cultural loss caused by parallel damage to the psyche is more difficult to conceptualise than physical loss. There was no way of knowing how fast a Chinese girl might have run had not her feet been broken and folded into small stumps. On a larger scale, it is difficult to project the loss accrued to Chinese society by the social, employment and personal costs of having women with mutilated feet. In the same way, once the psyche is mutilated, bound or deformed, we don't know what might have been achieved if it had been allowed to develop normally.

Comparably, it is impossible for the individual victim to understand the range and ease of thought, and emotional joy and sense of wellbeing, enjoyed by the intact psyche once they have been psychologically damaged. They may ponder the ease with which undamaged people seem to be able to negotiate their lives but; in a culture where barbarism is dominant, they are likely to blame themselves for their suffering and difficulty. For barbarians, an ignorant victim is the best victim. The best 'business opportunity' is when the customer is ignorant of their resource value because they can be bought cheaply.

Acknowledging the Inner World

A first step in understanding the realm of the psyche and the damage that can be inflicted upon it, is to acknowledge the full spectrum of human living and experience. For ease of conceptualization, we can understand all human existence as occurring concurrently in two worlds – the inner world of experience and the outer world of physical objects. Only the external world is visible but all human experiences in the outer world are concurrently experienced and recorded in the inner world. The fact that human existence occurs concurrently in two worlds is patently obvious but rarely socially acknowledged.

The existence of the inner world mainly comes to the fore of our consciousness and perception of reality when our own inner landscape suffers some wounding or devastation. When this occurs we often cannot be externally 'present' because our internal world demands all of our attention. This level of absorption only occurs rarely in the external world and only where all other aspects of the physical world are excluded. The absorption of fixed focus on the Superbowl or an AFL final on television is one such example. The determined set of the individual's focus can render someone, for all intents and purposes, unconscious to anything else happening and therefore not really present to the rest of the external world.

Even at a lesser level we can validate the reality of having an inner and outer world. Most of us have had the experience of being at a party or a social event but being 'pre-occupied' with affairs happening in another part of our lives. We tacitly acknowledge the two worlds of each individual's existence when we say, 'I'm sorry, I'm not really present' or, 'I was off in my own little world.' Others reciprocate the tacit social knowledge of the binary worlds of human experience with such common rhetoric as, 'Earth to Harry! Are you in there?' (acknowledging the inner world as 'there') or 'Snap out of it! I need you here' (thereby acknowledging the outer, shared social world as a separate space from the inner world which is designated 'here'). In these situations, the person is physically present in the external world but they are mainly present in the inner world of the psyche. When we are pre-occupied with our inner world (particularly with fears and worries...) the external world loses its predominance. When traumatised we are immersed in the urgent mental and emotional energy demands of the damaged ecology of the inner world.

The above-mentioned example illustrates a rare time in modern living where open acknowledgement is made of the fact that human life consists of two planes of simultaneous experience. When traumatized or distressed, we must acknowledge the unseen, co-existing inner world of our experience. In many realms, and particularly the constructed industrialized work world, it is taboo to acknowledge the inner world. Inner world absorption can make us less accessible to other people's demands upon us, which makes their 'outer world' of us as a resource, less pliable. Less mental accessibility is considered disastrous to profiteering enterprises who want to drain both the inner and outer world resources of employees while paying for only outer world contributions. This is one of the reasons there are so many taboos around discussing, honouring and acknowledging emotions, experiences, perceptions and many other aspects of the inner world in the external work and social world.

Damage to the Landscape: Trauma

Most of us have had the experience of having some loss or terror where our emotions were so overwhelming that we couldn't cope with, or relate to, the external world. When we are in high distress our inner world goes into hyperdrive trying to process negative experience so it can help us move back into a state that is less painful. During this intense type of processing our inner world is not only out of synch with; but often does not have the resources to cope with; the levity of casual social life and superficiality. With trauma, absorption with the inner psychic world does not have the same component of choice attached as in the example of the football game; because the central operating system in the brain simply overrides all other systems in an automatic emergency system response to commandeer all available resources and direct them to the damage.

Psychological trauma creates a 'brain injury' where the brain impedes all other processing until the trauma is addressed and homeostasis is restored. This is why school is a wasted activity for traumatized children. Maths is not their brain's urgent priority when their mind is engaged in a battle for survival and sanity.

To understand this phenomenon, people who have had a privileged upbringing and who were not traumatized can have some sense of the barriers to functioning for a person who lives with a damaged inner world if they think of a time they had severe toothache or migraine. This sharp, unrelenting physical pain makes it impossible to complete even the most routine of tasks and is similar to the internal pain when someone is traumatised. Brain processing of trauma takes such a high proportion of available brain resources that it can be almost impossible for traumatised people, coping with inner world damage, to complete the routine tasks of daily life, even though there is no visible physical injury.

The Insentience of Comfort

The refusal to acknowledge this dual reality of human experience often leads to the perpetration of great cruelty onto people whose inner world has been damaged. Privileged people will often set standards that are unachievable for those who have been harmed and sometimes; in a double oppression, will punish those people who cannot meet their standards. Many of our intractable social problems come because we ignore inner world damage and pose solutions which are unrealistic because they require psychologically wounded people to function at a high level. Their inner pain preoccupies most of their resources and makes such performance impossible. At best the psychologically damaged person has short spurts of high level production functioning followed rapidly by system shutdown for recovery. Baudelaire and Van Gogh were examples of such people. Those who have had a privileged upbringing will need to draw on their own experiences of physical pain to conceptualize the next sections. For those who have been less fortunate it is hoped that these sections dignify some of your struggle.

People who live in the west, who are reasonably well off, and who have little trauma in their lives can sometimes forget the existence of the internal world because their external world is comfortable and there is not enough pain in their internal world to distract their senses from immersion in, and total identification with, (absorption in) the external world. On the other hand, people who have been traumatized (from events such as domestic violence, rape, conflict or ongoing oppression or hardship of poverty, racism etc.) are well aware of how difficult it is to be 'present' and to cope with the sensory demands of the external world when the internal world is devastated and when internal pain is overwhelming in its demands.

The prosperous who crow that their success is all attributable to their discipline and personal efforts do not understand the great unearned benefit they have simply because their capacity to focus at will, or to relax at will, has remained unmolested. Success in the industrialized world relies heavily on these core (inner world) self-regulation capacities. The development of these capacities, or their destruction, occurs primarily up until the age of 5 when; in fact, we have very little choice about what happens to us and when kindness we experience is simply good fortune.

Outer World Focus: Core Barbaric Propaganda

For the purposes of this text it is important to note that barbarism primarily acknowledges the external physical world not the internal resources of the psyche. This is not always purposeful but has strategic benefit. Human sense of self resides in the inner world as do joy, wellbeing, happiness, peace of mind and fear, worry, panic and dread. We live with whichever of these predominates in our past and present experience. When we are safe we can work in a positive, purposeful way because we are immersed in; and can draw upon; the soothing and enchantment of the living landscape of the inner world. Alternatively, when we are under personal or cultural attack, we are often immersed in the horror and anxiety of the damage being done to inner world resources (peace of mind, calm, happiness and personal dignity). This is why barbarian incursion targets not only people's external resources but also peoples' intrinsic sense of core safety and wellbeing (the inner world), particularly of those who are relatively defenceless. This is due to general barbaric tendencies of lacking pity or compassion for others; being prepared to act with great force or intensity in a merciless manner; being able and disposed to inflict pain and finding satisfaction, and a sense of superiority, in witnessing the suffering of others. Those who are experienced in inflicting hardship on others or criticizing savagely, know that the stimulation of fear increases a person's malleability.

Barbaric strategies capitalize on the reality that, the fewer the resources a person has, the easier it is to threaten their sense of security, invade their inner world with anxiety and therefore to increase the likelihood they will conform to labour and other external demands. Once a person is in a highly aroused state of fear or stress (brain homeostasis interrupted) they are less able to marshal their psychological self towards resisting unreasonable demand or exploitation and therefore less able to protect their resources, no matter how few. It is important that we understand how some of these inner world attacks occur. Our inner resources of sense of self, inherent inviolable dignity, and sense of safety, in the world are the final frontier for maintaining our lives. When our inner world and sense of wellbeing is pillaged there is nowhere for retreat.

Therefore, in the recent barbaric incursion Australians and Americans were urged to focus on share profits, investment portfolios, rising housing prices and booming economies. This was the dream. The rise of barbaric social norms, increase in labour and time demands on the population, and subsequent increased pressures, eroded and destroyed the inner world of wellbeing and sense of safety for many. World Health data shows that, also during this time, 25% of Americans and 22% of Australians and Britons were suffering mental illness in any given year; their nations had some the developed world's highest rates of illicit drug use and some of the lowest rates for child wellbeing. While a comparative few Australians and Americans were basking in the illusions created from media bombardment promoting the economic 'boom' we were concurrently being threatened by rising financial sector decay, escalating child abuse and mental illness, increasing incarceration rates and an explosion in the prescription of anti-depressants and other mood-altering medications. The dream for some was therefore a nightmare for others. We could ask ourselves, what did these concurrent trends tell us about reality and what do we need to do about it? We can start by counting the full costs of systems based on competitive aggression and dominance.

CHAPTER 5: BARBARISM & CHILDHOOD

Controlling children's behaviour by using an ice pick to damage their frontal lobes is no longer in vogue but there are barbaric ideologies which perpetrate similar damage. The long term effect of harm inflicted in early childhood can wreak havoc on a person's inner world for life. Capturing the full picture of what can happen to children during a barbaric insurgency requires deep understanding of visible, less visible, and invisible, aspects of human existence. These include not only brain wiring and limbic system functioning but also the finely tuned sensitivity of small children's sensory systems, the high absorbency of their emotional world, and the fragility of their permeable, developing self.

Children need to be well loved. Their intrinsic dignity as a human self demands that they be nurtured and protected by adults who love them and by adults whose personal sense of happiness is directly affected by the child's. They deserve to be raised by people who are closely bonded to them, and who use the relationship of care to gently guide their development. They deserve to be raised in villages and communities of care, existing in a global circle of sustainable adult approaches to development and life. Children deserve to only be brought into this world by adults who are willing to fulfil these commitments.

All infants are born with natural empathy, ebullience, intelligence and creativity. Some call this resilience, but the focus on 'resilience' sidesteps the issue of preventing harm. The core question is not why only some children have these qualities but what has been done to children who no longer exhibit them? Barbarians proselytise that humans have always been subjected to violence in childhood, that children survive cruel adults, and that many grow into reasonably well adjusted adults. The critical words are 'survive', 'many' and 'reasonably.' Why would we make this our baseline? The focus on children's 'resilience', ie: how they 'bounce back' from harm, sidesteps the critical issue of why they have been unnecessarily thrown against a wall in the first place. The human talents for resilience, healing and survival should be kept for the unavoidable vagaries of human life and not evoked by needless, preventable cruelty. Brutality peddled under the rhetoric of 'toughening kids up for the real world' ignores the reality that much of the 'real' world has been created by those who were brutalized themselves. Brutalizing children to 'fit' the current system is a procrustean move that ensures barbaric continuance. It confounds what 'is' with what could be. The care of children is linked inextricably with human capacity for change and accelerated evolutionary development.

Tender Systems

The newly developing systems of small children are delicate, raw, and hypersensitive. As adults, we can forget the terror that is evoked when you are very small and threatened by an enraged, omnipotent adult. Children have a more porous emotional system than adults so that the behaviours of others are not experienced as external to them, but rather as part of themselves - absorbed into their developing sense of self. If we use the analogy of amphibians to conceptualize humans dwelling in both inner and outer world, then the child is the tadpole living inescapably in the inner world pond of feeling; a pond easily overheated by emotional violence. The adult is the frog who can escape the pond and survive in the outer world for periods of time. Adults can easily penetrate the pond of the child's inner environ and leave the child's permeable, untoughened 'tadpole' self, mired in toxins. All pond pollution is absorbed into the child so that adult cruelty, harshness or neglect, becomes embedded into the child's sense of self. Soothing care keeps the pond cool and clear.

Understanding this reality of inner and outer worlds is central to being able to conceptualize the way a child's physical, emotional, intellectual self systems soak up whatever is happening in the external social system. In the same way that the bones in a child's skull are soft at birth and the brain can be more easily penetrated and damaged, the internal world and self system and soft, and fragile, when children are young. The boundary to protect the vulnerable self from impact only develops with time. The basic toughening of a protective 'fence' around sense of self and inner world takes 3-5 years. During this time, the person's self system is highly exposed and can be easily damaged by the behaviours of others. It is critical that culture, community and family protect the child while their self system is fragile while their porous developing self can be readily polluted or broken by harsh behaviour. Sense of self can even be split irreparably into pieces (multiple personality, schizophrenia etc). Cruelty to small children throws garbage into their internal pond which is then absorbed into their sense of self and which remains in their internal world after the outer self boundary has formed. It is then experienced entirely as the self, not as abuse or care. When a child is harmed, they not only suffer emotionally and physically but their living brain wiring is destroyed while simultaneously, their wellbeing and sense of self is decimated. In effect we can mutilate the living psyche.

We now have complex brain scanning technology that gives a visual map of the damage which is inflicted on a child by violence, neglect or cruelty. Obviously, however, we cannot afford to remain the level of impeded intelligence which requires a brain scan to understand children's vulnerability, our power over them, and our capacity to affect them. Compassion and empathy give us a good enough scan on which to base our actions. The defining characteristics of barbaric behaviour such as enacting warlike, savage insensitivity towards other human beings and towards life sustaining systems, have powerfully toxic impact on children. Cultural acceptance of hard hearted, indifferent adult insensitivity promotes cruel, harsh norms for interacting with children which; in turn, promotes behaviours which damage their sensitive systems and developing capacities. Systems filled with competitive aggression flood the system of the developing child and are absorbed by it. It is not feasible to render visible to the naked eye the imprint or harm on a living child's brain of each aggressive or unkind experience as it occurs and nor should it be necessary. Each of us has had experiences of being assisted or harmed by powerful others. These experiences are enough data for us to recognize and understand the suffering of children. We have total power and impact on a child. We rule their world.

Without meaning to insult the high priests who believe technology is the spaceship that will preserve the species, we must respond at the common sense level of understanding the impact of cruel, savage, harsh, vicious, unfeeling, competitive and hard hearted behaviours on a living child. Intellectual 'scientific' (left brain) thought is much slower than the right brain at processing. We can't afford to wait for intellect to catch up if we are to respond quickly enough for species survival. It will take science a thousand years to discover what compassion has always known.

We can be unapologetically clear about which experiences harm, and which nurture, children in order to foster an anti-barbaric movement for this generation and for those to come. Powerful human change is simply about focussing, increasing our sense of urgency, making clear choices, and refusing to have our will eroded by distraction and titillation. Creating kinder, protective, child friendly societies could transform our species in one generation. The following section explains some basic neurobiology, brain science and present data we have about the acute sensitivity, permeability, and malleability, of the body and self systems of small children. In order to foster public willingness to counter and resist barbaric incursion into the living self of the undamaged child, the following section explores neuroscience realms as they relate to child development, and to our early experiences as humans.

BASICS OF CHILD DEVELOPMENT

Brain Facts

There is always a great deal of damage that can be perpetrated on humans but the damage which can be done in childhood is the most dangerous because it can disadvantage people for life. The earlier the harm is done, the greater the capacity for damage. This is for two primary reasons. Firstly, up to the age of three, our brains are still forming, like a fruit that is still growing. The changes in the human brain from birth to age three (tripling in weight) are comparable to the difference between the cherry size tomatoes that form on the vine and the large plump tomato purchased in the store. A child comes into the world with this cherry size 'brain fruit' and by age three this fruit has tripled in size to reach a brain which is 90% of its adult size. If, however, the brain is starved of critical experiences or if the child is harmed, then the final 'fruit' of the brain (growth which encapsulates a person's overall sense of safety, wellbeing and possibility) will be stunted, small and under-developed. If a child is treated cruelly, not only do they suffer in the moment but, because their brain wiring is simultaneously impacted they will also suffer in the future.

Tripling of size is a phenomenal rate of growth for any organ. Because our brains are the centre of our experiences and will only grow another 10% in size in our lives, our early childhood experiences are critical to our capacities and experiences for the rest of our lives. Our brains represent our minds. The recording of our lives and experiences in our minds, create memories which will either assist or handicap as we face new experiences. The experiences hardwired into the brain when we are small dictate the superhighways for the brain to use, which; in turn, dictate the things that will be easy or hard for us. Early damage is more extensive its effect than late damage, because it harms a building block upon which the next step in brain development depends. Subsequently the younger we are, the easier we are to mold and shape through intimidation or nurturance, and the more lasting will be the effects of learned fear or confidence.

As the brain is growing, it is plastic, somewhat like wet clay, and so it can be easily sculpted. Once early brain hard wiring is complete it becomes less plastic and in some ways the brain hardens (like clay hardens as it dries) so that early shaping or damage becomes part of the solid brain structure. Like a tree, once the brain is out of the malleable sapling stage, the direction in which it has been shaped is difficult, and sometimes even impossible, to reverse. In effect, childhood years are the critical years for affecting how we view life. We experience this permanent shaping done to us as our expectations of life, our sense of hopefulness, our optimism or pessimism, and the irrational fears and dogmatic beliefs we may cling to even in the face of contrary evidence. Trauma can particularly damage and halt next steps in brain progress because the mind gets stuck trying to process the unthinkable. This 'sticking' when, experienced as an adult, results in Posttraumatic Stress Disorder, Panic Disorder and other unpleasantries. When experienced as a small child, it can cause the brain to get stuck running around and around a limited set of experiences for life. The more forceful impact of trauma on the highly sensitive and delicate system of a child explains why it is possible for adult humans to be walking around in adult bodies locked in inner world experiences of age 2, 3, 5 or 10. Human brain development is programmed to progress normally only under conditions of kindness, responsivity, compassion and care; not under conditions of duress, neglect, viciousness or cruelty.

The amount and type of experiences given to the small child (caring or insensitive) determine the shape the brain takes and; in the majority of cases, the shape it remains. The dependency of human children for longer periods than any other animal means that, we have little choice to resist, and how adults treat us has permanent effects on our perceptions and our capacities. The reality of human physiological development means what happens to human children will leave them with healthy, prolific and efficient brain wiring and capacities, or with handicapped brain circuits. The tender, fragile and raw developing self can have great unhappiness inflicted or great confidence, hopefulness and calm. Any damage caused while we are in the uterus, by any of a number of teratogens, including alcohol, drugs or disease, has the greatest effect on the brain and self. Humans can recognize this when a child is born with the physical damage of Downs or HIV but have greater difficulty recognizing psychological damage and limitations caused by human cruelty and aggression inflicted on the keen sensing systems of small children.

The brain is an amazing organ which adapts itself to deal with injury and inefficiency, but any adaptation process required to circumvent early damage draws from the brain's limited energy and renders the completion of other activities, such as formal schooling, more difficult. It also makes routine development in areas such as social skill more difficult, and energy consuming, than for nurtured children. This is one of the reasons that abused, impoverished and neglected children are less likely to succeed in the so-called 'level playing field' of competitive education and employment. By age of three we are effectively psychologically and physiologically (intellectually, emotionally and physically) handicapped or advantaged. For those lucky enough to be nurtured in childhood, this is a first layer of taken-for-granted, unearned privilege.

Trespass In The Psyche

Sense of Self

Damaging or advantageous experiences we are given during the early years are integrated into our sense of self and we commonly think of them as simply being a part of who we are. In reality, much of our core sense of self and beliefs were developed from experiences over which we had little control. In terms of the psyche - the living self of the child - neurobiological studies have demonstrated that early damage is deeply embedded into the core wiring of our brains and, unless addressed, can therefore define and shape all of our subsequent relationships. Early wiring is so central it becomes unconscious (stored in the right side of our brain) and we are not aware of it unless we do some focused work which, because of the pain stored with painful memories, will also be uncomfortable and often difficult. Our early wiring becomes like the window from which we view the external world but because this window and our inner world has been with us since before we could talk, we experience it entirely as the 'self.' Once this reality comes into our awareness we can work for change.

In summary, adults literally leave their mark on the delicate self and sensitive brain of infants and small children in their care; determining the direction and to which extent the person grows, whether they are hurt and whether or not the developing sense of self is cauterized or mutilated. This is not like the trivial effect of leaving one's fingerprints on a glass. It is literally leaving marks on another person's being and the inner world that determines whether life is enjoyable or painful; difficult or easy; exciting or frightening. In turn, this perceptive framework will determine much of a person's future life experience as the inner world is the space where a person's capacity and ability to function in the external world reside. Early experiences, over which we have no choice or control, are just one of the many layers of unearned privilege or disadvantage which barbarians conveniently ignore.

Marking the Child

There are two critical things to understand in relation to barbarism and childhood: Firstly, as mentioned before, the future of any society rests in its children and in its treatment of its children. Secondly, the unconditioned child is a threat to barbaric imperium, and to the continuation of barbarism as a shaping force for the species. Control of, and harshness towards, small children ensures the implantation of a controlling force in the psyche and a tendency towards acceptance of barbarism as inevitable once that person is an adult.

Specifically, an unbrutalised child is less likely to be willing to savage others when he or she reaches adulthood. The earlier that brutalisation or neglect of a child occurs, the more likely it is that lack of care and aggression will be inculcated into the child's unconscious sense of self, therefore becoming part of the individual's unquestioned worldview as 'the way things are' or 'the way things should be.' Unquestioned compliance to the barbaric creed is essential to its continuance.

The hardening and barbaric inculcation of children occurs not only through parental violence or neglect, but also through harshness and viciousness experienced in school systems, overly rigid socialisation, and/or the exposure of children to the brutal norms of the wider social context. It is the day-to-day exposure of children to adult viciousness, greed, bad temper and interpersonal aggression, either as the direct experience of the child or the witnessed experience of the child when observing interactions between adults, which firmly indoctrinate them into barbarism.

Repetitious witnessing of, and direct or indirect experience of, aggression gives children forceful messages about survival in the culture, and what methods 'succeed.' In the absence of protective parental influence, whether due to parental neglect or overwork, children are even more impressionable to social indoctrination. In the presence of parental violence or abuse, the child's entire world becomes permeated by the rule of barbarism, their perceptual system is swamped with toxicity, and it becomes difficult for them to survive, let alone conceptualise alternatives. Although this can foster criminality, it can also foster self destructive patterns and lifelong suffering, depression and other deprivation. Indoctrination can occur through identification with the oppressor, i.e., acceptance and valuation of barbaric philosophy and the decision to similarly become a barbarian (oppressive, domineering, inhumane), or through dis-identification and concomitant sense of powerlessness (suicidality, self-devaluing, depressed). A child's internal resistance is easily overcome through physical or mental brutalization. Children who try to resist adult barbarism learn to associate helplessness and hopelessness with such efforts and can conclude that barbarism is omnipotent. This critically impacts on his or her willingness to engage in later acts of resistance and, en masse, this is a critical factor in maintaining cultural apathy and in preventing social change. During barbaric insurgency, an adult individual's refusal to use barbaric methods is often made with a sense of resignation that resistance will result in less personal and social power.

Prevention: Preserving Unspoiled Inner World Habitat

While traumatic experiences are painful for both adults and children, the difference is that the adult brain is not literally shaped by the experience – becoming a different shape or size. The adult brain can recover from negative experience in the same way that the skin recovers from a cut. (The exception to this is when the adult was traumatized in childhood so that their early trauma is reactivated by negative experience and they have little recovery brain wiring to utilize for self-repair). For a child, neural highways determining their physical brain capacity as well as their perceptions of self (their first and primary resource as a human being) are laid down as determined by kind/nurturing or hostile/aggressive experiences in their early years.

Seventy percent of the brain mass is developed by the age of two and ninety percent by the age of three. The increase in the weight of the brain in early childhood is mainly due to myelination and the development of new neural pathways. Myelination is a process of laying a special coating down on nerve pathways that enable the brain message to move faster, very much like putting down bitumen or asphalt to enable faster movement for the 'message-mobiles' of the mind. Brain freeways get the brain from point A to B as quickly as possible without crossroads, stop lights or pauses; which creates automatic, sub-conscious behaviour. The speed with which the brain takes this superhighway is faster than conscious thought. You can tie your shoes, brush your teeth, stand, and walk and talk without having to think about it, because these behaviours all have myelinated pathways in your brain. The primary increase in brain weight in small children to the point of age 3 comes from the growth of these brain 'freeways' which the brain will find the most energy efficient to use for the rest of the person's life. If those pathways are destroyed then suddenly such effortless 'unconscious' processes require a lot of hard work as the brain labours to carve a new path. Stroke victims can attest to this.

Therefore, our childhood experiences create structure and habitual pathways of the brain which are real blood, neuronal, chemical and tissue differences in the brain. Super-highways are the fastest and most convenient paths for the brain to use, so fast they are often unconscious or subconscious. Our first learnings about self and the world are in this automatic category. The impact of aggression or nurturance on the developing person is myelinated fast enough to be subconscious. When early experiences are of uncaring, neglectful, harassed, or distant, adults the subconscious learning is one of deprivation and lack. When early experiences are of being overpowered by a violent, aggressive or hostile adult the subconscious learning is helplessness and hopelessness. When facing new experiences or others with authority the brain will automatically go to these experiences to know how to behave. When experience is inculcated into the brain along with strong emotion it makes the 'groove' of the superhighway even deeper in the brain. Because small children have such fragile, sensitive systems and little emotional control, it is easy to overarouse them and to create deep emotional learning. The presence of a caregiver who can soothe a child and help them to calm down is critical to healthy development of small children.

Neural pathways utilised during early childhood are strengthened and become like a superhighway; for good or bad. Those that are not used actually retract or wither and atrophy. This 'Use-dependence' is a functional adaptation to enable the brain to learn and to efficiently adapt to the child's environment. This is a wonderful thing if the infants' environment is good because the person's brain adapts in a positive and healthy direction. It is terrible if the environment is damaging because the child's brain literally adapts to, and grows into a shape molded by, negative experiences or trauma so the child's brain becomes 'efficient' only for trauma. The brain is shaped by the experiences given to the child with high emotion experiences, either fearful or pleasurable, leaving the greatest marks. We therefore mark a child by fostering their self development with loving and caring behaviours or by cauterizing their brains with unresponsive, cruel, aggressive or abusive treatment of them.

A child whose parents have multiple resources (emotional and social as well as financial) will be raised in an enriched and supported environment and will experience rich and supported brain development with multiple functional synaptic connections and efficient neural pathways. Conversely, the brain of a child raised in an impoverished or stressed environment will reflect these factors in brain disorganization and attendant reductions in his or her learning and capacities.

Educational Foundations: Trauma, Neglect and Learning

Trauma and neglect have specific, serious consequences for the developing person. Children impacted by deprivation and distress not only develop less efficient pathways for information processing but, more seriously, have brain pathways functional for crisis and trauma but inefficient for other experiences such as the non-trauma situations of friendship, school and work. Neurophysiology suggests that, at least in his foundational assumptions about the impact of early experience brain pattern becoming unconscious, Freud was on the right track. Barbarism towards children can create a generation that is brain wired for aggression and trauma (avoid or engage), but not for productivity and healthy relationship. More importantly, if a child is neglected or traumatised their inner world is shaped by misery. They suffer.

Trauma also creates life-long ill-health effects and higher health risk behaviours for that person for life. Any former smoker, heroin addict or gambler can confirm the difficulty of challenging ingrained habit patterns (myelinated pathways), even if they are more behavioural than emotional. Any new habit will initially be less efficient for the brain, just as it may be possible to drive a Volkswagen through an uncleared forest rather than use the highway, but the movement is slower, more circuitous, more difficult and less efficient. It is possible to develop new habits but the temptation for the brain is always to take the easier, quicker road of the well coated myelinated freeway built by early, powerful experience.

Because of the delicate nature of our raw developing systems when we are small our earliest experiences are well myelinated and often have the slick asphalt of deep emotion attached. Adults often don't want to identify or address early childhood patterns ingrained deeply on their neural pathways because it can be a lot of work and; if the experiences were traumatic, often will re-evoke terror and discomfort of the original experience (the automatic learned response), as new learning occurs. Therefore, we cannot afford the energy waste caused when barbaric philosophies are laid as a superhighway in a child's brain. Prioritizing care and nurturance of children and promoting pro-social norms towards them could effectively address many of our social problems. We can only imagine the human energy, effort and potential which could be possible if we took greater care of small children and laid better superhighways in the brains, minds, hearts and souls of our next generation. It would seem a logical path for an intelligent species to pursue.

Trauma: Cultural Costs of Invading the Right Hemisphere
Damage visited on children in early childhood has serious implications for future social and cultural well-being, as well as for national and individual health costs. Brain and self disfigurement visited on people in early childhood creates cumulative damage and social costs over time. When children lack essential foundational resources they are handicapped in subsequent developmental tasks such as being able to interact well with others, tackling new experiences, managing education and employment, and ultimately parenting children of their own. Therefore, financial investment into supporting and protecting human development during infancy and early childhood has a far greater impact on health, welfare and crime spending, than when invested in any other point of the lifespan. Conservative estimates put prevention as saving $7

for each dollar invested. More importantly, the great motivating factor for any humane society in ensuring the protection and nurturance of children should be preventing a lifetime of unnecessary suffering, hardship and misery for any human person, and preserving this safety for all citizens.

Unfortunately, as small children are voiceless and voteless, they are often the population that receives the least of society's financial resources, particularly during a barbaric era. If you want visible evidence of this, compare the vast corporate skyscrapers in any modern city – built to provide comfort and opulence for businessmen and the most powerful – with the resources in any daycare centre. Compare the vast amount of money invested into adult luxury and comfort, from golf courses and health clubs, to elite vehicles and holiday resorts - with the resources invested into the homes, carers, health and living environments provided for our smallest citizens during the decades of barbaric resurgency and, most particularly, in the environs of those born into poverty. Barbarians will claim we cannot afford to subsidize a child's life in the realms of childcare or healthcare or education but have no problem funding financial rescues, propaganda, new industry, or conflagrations.

Barbaric Attacks on Childhood

Adult Responsibility for the Next Generation

The first priority then, in addressing the damage that barbarism has wrought in our societies, is to attend to the damage that has been done to our children. Because of barbaric valuation of competitive aggression and dominance, barbaric systems don't consider the developmental needs of children as part of the species, and worse, create environments and systems, which harm children and cause long term developmental and emotional damage. The concept of child-friendly societies is seen by barbarians as unnecessary and foolish. Barbarians primarily conceptualise the issues of childhood under the schemata of socialization and indoctrination. That is, barbarian main focus with children is ensuring that they obey and conform to the barbaric social structures, not considering whether those social structures harm the child.

Children's expressions of distress, or inability to cope, usually give rise to barbarian aggression and violence towards children – rationalized as 'discipline' but usually far more about using terror and brutality to force the child to conform to barbaric rules and indoctrinating them that expressions of distress will not be tolerated. The viciousness and harshness of barbarian philosophies towards children asphyxiate the intelligence, skill and creative potential in children which could be used for human advancement if it were allowed to progress and develop. The impact of cruel, uncaring and vicious behaviour to children is listed first because childhood is the inseminating level of consciousness; the crucible in which the barbarism or humanism of the future is forged; and the domain where barbarism inflicts the most pain and suffering.

Children's Rights

Because children do not vote they are rarely accorded their full human rights. The United States has not ratified the convention on the rights of the child and the Australian report card is poor. If we have difficulty recognizing the full citizenship of children it is unlikely that we possess the depth of respect for their humanity to nurture them fully and well into adulthood, and certainly, we lack the capacity to draw on their perspectives in ways that could contribute to healthy democracy.

Besides the humane imperative to prevent any human from a life of misery there is a species imperative for preventing brain cauterization and harm to the developing person. As we face critical survival challenges, we can no longer afford to damage and waste the human brain capacity which could generate the alternatives we need for species survival. We urgently need conscious and protective strategies for young children and to change our perspective on their needs and value.

Each of us living in aggressive cultures needs to be constantly alert for evidence of our own infiltration by barbaric norms and to address our own early inculcation into the barbaric code. We need to guard against the delusion that we own our children and base our interactions with them on caring relationship and on our deep responsibility as guardians. Barbarians focus on concepts of owning people and bonded labour and use coercion and control to keep people close at hand. Parents don't own children. If we don't own our children, then relationship becomes the basis of all of our interactions. How we treat our children is then on the basis of nurturing them and on caring relationship. Wise parents understand that coercion and control have a limited timespan of effectiveness in enforcing ties between parent and child.

We can challenge our own belief in barbaric tenets and ensure that our behaviours do not slide towards the cruel or the hardhearted in our interactions with others and particularly with children. We must resolve that any increase in our own tendency to be willing to inflict pain, suffering or hardship on others, to criticize another savagely or be interpersonally aggressive, is halted and eradicated. We can ensure that each of our personal interactions with children consciously nurture, ennoble, and support, them and that we stand firmly and resolutely against actions and social norms which are harmful to children, including increases in social acceptance of competitive aggression in a culture.

We cannot avoid exposing our children to the realities of the wider cultural norms but we can insulate and protect children from their effects. Although many fundamentalist religious sects seek to isolate children from the culture, this can foster a naïveté that makes their members particularly tasty morsels for predators and/or incapable of surviving outside of the religious group. Right wing conservatives tend to get fixated on limiting children's exposure to interpersonal violence on television and on the Internet because, for conservatives, this is in line with their preferred influence tactic of increasing social control and control of others' behaviour. Conservatives ignore the more powerful ingraining effects on children of experiencing, or observing, repeated successful social aggression, including that used by conservatives themselves in forcing others to conform to barbaric mandates.

Newborns will cry in empathy if they hear another baby crying. This means that fledgling humans must be taken a long way from their newborn state to be inculcated into barbarism. Young children, before they experience the stringencies of harsh socialization or our schooling system, have an almost dazzling clarity about human problems and the possibilities for their resolution. While barbarians tend to see children primarily as a liability, in truth, were we to properly value our children they would not only be a future resource but also an invaluable aid in the task of enabling humane species consciousness. In just one example, Professor Emilie Smith, conducting a study about racism, questioned young children about race and what it meant. One child matter of factly responded with, 'Well, we're all just blood and guts... right?' It is this type of piercing clarity that is essential for us as a species in the confusion and manipulated information era of the 21st century.

Systemic Barbaric Oppression of Children

Brutality perpetrated on people when they are children is the most effective tool in the barbarian arsenal for perpetuation of self interested, ego-based rule. Barbarian focus on economic elite adults, low regard for human vulnerability, and valuation of aggressive dominance, means that they often create systems which are hostile towards children, deprive them of necessary care and support, and force them into adult levels of independence before they are developmentally ready. Barbarian leaders typically express little care or concern for the welfare of children, except in a kind of patronising, 'read a story book for the media' kind of way. Childrens' vulnerability means they should be a top priority in all human planning processes.

Barbaric systems lack the protective mechanisms and structures that could foster children's development in healthy, sustainable and supportive ways. At the worst extreme, barbaric systems exploit the vulnerability of childhood for the purposes of profit and self-aggrandisement. The common barbaric practice of forcing children into independence, whether through poor and inadequate child care facilities, forcing the primary caregiver into work without providing appropriate care, or any of the myriad of other barbaric policies and strategies designed with no thought of the impact on children, can cause levels of intrapsychic damage for children which can halt their healthy developmental progress. There are a wide range of barbaric methods, laws, perspectives and processes which can perpetrate damage for children. Some of these are explored in the following sections

Strategy A: Reify Production — Deride and Dismiss Human Need

The current, quasi-fanatical, reification of markets, production and economics has fostered barbaric incursion into the realms of childhood. Our societies have invested heavily in technological advance and very little, comparatively, into the psychological, emotional and social development of the species, particularly during the critical formative years of infancy and childhood. The reasoning behind this choice is elusive, but the results are patently clear. As a species, we now have the technological capacity to destroy ourselves but we lack the complex psychological and emotional skills to respond effectively to this reality.

Our investment in mechanised, technological advancement is partly the result of our mass inculcation into the well marketed mythology that increased technology, production, and mechanisation, are the primary vehicles that cause species advancement and increase in the quality of human life. Unfortunately, no one was monitoring to identify the zenith point at which mechanised production ceased to add to human quality of life; thus allowing the point at which production began to be detrimental to our daily lives to slip by unnoticed. Our almost exclusive production focus is also partly a result of the barbaric tendency for action without adequate planning or complex thought. A market focus deifies production and economic growth and places human life in subjugation to the profit deity. This belief system encourages casual acceptance of Tenets I and II of the barbaric creed: Destruction of life systems and survival of the 'fittest.'

The widespread lack of public understanding about the importance of childhood is an example of the ignorance fostered by our limited investment into the psychological and emotional realms which, in fact, represent the majority of human lived experience. Public attention is rarely directed towards the vast neurobiological and neuropsychological knowledge we have describing how easily we can advantage or damage an individual's lifelong capacities by the experiences we give them during childhood. Sub-standard, poor public understanding and limited dissemination of information about the type and extent of damage which can be inflicted on the brains of children is as much of a threat to the species as nuclear arms and global warming if only because such harm creates damaged adults with impeded impulse control.

Exhibit A: Australia

In Australia, the phenomenon of damage to children and the realm of childhood that is caused by barbarism were exemplified in the recent 'economic boom' by escalating rates of child abuse, juvenile arrests and interpersonal violence. Barbaric social norms instituted and reified during this time had direct effects on children, increasing the hardship, deprivation, violence and cruelty to which they were exposed, especially those who were born into the lowest SES and the most vulnerable strata of our society. Recent statistics released by the Australian Institute for Health and Welfare (2007-2008) provide one small window of the full panorama of the effect of the barbaric reign on children. This report notes that the numbers of notifications of child abuse or neglect more than doubled in the last decade. Specifically, the following statistics were reported:

- The number of children on care and protection orders rose by more than 100% from 30 June 1998 to 30 June 2008.
- Across Australia, the rates of Indigenous children on care and protection orders were more than 7 times as high as for other children.
- The rates of children on care and protection orders in Australia increased from 3.5 per 1,000 at 30 June 1998 to 6.9 per 1,000 at 30 June 2008.
- The number of child protection notifications increased by 26% over the last four years, from 252,831 in 2004-05 to 317,526 to in 2007-08.
- The numbers in out-of-home care rose by almost 115% from 14,470 at 30 June 1998 to 31,166 at 30 June 2008.
- The average rise over the period 1998 to 2008 has been just over 8% .
- The rate of children in out-of-home care in Australia increased from 3.1 per 1,000 at 30 June 1998 to 6.2 per 1,000 at 30 June 2008.
- The rate of Indigenous children in out-of-home care was almost 9 times the rate of other children.

These nameless statistics represent 317 000 small and vulnerable children whose suffering was so severe it was publicly witnessed to the very serious extent that is required for state intervention. We should consider therefore, that these statistics represent the tip of the iceberg of child suffering during the 'boom.' When economists boast of rates of economic growth they should concurrently be required to report the correlational increases in harm to children so that the public is given a fuller picture. A 5% economic increase fed by an 8% increase in the numbers of children abused is a much more composite picture of the past decade in Australia. While empiricists may quibble about correlation not implying causation it would be unethical to conduct the type of mass experiment from which to deduce causation. It would also be redundant given that history gives us a more than adequately sampled human population.

As previously mentioned, these serious child abuse statistics are not representative of the full scope and extent of damage occurring for children. Australia, as at the time of this writing, does not rank well in its treatment of children and we must soberly face the reality that most damage to children goes unreported. Firstly, because damaging children is often socially normalized and considered acceptable. During barbaric insurgency it is even considered socially desirable. Secondly, most abuse of children occurs in the domains of the home or the school, where adults have absolute power, control and sovereignty. Children's age and dependency means they can rarely self-report even if they had the means, let alone the complex conceptualization capacities, required to do so. It is only when the significant injury or violence perpetrated on a child is witnessed by a concerned adult member of the public and validated by the state, that a child become one of the recorded child abuse statistics. While significant physical violence also perpetrates damage on the inner world it is only one of the many levels at which the self and psyche can be damaged, cauterized or mutilated. We can gain a few insights into the world and suffering of our children during our economic 'boom', by considering what the data below might mean in terms of the misery of a small child whose whole reality and day-to-day life is represented by just one of these 'stats.'

The UNICEF ranking of factors related to child wellbeing placed Australia 17th in its ranking of the treatment of children across 22 wealthy nations. Our children have a 1 in 4 chance of living in a home where there is adult mental illness and 680 000 of our children live in poverty. We rank 20 out of 27 nations for our infant mortality rate and this death rate is doubled for indigenous babies. Our youth road deaths are 12 times higher than Portugal. Australian children are 12 times more likely to live in a jobless household than those in Japan. Indigenous teens (suffering double disadvantage) have some of the highest pregnancy rates and our indigenous youth have the second highest suicide rate in the OECD. Fourteen percent of our youth (aged 4-17) have a mental health problem and ten percent of our children (aged 10-14) are reported as having long term entrenched mental health and behavioural problems. Our teen pregnancy rates are much higher than the OECD average.

Ranking the Value of Children in Barbarian Priority Systems

Because children are vulnerable and have little power barbaric philosophy pays little time or attention to their welfare. They are seen as of little importance, of low value, and as meriting few resources. Within barbaric philosophy, violence, aggression and harshness towards children is standard practice and considered part of 'good socialization' for their role as future barbarians. As with most realms, barbarians are ignorant of the real limits for children and the developmental damage which can be inflicted if those limits are exceeded or overrun. Even when barbarians are made conscious of the enormous suffering which can be inflicted during early childhood they tend to respond only in ways which assert their power as the authority and are careless about the complex and difficult work needed to ensure the appropriate care and nurturance of children. The knee jerk Northern Territory intervention implemented by the Howard government is a prime example.

In terms of barbaric focus, policy, and economic investment, children as a group are rarely considered unless it is to deal with the 'nuisance' that childbearing causes to profit making and; in poor populations, in interrupting the flow of accessible low paid labour. Barbarians' primary concerns in relation to childhood are usually related to finding the cheapest possible ways to provide childcare so that the parents of small children can be coerced or enticed back into the labour market. In the past two decades, both Australia and the United States removed welfare protection for single mothers and their children, often forcing children's sole caregiver into the low paid workforce. In Australia new 'work for the dole' programs forced single parents into the workplace without any guarantee of provision of care for dependents.

Single mothers are less likely to have the type of social support which would assist them in their work and caregiving duties, are more likely to be poor, and to not be able to access good quality care for their children. Once forced into the workplace they have less capacity to protect their child and no control over the quality of care their child receives. Subsequently, the children of the poor are most likely to be the children who have not been given adequate care in their most crucial developmental years from the ages 0 to 5. This means that many are not ready for school when they enter the education system. The damage to their capacity to learn is then compounded through their school years, effectively preventing them from getting an education that would enable them to join economic elites, thus trapping them within the same cycle of poverty as their parent. Then then bear the marks of early deprivation for the rest of their life. Erroneously, this damage is often blamed on the individual mother rather than on the social burden she is forced to carry.

Barbarism seeks the most vulnerable victims. Children who have been abused or traumatized in early childhood often end up being ignored, categorized as dumb, ridiculed, punished or failed, in a schooling system which does not acknowledge the reality of child abuse. Academic failure or inability gives the child an external liability which impacts on their opportunities for the rest of their lives and spreads the internal disability into limited external capacity. Abuse is compounded and the child is doubly abused by being penalized for having pain as a result of trauma. It is easier for individual teachers or society to categorize a child as 'dumb', 'lazy' or 'disruptive' than to take the time to find out why children are doing poorly and, to take the adult responsibility of ensuring that the inner pain of all children in the school system is at a low enough level for them to be able to learn. Barbaric myths that not all children are capable of learning facilitate this second oppression.

Conversely, the care, wellbeing and developmental needs of poor children are not of concern to barbarians. The short term and self-centred nature of barbarism means that barbarians are focussed on maximum profit and exploitation in the moment. They do not concern themselves with the concept of the future or of the intergenerational effects of their behaviours. Barbarians are typically uncaring about the suffering that coercive and aggressive environments and behaviours can inflict on small children and ignorant about the developmental damage that can occur when there is inadequate care.

The Case of Australian Childcare

During the recent barbaric insurgency in Australia a milk distribution entrepreneur realized that the enforcement of workforce participation by the regime, accompanied by the abolition of public subsidies for nonprofit day care, made childcare a new boom area for profiteering. The introduction of work regimes for single mothers and increases in land and housing costs for couples made childcare a service needed, as he stated, 'much like milk distribution.' His experience in establishing market dominance was combined with the advantage of being able to combine share market power with the public power of taxpayers' money. This was provided freely by a conservative regime bent on privatising childcare, irrespective of the standards this fostered.

By targeting childcare properties in prime locations, single day-care centres and smaller child-care networks and then using aggressive market tactics against small operators who were unused to being in the competitive market, this lone businessman was able to take over small, privately owned care centres. Small centres were undefended and unequipped to resist barbaric market aggression, irrespective of their longevity or the quality of care they provided to children. Using the competitive, franchised, market model this lone speculator set up over a thousand centres across the nation which took on the franchised 'care' of approximately 120 000 children. His company became Australia's predominant childcare and the world's largest childcare provider.

Critics pointed out that these centres were making private profit from public monies. In one year Australian taxpayer's monies represented $128 of the $143 million profit. The founder's personal wealth skyrocketed to approximately $260 million while staff in these centres were paid between $12 and $27 under award conditions. The government privatising childcare paid no heed to how this might affect the care provided to our most precious national resource, our children. After huge profiteering, to the tune of $2.5 billion dollars of market capitalisation, the company went into receivership and the incoming government had to provide $56 million dollars to keep the outgoing conservatives' newly 'privatised, share owned' childcare centres operating. The public has had to pay twice for a resource that is now gathering profit for private individuals. The public also paid $15 million dollars to aid a new purchaser when the childcare centres were sold by 'bid' to the highest bidder. While much palaver has been made over the financial losses fewer questions have been asked about this aggressive takeover of non-profit Australian childcare.

Critical social questions for us might be: How is it that barbarians were able to relocate the domain of caring for our small children into the aggressive, competitive, market sector? Why did Australians even countenance the notion of child care as profit-producing market stock? Subsidised by public money it was obvious that pirates would be attracted into the now lucrative realm of 'childcare' with or without any real sense of care for the wellbeing of children.

While profit explains some of our apathy we still must ask why Australians allowed such an incursion into the important realm of our most vulnerable citizens. Our easy acquiescence illustrates our own barbaric infiltration as a culture and some of our national indoctrination into the barbaric creed. Our lack of assiduous care and prioritizing of children's needs; our parallel lack of investment into their care, their developmental needs and their nurturance, demonstrates a barbaric apathy. In the main, the market profit generated by privatising child care has been paid for by taxpayers' public money; the loss of many carers motivated by commitment to the wellbeing of children rather than to profit; and the suffering of children when placed in mass produced, franchised services without attendant regulations focussed on care motivation. Widespread dismantling of systems of care is a marker of barbaric reign, as is decreased choice for families and caregivers, and increased pressure to participate in the competitive work market. All of these factors lower resistance to barbaric insurgency.

In short, the indicators of the health and wellbeing of our children are a national shame. The fact that child wellbeing has declined in the face of a boom in economic prosperity is an indictment on our adulthood as a nation. One might ask, Do our children feel 'prosperous' if they were born during this recent economic 'boom'? What is like to be a child in Australia? The following national sections explore this query.

Cultural Norms: Silencing the Child

What happens when children then use the only vehicles they have to express distress at quality of care or painful experience: negative emotion and behaviour? In Australia, when our children express their difficulty coping with frenetic pace or with surrounding social or adult aggression, such as that experienced with barbaric cultural norms or even poor childcare, we have a high propensity towards drugging them. Australia has at least 50,000 children taking stimulants for Attention Deficit Hyperactivity Disorder (ADHD) alone, without including the numbers of children on other psychostimulants and mood altering medications. This rate is one of the highest in the world. Internationally and nationally, we have very poor systems for the monitoring of drug side effects for children, let alone the effects of powerful psychostimulants. Because of their developing (and sometimes damaged) cognitive and language capacities many of these side effects will be borne by the child alone in their 'inner world.' The external world for adult is however, rendered more 'pleasant' in that the adult no longer has to deal with the distress of the child. We should ask, what is the experience of being 'more controlled' in the inner world like for a small child who was experiencing distress about the way the external world was functioning? What happens when, agitated behaviour; his or her only vehicle to express distress; due to limited capacity to talk and reason; is silenced and chemically strangled?

What happens to the physiological, homeostatic and psychological systems of a child when their behavioural expression is forcibly chemically subdued? We have no data on the impact of behavioural suppression on the development of the child's other regulatory systems. Teachers and adults routinely report psychostimulants as being 'highly beneficial' because up to three quarters of children become 'calmer and more controlled' which increases adult comfort, but we don't have any data on the long-term effects of these stimulants on a child's developing brain and nervous systems. We do have data which shows that children on psychostimulants to combat ADHD are ten times more likely to perform poorly at school than non-medicated peers. In other words, the drugs are not primarily for the wellbeing or educational capacities of the child.

This is one example where acknowledging the human inner world and children's vulnerability is critical to gaining a full understanding of the effects of our adult power. There are other consequences of medicating our children at such high rates. In one Australian state: Western Australia (WA), where rates of ADHD drugging are up to five times the rates of other Australian states there were almost 4500 child drug offenders caught in the twelve month period of 2007-2008. Children aged 5 and younger were picked up with amphetamines and cannabis. One in six Western Australian children is affected by mental health problems in a given year. In 2008 alone, 366 Western Australian children (not adolescents), some as young as ten, presented to emergency departments for alcohol related injuries and illnesses. This presentation would represent a very small slice of the number of our children who are drinking. While this certainly presents a problem for the outer world of adults, we must begin to consider what the inner world of these children must look like. It is not a Tuscan landscape.

Further Calculations of Inner World Damage

Statistics show a steady quarter of all 12 – 15 year old Australian youths are drinkers and the amount they're drinking is continually increasing. Binge drinking, long a social norm among Australian adults, is now normal for adolescents. Western Australian Emergency Departments have reported increases in presentations of intoxicated teenagers who must have their stomachs pumped because of alcohol poisoning – some with blood-alcohol levels of more than 0.15 percent. Our children are telling us something about our way of life and our social 'dream'.

The aforementioned statistics represent just some of the recordable, visible damage from which we can gather data in the external world.

Such data is often simply making visual the flow on effect of much greater inner world damage. If we begin to consider the full (both inner and outer world) costs, that children might be bearing, we must use a different accounting system for weighing 'prosperity' and for calculating the full costs of relying on the barbaric creed. We will need to take damage to the psyche and the inner world seriously to have any real effect on these types of social problems and social decay. We most certainly can't afford to allow barbarism to wreak havoc on the inner world of another generation. If, as a nation, we claim to want to nurture the next generation and to foster species advancement, then the care of children should be our utmost priority.

Marking the Child: Barbarism and the School System

Barbarism is based primarily on the use of aggression, intimidation and coercion to arouse fear so the dominator can establish or perpetuate control over others. It is a system therefore, which is fundamentally opposed to the processes of human empowerment. Under barbaric rule, the domains of education, health and welfare become subjected to increasing scrutiny and reporting requirements. During the recent economic 'boom' businesses had their legislative and reporting requirements diminished, while health and human professionals found themselves under increasing levels of surveillance, increased monitoring and reporting regulations, and increasingly required to justify their existence. While businesses should be required to justify their existence; health care and educational systems are part of human rights and should be exempt from such processes.

Under a barbaric regime the focus of education becomes bureaucratic compliance and linear outcomes, rather than good educational processes. The interpersonal, relational and concrete approaches that foster children's learning and increase their comfort and capacity in a learning environment are ignored while bureaucratic regulations are militantly enforced. Childcare privatized in franchise systems of low paid labour are the scaffolding to feed children into an uncaring school system for further powerful indoctrination into calloused behaviour.

With a barbaric external outcome focus, schools that do not produce outcomes (reading, writing and arithmetic), irrespective of their funding, population cohort, or resources, are punished. The inner world of the child and their experience of the education process become considered irrelevant. Schools that produce good outcomes, even if they already financially advantaged with private funding and wealthy populace, are given even more cash as reward for being 'on top', superior, and elite. Thus the advantaged receive more advantage. The priority is on rewarding dominance, not on the care of all of the population, or on assisting the disadvantaged. During the Howard neoliberal era, funding to private schools reached obscene levels while funding for public education was slashed. Concurrently, there was an increased focus on the testing of children, comparison of test scores across schools (private vs. public, high vs. low socioeconomic areas) and increased bureaucratic reporting requirements for teachers. The reporting was not to assess teachers' capacity to nurture children's intelligence or teachers' interpersonal capacity with, or affection for, children; but to monitor and enforce paperwork and bureaucratic conformity.

Barbaric After Effects

After a long tenure of barbaric rule therefore, the education system may be primarily composed of people whose primary focus is on control, career advancement, and bureaucratic adherence. Unfortunately, barbaric approaches to education advantage those professionals who use coercive control in their classrooms with children. These people advance through the education system hierarchy during barbaric insurgency, because they enjoy bureaucratic process and are willing to commit time to the paperwork and the self-aggrandisement that will enable their personal advancement even if their teaching suffers. Bureaucratically oriented teachers are also more than pleased to conform to barbaric methods of increased testing and labeling of children, authoritarian stringency in the classrooms and aggressive professional competition amongst peers. Less barbarically oriented teachers may resist these techniques and will often pay the price in terms of career advancement. Bureaucratic and power oriented teachers often achieve greater rank under barbaric dominion, and this poses a block to positive educational change once there is a change of government away from barbarism. The legacy of barbarian rule is often left in the highest decision making echelons of systems which may be populated by those who took advantage of barbaric infiltration of education, health and welfare systems, to competitively advance themselves. Such individuals actively block or slow progressive change counter to maintaining dominance and their own position of power. President Obama experienced the full force of this phenomenon in his first year in office.

Teachers who focus on the day-to-day and moment-to-moment interactions with children and who are highly skilled in the complex reflexivity which fosters the well-being of children have less time to commit to bureaucratic endeavour. Their time goes primarily into fostering relationship with children and attending to their needs. They have less time to devote to the type of bureaucratic rigmarole that allows advancement during barbaric tenure. Teachers who entered the profession because of their love of children and who have a creative approach to the learning process are often forced to leave teaching during a barbaric reign because of the increased hostility, competitiveness, and bureaucracy, within the education system. The consequence of this is that there is an increasing likelihood that young children entering the school system will be being taught, and under the daily control of, harsh, coercive and punitive adults who entered the profession primarily because of the opportunity to exercise power over others, rather than for their love of children. Indeed, barbaric incursion into the education system is such that teachers, who themselves accept and use interpersonal aggression, are unable to address the increased incidence of bullying and aggression among children in our school systems. If a society holds up the rule of abusive people as an inviolate right then the child has no hope.

Practical Approaches to Preventing Barbarism in Schools

Some of the nicest people in the world are teachers, and some of the most sadistic bullies are teachers, because the role gives huge control power over vulnerable people who have no voice and cannot resist. We must diligently screen teachers as part of our adult responsibility to protect children. From a longer term perspective, the practice of using university score as the only tool to determine entry into a teaching program is inadequate. In Australia, the fact that only a low entry score is required and that the teaching profession offers long periods of vacation and lucrative pay, can encourage uncaring people into the profession. Part of our adult responsibility is to ensure that those who enter the teaching profession are empathic, caring individuals who enjoy children and have a high level of complex interpersonal skills. Anything less is a failure of a duty of care. When you consider the absolute power a teacher wields over a child in a classroom, the opportunity for positive or damaging influence over an individual's entire life is enormous. Coercive, controlling individuals with a mean streak should never be left with authority over children. Screening for such tendencies should be mandatory within education, health and welfare; not with a punitive focus towards individuals, but definitely with clarity about adult responsibility to protect children. Individuals who are coercive and controlling should be given limited social influence, retraining and encouraged into professions where they are not working with vulnerable humans or humans at any point of vulnerability in the lifespan (including the elderly, the young, the sick, or the disabled.) There is a wide range of mechanistic or technology oriented professions, where precision, control and obsession with detail, are actually advantageous.

The great Spanish cellist Pablo Casals, himself a fugitive from a barbarian insurgency, made the following observation about the distinction between barbarian (external world) and empowering (internal world) approaches to education:

> What do we teach our children? We teach them that two and two make four....When will we also teach them what they are?We should say to each of them: Do you know what you are? You are a marvel....You may become a Shakespeare, a Michaelangelo, a Beethoven. You have the capacity for anything. Yes, you are a marvel. And when you grow up, can you then harm another who is, like you, a marvel? You must work, we must all work, to make the world worthy of its children.
> Pablo Casals

The importance of preventing ongoing human inculcation into barbarism is captured in the statement, 'Yes, you are a marvel. And when you grow up, can you harm another who is, like you, a marvel?' If adult humans developed the capacity, the will, and the discipline, to hear emotional suffering in small children and would witness the pain, suffering and psychic mutilation, of many of our small children in the preschool years, it would put modern horror movies to pale. The fact that we force the psychologically deprived child to compete against the psychologically well fed child is the school system is one reason we have so much difficulty advancing so-called disadvantaged populations. Placing traumatised children into the care of harsh, hardhearted or unfeeling teachers only compounds their difficulty and prevents educational progress. As Casals notes, children are marvels and if we will simply protect them; prevent and address inner world damage; and nurture them, we will create a human race of mind blowing capacity. It is up to us, as adults, to make the social world worthy of the capacity and loving self that is the undamaged child and to prevent the ongoing barbaric indoctrination which is blocking our species progress.

Summary

The brain and the psyche, coexist, and in some ways, symbiotically create, the inner world in which the self is nested. It is this space that a child uses to experience the outer world. It is possible for other humans to mutilate or enhance our sense of self when we are small because our physical helplessness and vulnerability combine with our neurological and brain physiological processes to mean that we have few walls to resist penetration of our inner world (fusion of brain and psyche). This is the period of life when other humans are easily able to enter our world and have a massive effect upon who we think we are. Adult choices and behaviors towards children during this time of early vulnerability can either nurture or ravage the inner world that a person lives with for the rest of their lives. In effect, adults around us leave their imprint on our living brains. Their kindness or cruelty towards us will enhance or impair (respectively) our capacity; sense of self, and the inner world, which is the vehicle for all of the rest of our experiences.

It appears that the human brain is set up for humane behaviours, not for cruelty. Similar to the outer physical world, adults can beautify, nurture and tend; or desecrate, despoil and uglify; the inner world of the child. This is the deepest level of the human self, the deepest resource of a person and the core of their human dignity. Barbaric cruelty in the form of cruel, unfeeling, hard hearted responses to children disrespects this deeply private space which represents the core of a human person. Barbarism can permanently trash a person's internal living room.

The quality of sensory stimulation, human warmth and tender care that is experienced in the early years doesn't just affect emotion but also affects the body's capacity to regulate critical body functions, to think and to interact with others. One of the oft ignored effects of children being traumatized is that a person who has been harmed in early life is investing considerable energy in ongoing management of that trauma through less efficient brain functioning. Humans are finite and we have finite energy (despite workplace propaganda to the contrary). Less efficient brain functioning or dysfunctional patterns drain energy away from the person's capacity for new learning, body repair and physiological maintenance. Inefficient homeostatic state regulation is linked to poor health outcomes and lower intellectual and relational productivity. This, along with the multiple external stresses they face, is part of why the poor suffer worse health than the privileged.

The experiences to which the small child is exposed will affect all domains of their life including health, relationships, work, learning capacities, adult success and achievements. Again, it is a wonderful advantage if the learned brain pattern response is optimism, curiosity and positive expectation; but terrible if the superhighway is trauma, fear and horror, because people feel these feelings before any conscious, rational thought is possible. Freud used the terms the 'unconscious' or 'subconscious', to refer to the paths in the brain which are travelled with such speed that we don't even notice them. They are the window through which we observe and perceive external reality. This is part of why adults find identifying and challenging early thinking and learning difficult. It takes a lot of conscious effort to identify a message which moves so quickly it that we often will only feel the emotion of it (usually fear or curiosity). Once adults identify an early learned pathway (from past experience) it takes effort to slow the brain down, block it from travelling familiar and easy routes and then to train it to take a different path. It can literally hurt.

Because barbarian systems focus on catering for the needs of competitive adults their policies, funding rules and social norms are constructed to benefit this elite population. The consequences of being born into a society with an aggressive, competitive, dominance focus are serious for children. Barbarian reign typically places children at such a low priority that funding for children's welfare becomes almost non-existent. Barbarians do not moderate their arrogant aggression or show mercy, even for the vulnerabilities of childhood. This results in many children, particularly those born into underprivileged environments, being exposed to unnecessary deprivation and suffering. Neglectful and inadequate, or, worse; cruel and inhumane education, family, social and care systems, are dangerous for children. These are the systems which get developed, funded and advanced during a barbaric era.

The exclusive focus on economic profit combined with the typical barbaric calloused and merciless attitudes towards those who cannot fend for themselves leaves children, and particularly poor children, without their inner world first skin of calm and sense of safety; their second skin of confidence; the protective shell of necessary family support and a safe outer world of healthy, caring systems, communities and cultures. Barbarians place little focus on early childhood and invest few resources in our most vulnerable and precious resources for the future—children.

CHAPTER 6: BARBARISM & CULTURAL LIFE

PROTECTING THE DOMAIN OF THE CHILD

Barbarism damages all systems which have sensitivity. This includes the nervous, physical and emotional systems of small children as well as the deep web of ecology and relationships upon which rich living is based. Because barbarism is a clumsy, unrefined and unintelligent code, it is unable to deal with complex, living or sensing systems. The barbaric creed, by virtue of its calloused nature and careless stance, is therefore a threat to any system which is living, delicate, or fragile. The ozone layer, in relation to the earth comparatively similar in thickness to the skin on an apple, is a delicate system. A child is a vulnerable psychological and emotional human system. Healthy families and communities are finely tuned systems of care which function as sensing, responsive, relational organisms. Due to our undue focus on industrial production and money making we have only crude understanding of the components and qualities of these complex systems.

When living systems are working well their mechanisms are generally imperceptible to our awareness and they reliably and consistently generate health and wellbeing. The sensitivity and delicacy of these systems is directly related to their complex, living nature. When they are broken or mutilated we usually have little knowledge of how to reconstruct or repair them. Once we have mutilated them, we do not have the capacity to bring them back to life. Only Frankenstein type creations can be revivified in a simplistic manner. For example, we cannot 'rebuild' a 50 000 year old Aboriginal culture in a few generations once we have decimated it. Thus, our stance should be one of diligent forethought and cautious care.

Our aim should not be to push delicate systems to their extremities to see how much they can take before they break, but to approach them respectfully and to be extremely circumspect about their use. Through lack of care, arrogance, violence and aggression barbarism invades and pillages the delicately balanced systems, not only of the environment, but of people's work, family and community lives. Invading and over-riding protective barriers, barbarians destroy precious sensing systems often without even being aware of their existence, let alone conscious of their central import. During short sighted 'profit making' moves essential boundaries are overrun, invaluable resources consumed, and indispensable systems destroyed. Money making is an inadequate justification for damage to life systems.

Child-toxic Societies

When work life becomes barbaric the constancy of home, family and community life is eroded. Precious and intangible elements of quality life such as sustainable pace, rhythm, ritual, relationship, community life, belonging, and routine, are destroyed. The critical contribution of such qualities to the healthy development of children isn't even considered in the stampede for profit. The impact of forcing children to move at the frenzied, manic, pace driven by adult greed and to achieve their developmental tasks under panic conditions has had incalculable effect. Each child's brain pathways grows at a rate and in a manner as individual as the child's fingerprint. Violently forcing the diverse and unique selves of children to conform to adult pace simply to make money is a classic example of the idiocy of short-term barbaric perspective.

We have lost much in the frantic race to be included in the lead pack. We have taken from our children the time and the right to sit aimlessly in the grass and watch insects walk past; to have their complex neuronal systems stimulated in equally complex ways by nature and leisure. In a ceaseless round of activities designed to groom children for elite competition we have taken from them the right to watch the clouds drift by, to think their own thoughts, to dream their own dreams, and to let their body and mind systems grow at their own pace. The regime of the external workplace has invaded the home space so that children are now regimented at earlier and earlier ages. As early as age 3 they must adjust to production line education with resulting impacts now endemic in our education system. The modern epidemic of ADHD and behavioural disorders in children too young to even begin their formal education is a national and international scandal directly attributable to the slide to barbarism and the overvaluation of the material status. Gentle predictable routine in daily life without freneticism, chaos and panic, provides an essential, soothing rhythm and steady beat for the growth of children's hearts, minds and souls.

In the frenetic goldrush of the 80s, 90s and early 2000s the largest portion of the booty was taken from the most vulnerable. The life worlds of children, the elderly, the poor, animals and undefended humans were the domains that were looted. Because of the creed's ideology of competitive dominance and 'fair game' there was no ethical dilemma for barbarians in pillaging defenceless life worlds. Lower power groups are seen simply as targets that require fewer barbarian resources to pillage. Low power is seen simply as an advantage: less capacity for resistance. Critical resources of care, time, and nurturance have been stripped from children and other voiceless groups to feed the insatiable appetite of the market and the purses of the wealthy. In doing so barbarism peeled back and destroyed many of the social and personal protective layers around small children. Just as peeling the hard shell of an egg away from the developing chick causes premature exposure which can damage or destroy the chick; the layers of sustainable family life, work life and gentle community living, which protect the sensitive developing systems of a child, have been peeled away in this barbaric era. The resources of time and care taken from parents and communities might only represent a new bauble added to the crown of a wealthy person but to the child they may represent life itself. Sustainable and enjoyable life has generally been extracted from the poor across developed and developing contexts. The wasteful and careless manner with which the essential, life sustaining resources of the poor, and of children, have been consumed by elites will go down in history as a mark of the severity of this most recent barbaric insurgency.

Cannibalised Culture

In Australia, during the Howard regime, a small but powerful group of legislators destroyed equal opportunity industrial relations legislation that had taken centuries of human struggle to attain. In a re-enactment of the centuries old power of the aristocracy the democratic struggle and sacrifices of hundreds of thousands of Australians were over-ridden by the legislative dominance of an elite few. The barbaric cost of the newly aggressive work environments has been mainly paid in individual's home and personal lives. Individuals were not recompensed for this loss, and, as resources were taken in a hostile takeover of legislative and democratic freedoms, resistance was made difficult. Individuals paid for these changes from the limited precious stores of their own time, energy, and personal life.

An increasingly barbaric workplace has meant increasing pressure and stress on employees who have been forced to work 60, 70 and more hours for their 40 hours of pay. Australia leads the OECD with the longest work hours. The imbalance of work/family life fostered by the new workplace regime and increased dominance over workers has meant additionally that Australians have not taken 121 million days of leave – worth approximately 31 billion dollars. Might this not represent some of our so-called 'economic growth?' Exhausted workers feed their kids fast food and then are attacked for creating an 'obesity epidemic.' A few elites accumulate the profit from the 20 to 30 hours of unpaid labour contributed weekly by individuals, and they profit in a big way. Multiply the pillaging of the life of the individual by thousands and millions of workers and billions of profiteering dollars result.

So what does this mean in real terms? Protective influence emanates from the family. Children no longer have a protective culture, community or even family circle around them. It means that often, the poorest children have been left in inadequate care while their caregivers have been forced into low pay exploitative labour to benefit the powerful. The parent returning home after a stressful day in an aggressive competitive environment is bringing home 20 to 30 hours of unpaid labour, now required, simply as a term of employment. Such a parent does not have time for the intricacies and care of relational life. No time to prepare nourishing meals, no time to listen to a child's rambling story of the day, no time to observe the developmental progress or damage their child has sustained in the hands of a carer, no time for the casual and tender exchanges that feed a couple's intimacy and relationship. The time that could have been devoted to these exchanges in a humane culture becomes consumed instead with the need to cram the unpaid tasks of creating home and relationship into the ever dwindling hours left intact after voracious barbaric pillaging.

In the past, the dynamics of time poverty and task overload have been observed in lower socio-economic groups, and particularly among single mothers who carry the double burden of the parent role and who are often uneducated, and in low paid labour. It is a new phenomenon to have this level of exploitation, time poverty and stress, spread to all echelons of the culture except that of the very elite. This has been a brutal blow to the quality of life and family life of the average citizen and, by extension, to the health of the culture. In effect, the right to family and relational life, rest, relaxation, and private time, has been removed from all but the very top few percent of the culture. Barbaros Ultimus.

Is it any wonder then that couples under pressure, spend more time fighting over who will do the unpaid work? They are fighting each other, when really the culprit for their stress and time poverty exists outside of the home. Partners may even divorce over the external tension and pressure displaced onto their home and relationship while the root cause of the damage to people's daily private life continues unabated. Once divorced, these individuals must continue to maintain home and family life in a cannibalised culture, where work extracts their private as well as their public energy. Increasing numbers of employees burn out, withdraw from the corporate world, or suffer mental and physical health effects but children pay the highest price of all.

Peeling Back Protective Layers: Family Life

A child's first wealth is a family rich in mutual love and care which can provide a healthy 'pond' to maintain the health of their inner world. The poor used to be poor in money and resources but had the advantage of their own time. They often used this time resource to foster and create networks of social support which provided other resources in time of need. Close relational networks of kin and neighbour could step in and help with childcare and other tasks if there was a sickness or misfortune in a family. In countries such as Australia and England industrial labour laws used to ensure that family time was protected and that employers who required people to work at night or on weekends paid extra. This was to ensure that the loss of weekend time, when parents and children could be together, would be materially compensated in a manner that would allow families to have extra time during the week for unpaid tasks and to carve out time together when needed.

Industrial Relations Laws and enforced work programs such as those introduced in Australia under the Howard regime decimated and exploited this final resource of the poor – free time. The poor are now forced into menial and poorly paid labour for the wealthy with no control over regularity or sustainability of workload or hours. Work which is required after hours and on weekends in time when children are at home is no longer required to be financially recompensed. When employees who refused to work irregular shifts at regular rates or who left inhumane

119

work conditions were given an 8 week welfare penalty we created a new form of bonded labour. As a result, the poor no longer have the choice and time to care for each other and to provide the buffer of social support which used to ease the impact of their material deprivation.

The underpaid servitude of the poor enforced under these policies had only one benefit – further wealth and profit to the wealthy in Australia and around the world. It has created a new servant class of maids, cleaners, and gardeners, who can perform menial tasks for the wealthy at low cost to their private purse. The social cost of such policies in terms of family breakdown, ill health, distress and behavioural problems for children and, ultimately, higher crime and social disruption, is paid primarily by those on the bottom of the heap – the poor. In effect these work programs are a way of further taxing and exploiting the poor in order to line the purses of the upper class.

When the Egg Breaks: Abuse of Children

In the west, people's lives have become increasingly pressured as they face increasingly hostile external and work environments where even the base level of resources they need for existence are under constant threat of being pillaged by aggressive others. In a barbaric environment marked by the absence of protective legislation; individuals have had to remain hyper-alert and ready to personally defend their own space and resources. Combine these types of pressures, with increased social acceptance of interpersonal aggression, myths of the disposability of individuals, and uncaring callused detachment; as the cultural norms for human relating and you have a tinderbox for family conflict, violence and divorce. The frustrated individual is encouraged to use harshness in their interactions with their children, spouse and intimate others, with the barbaric cultural mythology running strong – 'People are disposable and powerful elites can always replace any who do not conform.' The lack of care, which can then manifest towards children is of the greatest concern and is the greatest threat to the future of democratic cultures.

The increased interpersonal aggression which accompanies barbaric insurgency increases the percentage of adults who do not understand, care about, or respond appropriately to children. The barbaric creed's impact on social norms results in increased numbers and rates of children being treated harshly, aggressively and inhumanely. When children experience uncaring, harsh and violent behaviours from adults at home, in school, and in all social interactions, this becomes the entirety of their absorptive world. They themselves become hardened and, in turn, more likely to become adults who advocate and enact barbarism.

While conservatives are quick to blame individual parents, in truth, the increased pressure resulting from barbaric oppression through the low paid labour market must also be considered. Poor and stressed parents who are placed in inhumane work conditions, with increased legislative control and punishment for nonconformity, are often unable to cope with the twin burdens of poverty and the increased aggression they themselves are experiencing in the external environment. Furthermore, in an environment which is lauding and promoting aggression, people who are experiencing ongoing social violence themselves in the workplace and social environment are more likely to be stressed and to resort to aggression themselves. This does not justify aggressive behaviour towards children but it is to focus attention on the barbaric antecedents that contribute to increased child abuse.

By the time children are five we know that if they have been subjected to violence and brutalisation the marks will be evident in their behaviour and difficulties. We are even able to predict criminality and likelihood of antisocial adult behaviour by observing pre-schoolers. In other words, by the time they are five, the damage to children and to society has been done. This should galvanize us into immediate prioritization of the early childhood period and into investing large amounts of resources into the support of caregivers and the care and support of children during the ages of 0-5. Forcing poor single parents onto the factory line should not only be seen as profiteering behaviour, but also as harming the resources of the future. Similarly, the media marketing and increased sexualisation of the young female body; without concurrent marketing of alternative icons, choices and contraceptives; fosters and then punishes, adolescent pregnancy and single mothering. Skectics are alive and well.

Humanitarian planning would acknowledge children as full citizens and structure their developmental needs into all planning processes. This rarely occurs. By default, societies are designed mainly for independent adult humans in their prime and children and the elderly are excluded and become socially marginalised and disempowered. Because of their vulnerability, they are then at even greater risk of being harmed or oppressed. In effect, our planning at the moment with its focus on economically productive adults forgets the elderly and children and therefore excludes at least a third of the population. When you consider other disadvantaged populations such as single mothers, the homeless, people with disabilities, people who are ill, ethnic and racial minorities, and anyone who doesn't fit the elite prototype you are arguably excluding the majority of your population from planning processes.

While the well-being of children is sometimes part of political rhetoric, it is not, and never has been, the central focus for policy and strategic planning at state, national or international levels. Most political planning focuses on adult economic advancement and subordinates the needs of children to this aim. A society planned and structured for adults only, intentionally or unintentionally excluding focus on children, cannot foster human potential, and sometimes even destroys the basic productivity of the next generation. The barbaric society, structured to pander to the needs and whims of the most aggressive, destroys children.

Barbarism and Culture

Cultural Sickness

Changes in Australia have affected our cultural system which now mimics the American model but without the protective advantage of America's history of 200 years of underpinning philanthropy and a founding constitution. We used to live in a culture that did not treat people as production units and which resisted the mythology that the wealthy are worthy of more dignity than the poor. Australian culture was built on social norms of mateship and egalitarianism with a large working class and middle class, all of whom could afford holidays, schooling and their own home. All of them knew how to work hard. When neoliberalism swept in, these Australians who were the back bone of the workforce transferred their capacity to work from the 37.5 hour work week to the new 60 hour week, with disastrous consequences for their health and well-being. The calluses on the hands of the Aussie battler do not exonerate us from our oppression of Aboriginal and migrant people or our racism. Pre-neoliberal Australia was racist with a history of very small, socially contained, elite. Hence, by and large, white Australians did not have complex understanding of the face and conditions of indentured labour and were caught off guard by the dismantling of protective industrial legislation.

White Australians lacked the complex survival intelligence fostered in black people over centuries of bonded and indentured labour and enforced slavery. I once read the account of a white man put to work on a road gang with a group of African Americans. He was shovelling vigorously in the sun and was approached by one of his black colleagues, who advised him, 'Slow down boy or you won't make it.' The black man was kindly sharing his intelligence about the inherent cruelty, and the lack of care, of taskmasters who can set work at inhumane levels with a captive population. The slower pace, and refusal to be driven when you are pacing yourself for a lifetime of oppression, is not lazy, but smart. When you face a lifetime of endless labour which will enable only subsistence living; with a workload set by powerful, uncaring elites; you must pace yourself for survival, not for taskmaster approval. Poor whites in Australia are just beginning to learn this hard lesson.

During the neo-liberal period, the Australian top ten percent increased prosperity to grasp 45% of the nation's entire wealth. The top 20% of the population now earn more than ten times the bottom 20%. Thus, the 'boom' was simply a reallocation of resources from the very bottom to the very top, with disastrous, widespread, negative social consequences. This removal of resources from the many has fuelled spirals in all social problems from homelessness to drug dependency, from mental illness to child abuse. The widening of the gap between the haves and the have nots in Australia has not only decimated the middle class, but caused a concurrent increase in the number of lower class poor. This group will now never own a home or move out of indentured labour.

During this barbaric insurgency Australia's global position in housing affordability went from being one of the best in the world to becoming the absolute worst. House prices since 1987 increased 123% over and above inflation to go from to 3 times the median household income to 7 times, an amount that globally is considered severely unaffordable. Housing grew at double the CPI, 300% from 1986-2006, with the primary benefit flowing upwards in cash streams to the top levels while the hopes of home ownership for the young and the poor, flowed down the drain at the same rate. The homogenous and heavily urbanized nature of Australian life means that it is harder for the poor to 'flee' because there aren't low cost States they can go to for relief (as in the US or Europe). Thus, this spiral in house prices fundamentally and irrevocably changed our culture. The new flow of wealth to the top caused an explosion in outer status symbols that previously, Australians would have hesitated to own for fear of public censure. As Mcmansions, yachts, and four-wheel drives proliferated, so did arrogance. A new class of elites emerged in Australia with disdain and calloused disregard for the newly burgeoning lower class. The poor, as a group, can no longer afford the dignifying basics of home and rest, and their lives are at risk of the predictable chaos fostered by oppression and exploitation. We now have 680000 disadvantaged children (www.thesmithfamily.com.au) who can't afford books, uniforms and basics for school, and who experience the shame and social ostracism we have reserved especially for the poor.

Concurrently, the dignity of Australia's accessible, non-punitive welfare was removed and changed to a multi-conditional system which provides only partial funding for a life below the subsistence line. One of the conditions imposed was agreement to provide free labour for employers (work for the dole). The current government is set to place even more control over welfare monies, quarantining them for rent and food in a draconian approach introduced as part of Howard's racially motivated Northern Territory 'intervention.' It is a stain on the Rudd government that they would even consider rolling out a policy that has received resounding UN condemnation for violating human rights and which has caused such widespread harm in vulnerable Aboriginal communities. Doctors in these communities are reporting near starvation effects, a tripling of anemia in children under five and dramatic increase in low birthweights. In other words, this punitive approach to welfare has had the greatest impact upon, and caused great damage to, the most vulnerable members of our most marginalised and oppressed population. It is clearly ruinous.

When umbrella public funding for the poor was removed some amounts were re-apportioned, primarily to Church NGOs. This enforced blending of state and religion overrode State duty of care to the poor. It ignored the fact that most churches; skilled primarily in theology and dogma, are not professionally skilled in the complexities of distributive or procedural income justice. State responsibility should not be delegated to private bodies, let alone those which openly profess a categorical dogma. As a result, value laden categorization of people into 'deserving' or 'undeserving' poor has become socially prevalent. Increasingly calloused and hard-hearted social attitudes abound such as the idea that the poor should pay for all goods and services to 'teach them to appreciate what they get.' Second Hand stores (Op. Shops), previously a low cost alternative run primarily by older women, with goods costing only a few cents, were corporatised and turned into profit making ventures, often utilizing the employment of the new free labour available from enforced 'work for the dole' program. These Op. Shops now charge almost as much at discounted prices in regular stores, effectively removing the main avenue for consumer goods for the most poor.

Youth

Increasing numbers of Australian youth now have a criminal record. In West Australia, as national cultural violence has escalated, from the boardroom to the playing field, the emphasis has been on the development of a police state, with a primary focus on containing and targetting youth, not adults. This punitive focus on adolescents does not have the acuity to discriminate between young people who are experimenting or have been youthfully foolish, and those who are heavily inculcated in antisocial criminality. Increased numbers of youth now have a criminal charge related to behaviour that is age-normalized in our culture. Overly harsh penalties meted out in pre-adulthood, ruin not only the future of the individual, but also of the culture. A heavy handed, control and punishment orientation towards our youth harms them. We have a high suicide rate and, in our young males (15-24) this rate has tripled over the last 40 years and similarly increased in young men 25-35. The criminalisation of youth engaging in behaviours that are socially normalized and endemic does not serve our culture well. We definitely need to change the norms, but we can use youth misbehaviour to reconnect, educate, and guide them through the transition to adulthood, rather than exclude them from major portions for life (leadership and international travel etc.) Dangerously punitive approaches include giving a criminal record or incarcerating youth for misdemeanours such as driving on a suspended license, using marijuana, having pills such as ecstasy or holding a party serving minors alcohol. These behaviours need to be addressed but giving youth a criminal record is a punitive, short sighted and ineffective strategy which inflames, rather than reduces the problem. Unrealistic policies such as those requiring youth to drive 120 hours with a parent to get a driving license, means those who don't have a willing or wealthy adult who can contribute this much time, are denied the first step to adult freedom. Youth who drive anyway, in defiance of the unjust bind in which adults have placed them, are criminalized. When we criminalize youth who defy the system in unpleasant, but relatively minor acts such as this, we foster the next level of aggression and may lose future, intelligent social change agents.

'Reforming' the 'Antiquated' Notion of Justice

In Australia, conservative regimes erased almost 200 years of human rights struggles with sweeping changes to industrial legislation, welfare and family law. Significantly, we are the only democracy in the world without a human rights or similar act, a position which facilitates human rights violations. Australia is still a deeply sexist society. Almost 60% of Australian women experience violence over their lifetime. They do more of the unpaid labour in the home than women in any developed nation. In the ASX 200 only 49 percent have one female board director, compared to US, 88 percent; UK 76 percent and South Africa 62%. Over the past five years the number of women in executive feeder positions for CEO and board positions actually decreased in percentage from 7.5 percent to 5.9 percent. Australian working women report serious fatigue, due mainly to the additive load of the burden of household, childcare and low pay employment; which drains their adrenal and autoimmune systems. The contradictions and paradoxes inherent in Australian culture are illustrated in the fact that globally, we are ranked number one in educating women, but 40th in employing them. In other words, Australia has no problem with women paying for their education but no intention of letting them use it. The illusion of equity is exploitative of women's hopes and naivete' and, in some ways, more insidious and damaging than open exclusion. There are severe social penalties for discussing or pointing out gender inequality in our culture. Changes to the status of women and rights of children; which reinstated their positions as subordinate to, and having less value than; males, received little attention. This is not an exhortation to deprive women of their liberty and human rights or to force them back into the unpaid nurseries and kitchens of the nation but to address inequity in labour distribution.

Cultural Autopsy

When we examine the cadaver of pre-neoliberal Australian cultural life we see the cancer of privatisation invading and choking the organs of public health and education. We see the fair-work- fair-pay employment system in cardiac arrest. We see cultural skeletal deterioration from undue obeisance to money making. We see the organs of the culture of equality represented by Sunday lunch for everyone, not just those with yachts; removed. We see children's rights to be cared for by their primary caretaker hacked off. We see the loss of non-corporatized spaces in the internal cultural cavity and the grey pallor of family and cultural life drained of essential time and energy nutrients.

Barbarism and Work Life

Power and Aggression

Wellbeing and sustainable living are central to processes by which humans will be able to experience provolution–an advanced evolutionary leap for the species. In cultures where profit is the primary aim; aggression, greed and unbridled ambition, come to be seen as strengths rather than as personal weaknesses. 'Let the economy rule' means that values of equality, human dignity, procedural or distributive justice aren't allowed to 'interfere' with unfettered mechanisms of greed and viciousness which are fostered by the barbarian tenet 'anything goes' in the achievement of profit. In a workculture where aggression and viciousness are honored it makes sense that, in a relatively short period of time, an elite emerges (management, CEOs), who were largely advanced through their capacity to be vicious and/or their personal willingness to dominate fellow workers. As the mantra 'anything goes as long as it leads to more money and power' permeates the culture, aggressive qualities become the criteria for reward and advancement in the workplace and a new SS emerges. The catchcry 'let the market regulate itself' means 'let viciousness rule the day and may the victor take the spoils'. Running closely alongside is usually the rhetoric, 'Those with the most deserve it and those without don't.'

In societies where competition, small mindedness and dominance are lauded and the values of the culture are cruelty, interpersonal aggression and nastiness, it becomes socially acceptable to be vicious. No longer do people feel the need to apologize if they lose their temper or are publicly nasty to a colleague. In fact, many carry this behaviour around as if it were a mark of honour and proof that they 'have what it takes' to succeed. They may have what it takes to advance in a race of viciousness but this is no more an honour than advancement through the ranks of the brownshirts and the SS in the 1940s.

Nastiness and willingness to use aggression is common in decision making circles and managerial positions at the moment because many good people left the competitive pond during barbaric insurgency, tired of having their position always threatened by circling corporate piranha when they refused to impose inhumane conditions on others. This included university lecturers who refused to force young people to forsake their education for profiteering models designed only to make education the second largest gross domestic product. The mass shallow instruction with a focus on regurgitation of information has, in effect, robbed the young of their education in order to fatten the old. Australian lecturers who refused to conform were replaced by lecturers from developing countries (primarily India and China) whose desperation guaranteed compliance. In the primary and secondary system, school teachers left who couldn't take one more bureaucratic piece of paper getting between them and their desire to nurture the minds of the children in their care; as did social workers who couldn't handle seeing one more broken child that they were not funded to care for; government workers who refused to penalize another person for their incapacity to work and doctors who couldn't take one more day of health system changes that reduced doctor-patient relationship to 6 minute cogs in a profit making machine. And so on ad infinitum.

It makes sense therefore that the hallmarks of the new breed of managers in the workplace are unthinking compliance with demands for increased productivity; and a willingness to use any tactics available; no matter how vicious or how serious the effects on their fellow man. Hayashi – death from overwork – was a phenomenon that emerged in the newly 'democratized' Japan after the Second World War. Employees were driven internally to work themselves to death as the qualities of loyalty and service to the emperor and family were transferred to the workplace and the employer. Here in Australia however, where kamikaze self sacrifice is not a part of cultural tradition, death by overwork must be driven by an unthinking, uncaring other – a line manager, branch manager or CEO who is prepared to drive the workers under him with no sense of guilt if it 'increases profit.' It requires the uncaring other to achieve the sacrifice of the worker in the Australian culture. Sadly, there has been no shortage of takers who stepped up to the line during the recent 'economic boom' eager and willing to impose unrealistic, unsustainable, and damaging, workloads on their colleagues.

The industrial legislation which has removed choice and which actively punishes and penalizes those who try to resist the workloads simply increases the power available to managers willing to be the brownshirts. It does not force them to drive their fellow man beyond the limits of sustainable or fair work for pay, it only gives them that option. It is common sense that forcing mothers and fathers to work around the clock, on weekends and evenings without financial compensation will damage their family life, their capacity to sustain family life, to sustain their relationship together and critically, to do the important work of caring for children. The 'new elite' of managers and leaders are encouraged to dissociate themselves from the role they take in imposing rules on their fellow man. External 'pressure' to be inhumane is seen as excusing them the personal choice to impose work pressure on employees without using the power of their role to be a buffer against the exploitation of those with less power.

As a result the workplace is increasingly sustainable only for the unfeeling. This is dangerous. Too many people are being given the experience of overwork, workplace bullying, and abuse - unnecessary acts of meanness and violence which can cumulatively break people's spirits. Many are beginning to consider subsistence living as better than the violent workplace and are withdrawing themselves at a time where governments need a later retirement age to keep the workplace viable. The costs of profiteering, and lack of reciprocal corporate loyalty, include increases in the daily stress of work where fear of being discarded pushes employees to over perform, or to conform with inhumane work demands. The sacrifice of the work culture where corporations returned employee fealty with reciprocal employment loyalty, has increased the levels of generalised anxiety in the population. As with all relationships, exploitation makes people nervous and stressed. The calloused profiteering that created these problems in the work culture has eroded the workforce needed to deal with the labour shortages ahead when baby boomers leave the workplace. This is another example of financial benefit for elites drawn directly from heavy public losses.

Barbaric Aristocracy

The past decades of economic rationalism have recreated the aristocracy. The power and priorities of this new aristocracy were reflected in the massive battle President Obama had in his attempt to introduce universal healthcare access to the American system. Aristocrats claimed that providing citizens with healthcare would 'bankrupt' the nation. These same pundits had no problem signing massive cheques for warfare and the financial bailout needed after barbaric pillaging of the economy. It appears that bankruptcy is a relative term and that barbarians consider some areas more 'bankruptcy worthy' than others. It is mendacious to sell the public the lie that Universal healthcare bankrupts a nation given all of the international data to the contrary. In addition, such a claim takes focus away from asking the question: what cumulative barbaric decisions could have brought this great nation to the place where it 'can't afford' to attend to the health of its own citizens? What would the founding fathers say about this collapse of liberte', egalite' and fraternite' into narrow aspirations of individual greed?

History tells us that the aristocracy don't give up their privilege easily – especially once it has been institutionalized and legitimized. Make no mistake. The new aristocracy firmly believe in their right to accrue resources through whatever means possible and spend little time in consideration of notions such as injustice, the dignity of human life, and the social change that might be required to foster that dignity. The vision of Martin Luther King reminds us that concepts of justice and the dignity of human life are essential if human development is to occur, 'I have the audacity to believe that people everywhere can have three meals a day for their bodies, education and culture for their minds, and dignity, quality, and freedom for their spirits. I believe that what self-centered men have torn down, other-centered men can build up.'

When increased production is automatically seen as positive growth then increases in crime, social ills, systemic disorders and poor health are not considered. It is not true that destruction of life systems for economic profit automatically brings benefit, or that it is the only way. Australians, who work the longest hours in the OECD, are also the highest health system users in the world. People drilled into being passive automatons serving 'the market' lose their capacity to take care of their own health, resulting in increased personal and social cost. The preferred 'quick shortcut to profit' for individual profiteers does not benefit the public, the country or the species. What if economic growth remained stable or shrank, but our quality of life and our health improved?

CULTURAL LIFE

Haiti: A Solid Example

Before free trade over-ran their economic system Haitians used to produce 90% of their own rice. The agriculture of Haiti, facilitated by six months rain a year, rich soil, and cultural and social norms which facilitate cooperative community life and work, was destroyed by so called 'free trade agreements.' These 'agreements' made the nation dependent on imports by flooding the market with products at a cost that local producers could not under-cut. Forced out of villages by the new 'unprofitability' of agriculture Haitians were pushed into city slums and into production and factory work to provide cheap export products. Haitians complained of poor work conditions in the factories, of being locked in until an enforced 'quota' was filled, and of having a minimum wage of $3 per week enforced by the President against popular will. Haitians, unconditioned in the brutality of barbaric production regimes, complained about factory work removing their right to have family and community lives. These complaints were ignored by the primarily foreign managers brought in to run the factories.

In the wake of the recent devastating earthquakes Haitians are asking that foreign aid be focussed on enabling them to return to an agriculturally based economy. This request is being overrun and ignored by barbarians with their own production agendas. 'Free trade partners' insist that Haitians don't know what is in their own best interests and offer aid conditional on the basis of Haitians re-establishing clothing and other industrial production facilities. This forceful, profit oriented perspective overrides the right of the Haitian people to choose their own cultural values and priorities. It is blind to the strengths of Haitian life. After the earthquake 450 refugee communities self-formed and peacefully organized their own security, the sharing of goods, and the equitable distribution of foodstuffs.

Haitian culture revolves around gifting and solidarity, with much gifting being done silently and without expectation of compensation or acclaim. People share what little they have with one another so that luck as well as loss is distributed. Strong cultural norms and traditions preserve human dignity in the face of material deprivation and ensure that those products available do the most good for the community as a whole. Systems such as Sabotaj; a sharing system used among women in the markets; Men ansanm and sol which are community generated financial assistance; and Kombit, a collaborative labour system to accomplish an outcome difficult for the lone individual. No one makes a profit from these practices and aid is given as needed, or on a rotating basis. Fair reciprocal sharing is an intrinsic part of Haitian life. The gap in cultural understanding was evidenced by the US and UN troops whose focus was on preventing food riots and who therefore used distribution methods that were cumbersome and awkward in comparison to the efficiency of the self-organized refugee communities.

Haitians have been far more effective in responding to, and dealing with, disaster than would be possible under the barbaric creed. Why then are we forcing them under our system of values?

With the earthquake many rural people have returned from the city to their own towns. Haitians are asking for a return to a primarily agricultural economy and to be able to use aid to, once again, become the bread basket of their region. They do not want their economic growth dictated by serving foreign markets rather than by the needs of their own people. Unfortunately, bottom up plans are not the focus of international intervention and the voice of the people is being ignored. Externally developed 're-development plans' for Haiti include reconstruction of apparel factories such as the Port au Prince T-shirt factory where 1000 workers died.

Our self-serving bias becomes even more evident when we acknowledge the latest (2010) WorldBank research demonstrating that agricultural growth reduces poverty among the 40% poorest three times more than growth in any other sector. In other words agricultural growth, Haitians preferred option, would also be the most effective for the poor. Why then are we insisting on Tshirt factories to supply our own populations? Is it possible that a barbaric agenda could be operating? Indeed, our economic salivary glands are clearly visible and drooling.

The Co-optation of Altruism to the Profit Making Motive
In effect the industrialized system, coupled with globalization and the corruption caused by having economic development as the core social value, have brought western societies to the point where altruism is a safe and wise behaviour only for the very wealthy and privileged. The pervasiveness of greed as a core social value (neoliberalism is just another word for giving social merit to the concept of greed) has infiltrated even the ranks of the poor where brotherhood and solidarity used to provide some safety for those who wished to engage in care of their fellow man.

We now have a social milieu inundated with social piranha – those ready and willing to use unprovoked interpersonal aggression and violence. This makes the social environment hazardous for non-aggressives who are seen as easy prey and a soft target for barbarian attack. The boss who abuses and exploits workers is lauded for 'increased productivity.' The organization that overwOrcs and exploits workers is applauded for corporate profits. High staff turnover and staff health and wellbeing are not even considered as part of the corporate report card. We have normalized stealing and violence in the market-place as 'an inevitable part of a free market system.' As we have allowed, tolerated, encouraged and normalized corporate piracy and corporate exploitation of the environment, indigenous and poor people, we have concurrently legitimized and validated violence at every other level of society. We have normalized violence at such high echelons in our society that we cannot protest its increase amongst the lower class unless we want to address it at higher levels. If we are going to validate and reward violent, inhumane, cruel and exploitative behaviours at corporate and government levels then we had better expect greater crime and violence at all levels, and in all facets, of our societies.

Why are we accepting this as truth nowadays when it was not a 'truth' 50 years ago? What has changed to make us so willing to accept so little? The poor and the disadvantaged are exposed to more violence than they were one or two generations ago. Why aren't we agitating for safer environments for the children of the poor? A civilized society is just that – civilized. It does not reward and bolster egotism, vanity, greed, deceit and excess. Any society that does so is consuming itself.

Greed versus Need

Privileged Western humans have lost the capacity to discriminate between greed and need. In Western Australia, palatial mansions of a scale that would have made them hotels in the past century have proliferated. These vast sprawling concrete edifices now crowd the river and water lines and gentrify urban suburbs. This proliferation of McMansions is linked to the mining boom and an increase in 'prosperity and material wealth' for some citizens. What is concerning, is that the average citizen no longer seems to understand that humans don't need palaces. They need homes. These mansions invariably are surrounded by high walls and the first floor has vast quantities of cement to prevent break-in or entry. From two and three-storey balconies, elites can entertain each other and look safely down on passers-by, while maintaining significant physical distance from anyone outside the wall.

While the ego may be gratified by the size and scale of one family or couple, occupying space that would comfortably accommodate 4 or 5 lower class families or 10 or 12 developing world families, this is not ecologically or socially sustainable. In addition, walled palaces destroy the social fabric of shared human living and belonging. Humans flourish and thrive in communities where they are acknowledged daily, and known personally, by others in the community. In observing the proliferation of hotels sized domiciles along the waters edge one can't help but wonder whether these hotel sized homes built by elites during the neoliberal era will be the hotels of the future. Maybe they are gifts to the next generation of communities, where the need for all humans to have the rest and refreshment of periodic stays by water will be recognized and facilitated. Perhaps in the future several weeks by the water will be provided to all people on a rotating annual basis and the rest of the year, we will live in small, caring, relational communities, where constancy and kinship will be central.

Community Life

There has been much focus on the loss of the natural world caused by barbaric incursion but we need equal attention to the extinction of human relational spaces. The free time and energy people used to have for relational community has been taken by longer work hours and frenetic demands. Relationships require time; time to spend with one another, to share the happenings of the day, the trivial and the immense, to sort together through the significance of daily events in order to find the numinous thread of meaning for each individual life. Restful, peaceful spaces in life are bound inextricably with humans having free time. Production energy should be harnessed towards enabling and fostering these aspects of human life.

When busywork can be demanded of the average citizen by landlords, bureaucrats, teachers, phone companies, banks and any other institution, people's lives become consumed in the mire. Precious downtime becomes consumed by reporting for no other purpose than that of surveillance or creating further profit for an anonymous individual. Property managers, the new spawn of the property market, demand busywork of tenants that they would never do themselves in their own homes. The great Maori culture has the following saying, 'Ki mai koe ki a au, He aha tem ea nui tenei ao: He tangata, he tangata, he tangata' which is translated as, 'If you should ask me what is the greatest thing in the world, the answer would be: It is people, it is people, it is people.' We are experiencing decreased richness of our quality of life because we no longer live in communities that are cognisant of, and emotionally supportive of, people. There are times when human life is meant to be measured by the tick of the clock, the rock of the chair, the sway of the tree and where mechanistic production energy is irrelevant.

The decreased valuation of people makes individuals fearful and desperate for wealth that can buffer them from social aggression and give them the feeling that their lives have value. Cults and fundamentalist sects proliferate during barbarism, breeding on the increased fear in the culture and the individual's desire to have value. Such groups foster mental illness with creeds that advocate arrogance, superiority, and detachment and separation from other members of the culture. We can't afford societies where individual people don't think they matter, or where they think their life is of less value than their rich neighbour. This is the real danger of consumerism. It devalues us all. We can only have things and not be consumed by them if we are living in a rich, deep fabric of relational life. Without this we struggle to find meaning and to feel that our lives matter and we are easily seduced by products that materially tell us that we do.

We accord each other's lives meaning when we treat each other with kindness, dignity and respect, thus demonstrating our recognition that their life matters, and what happens to them matters. This decreases the levels of generalised fear in a culture, because individual humans are then surrounded by a pervasive sense of safety and the assurance that multiple others would come to their aid, if they were attacked by foe or misfortune, as in the Haitian example. Thus, the full costs of homelessness are not only the tragedy and suffering of the individual human forced to pretend they are expendable trash, but also the assault to the generalised sense of safety and care in a culture. This sense of safety is essential to keeping generalised anxiety low and to fostering productive creativity, which can then be used in the service of the many.

Loss of Local Culture

To consider fully what we have lost in domain of community wisdom and culture peruse any 'Old World Library' or National Geographic series from 50-75 years ago which documented and catalogued places with their own distinct cultures, community life and traditions. Compare these recorded tableaus with the concretized, homogenized, franchised norms of stores, products and interpersonal aggression now evident in most cultures across the globe. Unique traditions and diversity have been bulldozed by corporate globalization and local life has been laid waste. Local culture has been interpenetrated, overridden and destroyed.

Global tourists now crave and hunt for, small idiosyncratic communities which still have remnants of unique cultural life. In tourist traps people search for the small place, tucked away in a nook or cranny, where individuals have escaped the mass production onslaught. They are looking for a rustic store, a charming, unexpected and authentic place where some human has put their own print and an expression of their unique individuality onto their product. Such a creation is often the result of an individual's whole life experience to this point. It is an expression of who they are and cannot be forced or mass produced. Any such attempt would lose the unique essence that creates its intrinsic value. It renews our own core vitality and recognition of unique life energy. The westerner travelling the world is desperately seeking this pre-homogenized sense of possibility and creativity. Ironically, this tramp of millions of human tourists around the globe searching for unique authentic culture destroys what little non-homogenized culture remains. If, instead, we protected children and allowed, fostered and encouraged each person to make their unique authentic expression as part of their work, our cultures would become rich tapestries of their own.

Alternative Models

The indigenous concept of elder is critical to the health of children. Carrying responsibility for the child with the full resources and responsibility of an adult is a much underestimated but critically important role which is not taken up often enough in our cultures. In the decades since the 80s childhood has become increasingly pillaged by the economy (consumerism targeting pre-schoolers), parents' desire to increase their own status (child's clothing, activities done to increase adult status), emotional pillaging and the lack of protection of children in schools and communities. Adult irresponsibility varies from overwhelming them with information they can't cope with (ie: global warming) because we are scared and don't know what to do about it; to the violent pillaging of sexual and emotional abuse. It includes not being at home so they must parent themselves when we are working for status symbols without also ensuring that they are safe and well nurtured. Seeing our legacy as cash is immature. The young need to have hopes and dreams and if we deny them this we deny them their future. Cash is a cold substitute. Cesar Chavez, the great Latino activist brings us back to reality, 'Our lives are all that really belong to us; so it is how we use our lives that determines the kind of men [and women] we are.' Exploitation of childhood for cash profit is disastrous and must be halted. Real caring means being prepared to do whatever that takes.

Investigating Alternatives

Stemming the Blood Flow: Leadership

The danger of the current system's investment of enormous amounts of money in marketing its own image is that it has done such a good sales job that we are not recognizing the danger signals put out by every human system on the verge of collapse (increased crime, social problems, suffering etc). Without this clarity, humans cannot correct the system and prevent collapse. It is clear, for example, that the care of human beings is not the central decision making tenet for the World Trade Authority, for the boards of multi-national corporations or for many decisions made at international and global levels. Instead the guiding principles may be profit, competition, self-interest or dominance. How can we expect systems to work for humans when tenets such as competitive dominance are the bases of decision making?

The structures of many current power systems actively screen out, demote, or actively oppress, those who hold human wellbeing as their core value. People who choose not to be aggressive or exploitative in their business interactions are less likely to 'make it to the top' and to be sitting in the echelons where decisions are made that affect millions, and perhaps the majority, of 21st century human lives. On the other hand, those willing to enact aggression, dominance, competitive greed, and/or exploitation of others, are more likely to rise in a system which rewards such behaviours and therefore to be at the levels where there is great power and few legal or systemic constraints. The norms of greed and exploitation which foster the rise of those who value dominance and interpersonal aggression also direct decision-making processes at higher levels. This ensures a circular system which enables power-holders to buttress their positions and to protect and increase their personal power and resources.

At the global or multi-national level, for example, there is little legal or systemic retribution for decisions made which destroy communities, environments or individual lives if such decisions profit the few power-holders who make them or the few shareholders to whom they are accountable. This not only creates an elite who can act with impunity across national and international law systems but also increases the vulnerability and likelihood of oppression for those who have little power. The average Joe or Joanne has less and less say over the decisions which affect their built environment, their work and their future – be they in Pakistan, the United States or Swaziland. Such decisions are increasingly concentrated in the hands of faceless, nameless power holders who hold little personal accountability for their actions.

The 'corporate body' is comprised of individuals who are making decisions. These decisions are anonymized by the concept of a board where individual decisions, and use of influence, are rendered invisible by the illusion of a group identity. We are encouraged to believe that 'Board decisions' are democratic and must not be challenged 'because they represent more than one person' but this is an over simplification of reality. A group or majority of barbarians will simply ensure barbaric group decisions. In addition, a group with even just one aggressive, dominant, vicious barbarian will often simply follow his or her command.

In reality, the concept of board gives facelessness to the perpetration of damage. When people can make decisions anonymously and without personal responsibility then gross violations of human rights can be perpetrated without any consequence for the decision maker. Theoretically, there is really no one at the helm of a corporate 'body' when board members are changed regularly. This is analogous to Frankenstein operating without a brain or sensing system. Damage is done by 'no-one in particular' as board members move on and carry no ongoing responsibility for the decisions that they have made and the consequences that follow. This encourages public fatalism about the acts of corporations and does not require people to carry responsibility for their actions. Individual board members must be held responsible for each of their votes and decision contributions, in an ongoing, manner with accrued accountability. Barbaric power without scrutiny or boundary ensures atrocity.

Stemming the Blood Flow: Regulation

We now need positive reform and public regulation of the free market system. In the artificial dichotomization of capitalism and communism, the market has been conceptualized as representing the many, but this is too simplistic. In reality, the market has now become controlled by the few and, in order to protect the freedom of the market and democracy, it now must again be regulated by the many (public government regulation) to prevent mass exploitation by the few. Social breakdown is costly, revolution is costly – preventive maintenance is cheap.

What people do for business within societies must be brought back under the realm of the humane and made subject to all of the legal and ethical constraints of civilized society and advancing culture.

What people do to make money must not be exempt from the constraints of the humane, civilized standards which sustain good relationships in any other domain; including that of family and community life. 'The market' or the 'economy' cannot be considered to be outside of the legal and moral constraints of every other part of civilized society. 'Making money' must not occur at the expense of other people's lives, freedoms and lived environments; but must contribute to the advancement of human society and humane civilization in the same way this is demanded of family, community and legal life systems. In an enlightened world, businesses would have to provide a greater raison d'etre than profit to be given the right to exist.

Barbarism encourages unthinking violence and animal like aggression towards other members of the species. It does not encourage the use of our most evolved and developed human capacities for conscious compassion and intelligent choice. Barbarism is an immature, unfledged philosophy which neither draws upon our most evolved capacities nor positions the species for the next stage of evolution. The puerile obsession of barbarians with domination and violence is truly a 'dog-eat-dog' philosophy which belongs firmly in the animal domain. If we begin to choose alternative, more effective philosophies for social advancement and to nurture and protect children then we will begin to have societies in which violence is no longer an inalienable part of life.

CHAPTER 7: BARBARISM DIVIDES AND CONQUERS THE SPECIES

Barbarism divides the human race against itself. Under the directives and beliefs of the Creed, the males and females of the species are polarized and pitted against each other. Through unfair competition; the subordination of females through legally or socially sanctioned exploitation of their bodies, or labour; and through physical and sexual violence against females; humans have created an artificial divide. This abyss, excavated to great depth over time, is a chasm into which the majority of species' transformational, synergistic options disappear.

Whenever we over-ride or desecrate the human dignity, body or self of another, we cause anger and fury. This is why it is difficult to enact bloodless revolutions. An enraged populace trying to recapture their own rights and boundaries will often overrun the boundaries of others and hence become the barbarian they seek to overthrow. Acts in which females are being used by males for selfish purposes have made us adversaries when we should be confederates.

Men do well to be cautious of the women's movement because the rage and fury generated by multitudinous acts of oppression and injury sometimes do lead to females seeking vengeance rather than reparation and equal mutilation rather than atonement. The socialization of females into caring roles does; however, make it unlikely that they will enact savage cruelty en masse because the compassion developed in such roles, typically makes people less likely to enact extremes of vicious barbarism. Conversely, female aversion to violence is part of the reason that, globally, women are still subordinated to men. Individual females, who personally adhere to the code are still able to enact savagery, but, as a group, females are less likely to fully identify with the creed.

Nonetheless, it is still behaviour that defines barbarism, not maleness. We don't want to move from a barbaric system administered mainly by males to a barbaric system administered mainly by females. Females are just as capable as males of embracing barbarism as a philosophy and, when they have power, are of equal harm to others and to species progress when they do so. The current difference is that, due to allocations of global power fewer females have had access to enough power to have mass effect. Women are disproportionately poor, owning less than 2% of world property and less than 10% of the world's wealth even though doing over 70% of the world's work. Abuse of power is less likely for females because they have less power. When powerful females are barbaric adherents their impact on life systems similarly deleterious to males although different in scope (See also section entitled, 'Mean Girls.') Anti-barbarism is about moving to egalitarian, enlightened societies where care and human relationship are protected, central, motivating and legislated values. We can address barbaric beliefs across the human race.

Barbarism is a creed which advantages males when gender is the categorization system, when the male of the species is considered to be the superior gender, and/or when males are given unearned power and privilege. Evidentially, the female barbarian pitted against a male barbarian, of equal power base in all other domains except for gender, will lose. Women are outnumbered 4 to 1 in legislatures around the world. They are two thirds of all of the illiterate and homeless. The species issue is clearly the unnecessary polarization of the genders and the imposition of the barbaric code in male-female relations. Barbarism fosters violence, inter-gender mistrust and hostility. This divides the species against itself and impedes advanced species' progress.

Using, abusing and exploiting people of any gender wastes valuable species' resources and creative capacity. Using gender as a rationale for injustice and inequity is invariably barbaric because it adheres to the creed and uses violence to maintain inequity. The bitterness and hatred generated in women by ill treatment at the hands of men makes it immeasurably difficult to foster species' advancement. Even though the proverb, 'Women hold up half of the sky,' is meant to assert the dignity of the female half of the species, it is too often used as an excuse to misuse female bodies as beasts of burden in every domain, including the marital bed. This creates a block of incalculable dimensions to species progress.

People are our greatest resource for real species' advancement. Importantly, injustice towards, and oppression of, women destroys creative possibilities for cooperative inter-gender synergy. The creative fusion which would be enabled if we preserved female dignity through equitable, mutually respectful interactions would catalyse species advancement beyond our wildest imaginings.

Taking women to the point of desperation is a risky and unnecessarily dangerous position which the human race has been enacting for too long. Females are more than 80% of the people trafficked globally with 79% of these being trafficked for rape. Over two million women and girls are sold as sex slaves each year, two every minute, into an existence where every day of the rest of their shortened lives is spent being repetitively raped by an endless line of men. Approximately 20% of all Nepalese girls under 16 are trafficked into India for sex slavery. Victor Frankl and Elie Wiesel, both of whom were incarcerated in the Nazi concentration camps, sorrowfully observed that when humans are repetitively pushed beyond the boundaries of their humanity by sadistic abuse they can regress to animalistic cruelty themselves. Arguably, Aileen Wuornos was one of those people. Even revolutions conducted on behalf of egalitarianism, such as the French revolution, had difficulty remaining bloodless. By and large, human females have conducted their movement without physical violence, but this should increase rather than decrease solidarity between men and women in the urgent work to halt barbaric penetration of females.

Body Differences

The male body of the human species is stronger than the female body. Because of these body differences, given general age and health parity, the average male can physically overpower the average female. Male control is supported by the greater body strength of males as well as by female vulnerability in sexual organs, pregnancy, and responsibility for small children. In most human societies cultural norms of female caregiving duties, and decreased mobility, increase the physical strength differences. Therefore, for the human female, maintaining the dignity of her body is conditional upon living in a country with laws and norms that penalize males who would use her body against her will. Existence of such laws, and willingness to enforce them, depends heavily on whether males and females are seen as having equal value by the culture.

An individual female cannot maintain her body integrity and autonomy unless she is protected by cultural laws and norms that proactively prevent males from violating her. Ominously, in the 21st Century, a female's body rights are no more guaranteed in the West than in the East. Institutional intimidation and systematic domination globally

143

guarantee male privileged access to female bodies. For a female to have body autonomy (the right to have control over her body and how it is used) requires a society which accords equal value and power to male and female, ensures equity and dignifies women by socially censuring exploitation or derogation of females. This issue of male control over female bodies is, at its core, about the misuse of physical, economic and social power to derogate and exploit, rather than just about gender. Body control is the first of many levels of domination established over women.

Barbarians ignore male and female physical body differences in domains in which they wish to perpetuate unfair competitive advantage. Athletics is one of the few exceptions. Male and female athletes compete separately in athletic competitions such as the Olympics because of open acknowledgment of species' body differences which are rarely acknowledged elsewhere. These body differences of increased male strength are used primarily to maintain male dominance and keep women in forced labour rather than to carry a greater proportion of species' work. From corporate structures to rice paddies, from carer roles in the west to factory work in the East, the male-female body strength differential is used to subjugate women not assist them. Women make up 70% of the 1.1 billion people living in absolute poverty. In developing countries women produce between 60 and 80% of all food but have no control of the land. In societies where women are accorded such diminished value, an individual female's capacity to maintain body integrity and autonomy can be non-existent.

The impact of half the species having limited controls over their own body self has inestimable impact on the capacities of the species. With country data showing up to 70% of women will experience physical or sexual violence from a male in their lifetime, mainly from their 'intimate' partner, father or close male family member, we begin to understand the rites of male barbaric subordination of females. Coercion, violence and control are socially normalized gender intimidation tactics across cultures. In some countries more than half of women report their first act of sexual intercourse was forced. From the exponentially increased use of rape as a weapon of war; to the 100-140 million females who have had their genitals cut out; to the 80 million female child brides each year; female bodies are attacked and mutilated without penalty. As previously discussed, a person's body is their first possession and the space in which they must live. When it can be pillaged and used by others with impunity, with no power to resist, this is an ultimate powerlessness. When women can be forced to bear unwanted children they are, as the great author Marge Piercy described, being 'used as a public sewer.' Critical, fundamental changes must therefore occur globally in male access to, and use of, female bodies.

Across the globe young males are encouraged and patterned to dissociate their sexual arousal from primary consideration of the female as a human person and to separate sex from relationship with its intricacies of care, compassion and reciprocity. Where there is coercion and manipulation involved then 'having' to have sex further de-powers rather than empowers a female. The etymology of the word goth (original barbarians) comes from the words meaning 'to pour', from the idea that Goth people were 'pourers of semen' who created men (first) and then 'people.' The import of these masculinist foundations cannot be overstated. The pouring of semen cannot be the one-sided focus of sexual activity. The female is portrayed as a vessel, simply a receptacle for sperm and male effluent of invective, dissatisfaction or aggression, rather than as a living being with creative capacity, will, hopes, dreams and desires. It is even more damaging to the species when the female also believes herself to be mainly a receptacle for male desire and has no sense of her own value or irreplaceable role as part of the species.

Relational Approaches

The devaluation of females ruins and impairs all male-female relationships including so called 'intimate' relations which are the highest areas of violence and murder risk for females across the globe. In the United States one third of all women murdered each year are killed by their 'intimate' partner with the rate at 54% for women in Australia and 74% for Australian Indigenous women. 'Love' is a dangerous place in the west and elsewhere. This is a clear reflection of the infiltration of the barbaric code into our understanding of relationship. Barbaric indoctrination has caused us to see imbalances in power, believing we 'own' other people, and coercion and control, as 'normal' in relationship. Even so-called 'modern western romance' feeds on imbalances in power with coercion and control as central dynamics. Imbalances in relational power cause problems because of the increased tendency to use coercion. If we believe we own others, then coercing bonded or forced labour, through sex and other avenues, are seen as our right, our droit de seigneur.

The concept of ownership as fostered through marriage is problematic when it depletes the sense of humane responsibility for the other person in the relationship. If we don't own people then we have to negotiate fairly and respectfully for what we want. We also have to maintain relationship with them if we wish to continue to benefit from their contributions. Our own resources are then directly affected by our capacity to convey respect and care and be fair and just. How we treat each other then matters materially as well as humanly. Sense of ownership of another person is fostered by power inequity. Male sense of ownership and prerogative over female bodies fosters violence and abuse. Gender inequity and devaluation of women putrefies relationships between individual males and females thereby infecting wider species' relations. A relational perspective keeps us mindful of our responsibility to tend to the wellbeing of the other. Relational health is fostered by kind, caring, empathic, respectful, cooperative, empowering behaviours between autonomous beings of equal dignity. Men of quality are not threatened by the notion of women having equal power. In the absence of the capacity to dominate, own or coerce another, equal power, then relationship comes to be of central and great importance.

Species Rights and Body Rights

Denial of species' rights to females is problematic in all domains but the issue of male control over female bodies is the most problematic. The question of male prerogative over female bodies may well be the question which decides the fate of the species.

Population control is now our most critical species challenge. It took us 10 000 generations to reach the 1950 global population of 2 billion people. In one human lifetime we have gone from 2 billion to 7 billion and by 2050 will possibly have 9 billion people on the planet. Unless this issue is squarely faced alongside the issues of social valuation of women, and global valuation of all human citizens; we will face the increased infanticide, forced sterilizations and abortions, resultant gender imbalanced population and steep increases in illegal sex trafficking which were outcomes of the Chinese one-child policy. All of which perpetuate increased devaluation of women.

At this time, the right of the majority of females to control their own bodies is subordinated to male desire. Obstinate refusal to educate, empower and respect women in every domain, including that of control over their own bodies, and in every culture, including developing countries and those of different faiths, is the primary barrier to achieving sustainable population growth for the species. Globally, an individual female person's right to control her own body is commonly denied through social and legal norms which prioritize and legitimize male access to female bodies and enforce childbearing. Across nations females suffer a range of restrictive life conditions and laws which ensure male dominance over, and access to, their bodies.

IN NO DOMAIN MAY THE TRANSFORMATION OF THE SPECIES BE SO HASTENED THAN IN THE DOMAIN OF SEXUAL BEHAVIOUR.

Sexual Behaviour

Currently, there is a tendency to regressed, animalistic beliefs in the area of sexual behaviour. In the domain of sexuality there is firm adherence to the narrowed barbaric view of humans as animals who advance through establishing dominance (Creed Tenet II). Media, scientific review and popular print urge us to conceptualize sex primarily as animal instinct. From this perspective humans are seen primarily as instinctual animals and only secondarily as conscious creatures with a living inner world. Using urge, instinct and arousal as the foundational basis of human sexual behaviour categorizes us with the orang-utan, dog or rat driven by mating heat to compulsively seek release. Muslims who insist that males are driven to rape a woman if they see her leg, hair or neck, are suggesting western men have more control over themselves than Muslim men. Belief in male compulsion to rape suggests that, in the domain of sexuality, humans are animals with no control or choice over base instinct.

Western conceptualizations are not much more helpful and often lead towards the faddish rather than the complex. The focus of popular magazines such as Cleo or even pornography is at high school levels of exposure and manipulation of body parts. Male and female adolescents are encouraged to focus narrowly on sexual urge, physical release of orgasm and the arousal that the female body self can elicit for the male. These are components of sexual behaviour but obsessive focus on these aspects is problematic as it excludes the unique possibilities of sex for conscious beings with emotion encoded memory and capacity for bonding. It does not even begin to explore the possibilities of sex for a relational species where relationship carries transformative capacity.

147

Insensitivity, inability to respond to others, domineering, harsh uncaring behaviours and habits are not a good formula for ecstatic, erotic, sex life. Therefore, barbarians tend to substitute number of conquests and sexual status of partner attractiveness, for actual skill and depth. It is a shame that females are increasingly buying into this shallow evaluative system. Young females, swayed by norms that encourage them to increase ease of male access to their body, may be unaware of the contrast between being left to live within the body which has been accessed without respect or care, and the casual and temporary male engagement with it. They must also live with the double standard for sexual behaviour which socially devalues a female who allows males easy access to her body and invokes economic and social punishment, now and for her future.

Current Australian statistics on the experience of unwanted sex for adolescent females suggest that, using primarily animal instinct and power brokering concepts of sex, young Australian males are increasingly viewing the female body as a space to relieve themselves - irrespective of the wishes or effect on the female who inhabits the internal world of that body. Significant increases in the numbers of young females engaged in binge drinking are also facilitating increased male access to female bodies due to the lowered capacity of the inebriated female to negotiate.

The endemic nature of narrow sexual focus and exploitative male sexual behaviour was highlighted when a 2009 study conducted within the United Nations found that employees who sexually assailed colleagues enjoyed impunity. If the world's foremost mechanism for asserting human rights cannot create an egalitarian environment safe from male invasion of female bodies then it certainly cannot handle the complexity of barbaric relations being enacted on the world's stage. In European Union countries between 40 and 50% of women experience unwanted physical contact, sexual advances or harassment. Women are five times more likely than men to experience violence. In countries across the globe up to 60% of women report that their first act of intercourse was forced. If the definition of force was broadened to encompass coercion facilitated by lack of female access to information about sex this percentage would be much higher.

Conceptualizations of sex that emphasize dominance and the satisfaction of base instinct reflect global, multilateral dysfunctionality. Sex is always a form of interpersonal relating involving the body. It is a unique form of relating laden with social norms of exploitation, relationship, violence, and use or abuse of privilege and power.

Orgasmic Potential and Body Consequences

Sex has different implications for the male and the female of the species. Sex for males invariably involves the intense pleasure of orgasm as he ejaculates. Unless he contracts an STI he may or may not have any other body or self effect. Sex for the male generally guarantees physical pleasure.

Sex has entirely different body implications for the female of the species. First of all, the physical act of sex does not guarantee pleasure for the female body. There are significant differences in arousal rates, patterns, and responses, between male and female of the human species. While males can achieve orgasm from reasonably short periods of touch females are unlikely to do so. The primary male sexual organ, the penis, has easily accessible nerve endings for stimulation. Even though the clitoris contains roughly double the number of sensitized nerve endings found in the penis, those nerve endings located below the skin are not as easily accessed and stimulated. Female sensory organ positioning and response mean that the layers of the clitoris embedded under the skin arouse more slowly and often only from prolonged touch and focus. There are sensitised nerve bundles similar to those in the penis in the entire body of the clitoris which extends down either side of the labia and has a knot of nerve endings at the top. In physical terms, the clitoris is a more diffuse multi-dimensional organ than is commonly recognized. It has extensive, supporting spongy tissue masses that attach broadly from the pubic arch to the urethra, vagina and labia, and bundles of nerves which run down the labia of significant size. Once these nerve endings are aroused, through stimulation of the nerve 'legs' running down either side of the vulva or of the clitoral hood at the top, female orgasm through intercourse becomes possible although ongoing clitoral stimulation is usually still required. This is because, contrary to popular myth, outside of the clitoris, there are few sensitized nerve endings in the vagina.

This is why Clitedectomy in the form of Female Genital Mutilation is comparable to cutting off a male penis in terms of damage to sensory receptors. One can only imagine the swift global response if some religion proposed a similar genital mutilation excision be conducted on males in childhood! Without arousal there is no lubrication of the female sexual organs which can result in painful sex for the female and tearing of sensitive tissue. For the human female, intercourse at best brings the pleasure of orgasm and at worst involves physical pain and tearing of flesh, with no physical pleasure at all.

Prolonged touch in the context of mutual sexual pleasure requires male willingness to attend to female arousal. Ideally, the male attends to the physical pleasure needs of the female in sexual activity but this requires choice and active participation of the male. In contrast to the female who can, 'Lie back and think of England' and still ensure that the male gains pleasure from intercourse, unless the male is willing to touch his partner and attend to her arousal; intercourse is unlikely to be physically pleasurable for the female. In the nineteenth and early twentieth century science and popular opinion asserted that females were, by and large, anorgasmic (frigid), and unable to experience orgasm. Actually, what was happening was that men were masturbating on women and Victorian women had no access to knowledge of their own bodies. Hence they were prone to anorgasmia, fits, fainting and bedridden pregnancy. Males who are sexually skilled and powerful don't need the vehicle of a female body when they wish to release sexual, physical or social tension.

Female arousal appears to be more complex than male arousal and hence addressing female arousal is not as straightforward as finding a female Viagra. The multiple global cultural and religious taboos against females thinking about sexual power and control are problematic. Globally, males can achieve arousal by thought and imaging but, except for a small proportion of elite westerners, this is unlikely for females. Some studies suggest that there is a part of the female brain which must be 'switched on' before she gets involved in sexual activity or physical arousal may be almost impossible. Hence, it is highly problematic that, across cultures and time, female access to information, education and controlled, safe, graduated sexual experience, have been largely denied.

Throughout history males have routinely had easier, and greater, access to information about sex and female body than females themselves. Such knowledge has always given males unfair advantage and control over sexual activity. When males have more knowledge of sex than women do they can use that knowledge to obtain sex without caring. Female arousal is affected by desire, which, for women, is often psychologically and relationally based. Throughout history, male knowledge of, and manipulation of, this knowledge, particularly when females are young, has given men unequal access to female bodies and sexual intercourse. The uneducated, disempowered young female, can be manipulated through feigned affection and by touch, into unwanted intercourse. 'Seduction' is actually coercion when the female doesn't have basic understanding which would give her any control over sexual touch, her pleasure, or access to her body.

Sex, Choice and Violence

The loss of control over the body in unwanted intercourse has far greater consequences for females than for males because the female body is penetrated by the sexual act. The female genital tract has permeable tissue running from the vulva to the cervix which allows viruses to cross directly into the bloodstream and means that the internal body system is exposed and perforated by intercourse. In contrast, males have a very small area of permeable tissue on the head of the penis which pales in comparison to the large area of the female body that is exposed to infection. Physiologically, this is why females are two to three times more likely than males to contract STIs and HIV from intercourse and why young women are 1.6 times more likely to be living with HIV than young men. In Sub-Saharan Africa girls make up to 75% of the infections in the age group of 15-24. This is not because these young females are promiscuous but because of older male sexual coercion, violence and unequal access to their bodies in the culture and frequent tearing of their bodies in forced intercourse.

Once a male has had full access to her body through intercourse the female human risks impregnation and the full consequences of this for her body self. The naïve, uninformed, manipulated young woman is unlikely to have used birth control. Faced with pregnancy females must choose one of two body traumas: Abortion or another human forming within her over ten months to become, literally, her 'flesh and blood.' If she chooses to remain pregnant the body costs she faces include the pain of labour and the intensive physical work of caregiving during the early years where survival is totally dependent on adult care. The financial and career costs will be significant and, in most countries, she will be expected to bear these personally. The female is usually held accountable for fulfilling the child's needs during the vulnerable early years in a manner not obligatory for males. The female then has responsibility for the welfare of this new person for at least a decade and a half and will often bear commitment to the welfare of her child for the rest of her physical life. Thus, the cost of losing control of the body self has lifelong implications for females. Practices that increase male capacity to coercively access female bodies carry significant risk and cost for women and girls.

Loss of Body Self: Marriage

Ironically, the ultimate loss of body control for many females across the globe occurs in the context of marriage where sexual violence and coercion are endemic. For women in many parts of the world being young and married is the most significant risk factor for contracting HIV. In Zambia and Kenya for example, a young married woman is at higher risk of contracting HIV than unmarried sexually active peers because of normalised male sexual promiscuity and taboos against married women using contraception. In some countries this means married women are at higher risk of contracting HIV than sex workers. In one Cambodian intervention attempting to address risk, married women were given condoms to take home to their husbands. One third were beaten for this.

Differences in body strength between male and female mean that females are at greater risk of sexual coercion, violence and rape within, and outside of, marriage. When there is rape or sexual violence the female body tissue is often torn or cut which additionally increases her risk of contracting a sexually transmitted infection. There is a period after HIV infection when seropositivity and infectiousness peaks so that a married man with multiple concurrent partners puts his wife at high risk of infection. In the United States, 70% of all HIV infections are heterosexually transmitted during the childbearing years and HIV is the leading cause of death for African American females aged 25-34. The physiology of the female genital tract means that multiple partners, with or without female consent, place the female body at higher risk than males. Therefore, if we were to fairly legislate sexual equity we would have to protect, and give greater control to, females.

The deeper dynamic of barbaric male-female domination and coercion needs to be addressed at the species level. Until that occurs we need to assist females to deal with unequal male access to their bodies by giving full education, contraception and access to safe medical and family planning services. Having 75% of the HIV population 15-24 in Sub-Saharan Africa represented by young females who had little choice over older male access to their bodies is at the scale of a crime against humanity. If females are not given control over who accesses their bodies, when and how they access them, and whether or not they can make a choice about growing a human being within their own personal body space, then the human race has no hope.

Control of Female Bodies

On the question of control over female bodies too often, in developing and developed nations, Muslim, Christian, Hindu and atheist, are united in their position that males should retain control over female bodies. Ostensibly this is to protect them, but such 'protection' is only necessary in a barbaric system where women are not accorded full human rights. In the recent barbaric insurgency Bush moved to decrease female control of their bodies globally and repealed all but the most basic reproductive freedoms for women. He re-imposed the Reagan-Bush Snr. Global Gag rule which, in the 1980s, inflicted immeasurable suffering on women around the world by effectively removing the only health resource in countries where medical care came through family planning clinics. Bush Jr. expanded the reach and the enforcement of the Gag by removing funding for any agency which offered, supported, or spoke about, abortion for women. He did this on his first day back in office in January 2001, sending all nations a strong message about the prioritizing of male bodies and desires, the subordination of women's body decisions to males and the pitilessness with which this would be enacted. Foreign NGOs who refused were denied assistance to provide any health services. For the women in the developing world who would like to space their children but who have little or no control over sexual activity and access to medical resources, this move was disastrous. Bush's Gag Rule increased the risk for millions of women of contracting HIV, of unwanted pregnancy or unsafe abortion. His gag idea is an extreme example of the damage that can be done by living in delusion rather than in reality. Thousand of the world's poorest, most powerless, and voiceless women, paid the ultimate price with their lives for this male power game.

Bush's senate also blocked ratification of the UN treaty on the rights of women and cut $34 million funding to the United Nations Population Fund which was estimated to directly lead to over 2 million more unwanted pregnancies, 4,700 maternal deaths and 77, 000 deaths of both mother and child. If criminals in western countries are held to account for one death, how much more should leaders be held to account for decisions which cause the loss of so much human life?

153

Only Abstinence?

Nationally Bush prioritized male access to female bodies by denying young women formal education which would increase their choices and control over where, and how, their body was accessed by males. Males receive much sexual information informally and in their socialization and enculturation into male culture. Females often must rely on formal channels such as health classes. The removal of these formal channels effectively removed female access to information which could assist them to retain control over their bodies and choices in the sexualised adolescent culture. Sex education has been shown to decrease female pregnancy, STI and abortion rates. The Netherlands begins sex education in pre-school and continues throughout this education through all levels of schooling, resulting in the world's lowest rate of teen births, an HIV infection rate eight times lower than the US and a teen abortion rate three times lower. In France, where sex education begins at thirteen the abortion rate is two times lower than the US and the teen birth rate is six times lower. Because all scientific evidence was overridden to implement a policy of significant harm primarily to young women it is obvious female wellbeing was not the focus.

Those decades saw young women being sexually exploited at previously unheard of levels. While barbaric rhetoric focuses on making the individual young female resist social pressure this conveniently ignores the social protections removed under barbarism which make girls and young women more vulnerable to predation. In cultures where social consequences for aggression are removed, this includes sexual aggression. Once aggression is legitimized and 'aggression and privilege without consequence' becomes the rule, it is inevitable that young women pay the price in increased sexual violence and exploitation. In the US, 83 percent of girls aged 12–16 experience some form of sexual harassment in public schools.

In the middle of a culturally and ideologically barbaric wasteland, where youth have not been given adequate care by parents and adults, the young will take whatever passion and highs they can – even if through alcohol and unsafe sex. The 'Abstinence Only' idea removed critical information from teens bombarded with increased cultural and interpersonal aggression which were decreasing female ability to negotiate during adolescence. While conservative barbaric control of women's lives is fostered by such ideas as 'promise keeping' this does not deal with the power and control issues of sex between genders. Girls lost access to information which would have protected and assisted them to independently negotiate sexual decisions while they had little sexual experience and while in an environment of increased sexual aggression.

The loss of sex education and choice increased the pregnancies of young, uneducated, women and further functioned to exclude female voice from the realm of the market and decision making. Bush's Gag rule and the requirement to have 'Abstinence Only' mumpsimus disseminated in high schools, when combined with barbaric propensity to blame the victim, provides a circular rationale for the oppression of single mothers. Young women who became stuck in the category of single mother, which is the single greatest predictor of living below the poverty line, lost access to housing and welfare subsidies which were subsequently axed by self-righteous wealthy politicians. Single mothers became increasingly subjected to work for welfare forced labour and separated from their small children.

The Gag Rule

It is no coincidence that President Obama removed the Gag rule in his first week in office. He understood the significance to global injustice and the increased male control over female bodies that the Gag facilitated. Possibly it was his partner, Michelle Obama who understood this but, in the 21st Century, her contributions to his leadership are rarely publicly acknowledged or accorded weight. Acknowledgment of her political influence as an intimate partner would be seen to 'emasculate' Obama. In fact, her open comments about his maleness during the election were quickly silenced by his campaign managers. In effect, the campaign managers were acknowledging that a primarily barbaric culture still refuses to be honest about female contributions made in marital and intimate partnerships. Therefore Ms. Obama's female opinions, perspectives, and strength as an equal partner, had to be censored.

The species must become more cognizant of its propagation. Overpopulation is arguably the greatest real survival threat we face and yet almost nothing is done about 'body terrorists' who refuse to allow women to make decisions about how their bodies are used and who actively block their means to do so. The Gag removed funding from agencies in countries where women have little or no control over sexual coercion and where intimate partner violence is rife. Those who enforced the Global Gag could be held to account for some of the millions of unwanted births and cases of HIV infection that occurred.

Relationship

Male control over, and abuse of, female bodies wastes the creative and productive potential of half the adult population and damages the possibility for integrity and dignity in human relationship. By reversing the gender roles of deep sea Angler fish we dehumanize females and erotic, passionate life suffers. No epic romance has ever been based on the idea of the disposability of the individual. The willingness to see others as irreplaceable, loyally cherishing them, and keeping them within our circle of care, is at the core of erotic relationship. Homo sapiens is outmatched by the wolf, fox, coyote, eagle, swan, osprey, hawks and even termites; all of whom are loyal to their mates. While human vultures prey on a range of human bodies, vulture communities in nature will attack a male caught philandering. In the domain of sexuality, some sections of the animal kingdom are more evolved than homo sapiens. The human orgasm, which comes from manipulating power over another, can never match the climax, ignited by people in deep, knowing relationship fed by bonds of loyalty, respect and care. Phenyl ethylamine can be switched on by passion, but it is fed by acts of care and will. Few humans have developed their self knowledge, their personal power and self control, to develop relationship to the point that their hormonal and blood systems respond to their will in cycles of erotic connection that they consciously feed and maintain. While the climax produced in this sexual relationship matches heroin in its hit factor, it doesn't carry any physical backlash and can't be reproduced by artificial manipulation. If you don't care for it, you can't have it.

Sixties Sexual Devolution

A real sexual revolution would have decreased ease of male access to female bodies, not increased it. The focus in the sixties was on sexual activity as liberatory in itself, rather than sexual choice as liberatory. Young women were told that 'free love', allowing multiple males to have access to their bodies, was part of their 'liberation' and this has occurred in the context of an adult vacuum of real information and realistic alternatives. The sixties resulted in increased male access to female bodies; particularly females in early adolescence and pre-adolescence who; if dressed provocatively, as encouraged by media and the prevailing culture, became 'fair game' for older predatory males. The so-called sixties sexual revolution ignored the fact that having to have sex is just as forceful and controlling as not being allowed to have sex.

Girl Culture: The Neutered Female

'Abstinence Only' exists in a mythologized realm devoid of any of the power dynamics in current male-female sexual relations or current female sexual conditioning in the culture. Whether it is the US or Saudi, men can still get away with raping women. Female bodies are sites of resistance where the species war of human aggression is being fought. Young girls are encouraged to trivialize their own bodies and to be flippant about things that matter as highlighted by Pink in the song, 'Stupid Girl.' Female sexual conditioning needs to revolve less around virginity and more around enabling young women to be aware of their value, their own pleasure, and the fact that their bodies are their own.

At the moment, exploitation of female bodies has reached unprecedented levels with rainbow parties, sexting, group sex and home porn, exploding in number. For a young male to be in his body is the experience of strength, capacity to overpower another, and to claim intimate personal resources from another. In Australia, between 40 to 60 percent of young women report unwanted sex. Our chlamydia rates have quadrupled in the past decade, and for many of our young women, being in the female body is an experience of capacity to be invaded and to carry inner world damage, which receives no external recognition, and evokes no external compassion. With body violation, it is the erasure of self that damages females most. Violations of the body mean that the inherent dignity of that human self doesn't matter because she is female. Males need to listen to, and respect, what it is like to live in a more vulnerable body. The scrawny, skinny, or short male usually has some of this knowledge. The female carries the greatest impact of the more vulnerable body self of the species in the risk of an unwanted pregnancy.

To raise some old questions: If the State raises young women to be naive and ignorant of the diminished social, legal and economic status of their gender; does not give them basic information or rights over their bodies; and concurrently feeds them mythologised, romanticised notions of male/female relations; so that such young women become engaged in exploitative sexual relations with males, does not the State bear responsibility for the progeny of such relations?

If the State raises young women to be naive and suffers their oppression in the home and schoolyard, and these young women become easy targets for predatory and violent males, does not the State bear some responsibility for the violence enacted against them?

If the State supports misogynistic notions of owning women and children, and doesn't provide any acknowledgement of, or respect for, caring and the role of carer, then shouldn't that society be held accountable when males beat, abuse, hunt down, and murder the women, or the children, they believe to be their property?

As long as a society allows the naive the gentle, the trusting, and the vulnerable, to be nothing more than a tasty titbit for the aggressive you have a society that can only degenerate not advance. Only with care at the centre can human societies flourish.

The Feminist Revolution vs. the Queen Bee

Female Culture

The culture of women used to be distinct from violent male culture but it has been pillaged and infiltrated by barbarism. Female culture has suffered a divide between barbaric and non-barbaric adherents. Women who enter the workplace and continue to care often find themselves exploited, overloaded with work, expected to do the emotional as well as the physical work of the workplace and home, and rendered ineffective, or burned out and incapable of contributing. Hence, some women, as men learned to do centuries ago, are learning to check their care and their humanity at the factory door and to conform to desire for production, status and advancement above all else. Females do this without the support system traditionally accorded to men and without the same guarantee of rewards. It is not an equal playing field and hence women who wish to be at the top must show their capacity to play the boy's rules with a ruthlessness that even males might hesitate to enact.

Hence, as women rose to world, national and corporate power positions it became glaringly apparent that barbarian high priests could be female. The female leader 'worse than the men' whose calculated cunning, cold ruthlessness and lack of care, leaves little room for humanity, knows that power positions for women are rare and she grips her territory with an iron fist. The traditionally masculine self structure emerges. These women adhere to the barbaric creed in willingness to advance at any cost. If feminism does not produce an increase in caring, humane behaviours and protection of those who behave in humane ways its utility to the species is limited.

The barbaric male culture has infiltrated the social realm of adolescents to an unprecedented level and exterminated many less barbaric social spaces which used to exist for young people. Although, at this historical time there is infiltration of male culture by barbarism, barbaric male culture must be distinguished from male culture as a whole. Furthermore, it is critical that barbaric male culture is defined and identified as distinct from the acts, beliefs and behaviours of individual males who must not all be tarred with the mass definition of barbaric. Just as there has been some resistance to barbarism in many realms, so, many males, often at great personal price, resist barbarism to live by pro-social values. Barbaric cultures that denigrate women mean that the man who is a good friend, husband, father and colleague, to women must swim upstream against his own gender community and often must forsake the privileges and protection of the 'brotherhood.' Barbarism makes decent relationships difficult for everyone. In this Feminism needed greater specificity.

Feminism's assumption that women who had the desire for equity between male and female also held values of power sharing and humane, caring behaviour was naïve. The fact that women can be as bad as men does not change the need for gender equity or the need for massive global changes for gender equity. It means that gender equity needs to be achieved quickly so that we don't lose the authentic remnants of indigenous female relational culture that remain. It means that the nuanced behaviour of power sharing requires solidarity around values of human dignity, equity, humane standards for behaviour and mutual caring responsibility. There are species females, some who call themselves feminists, who value barbarism and who enact vicious cruelty to others. Women who do this are just as problematic in leadership positions as men. The root of the problem is barbarism. In the instance of sexism, the barbarian uses the relative physical weakness of the female of the species as a means to increased exploitation and accrual of unearned advantages. Unless barbaric violence and exploitation is seen as the enemy then dominance and aggression can become mixed into feminism's pure desire for liberation for the female of the species and cause aggressive infighting and/or cruelty or domination of males of the species.

Barbaric behaviour causes non-barbaric females to distance themselves from feminism and the aim of equality for the genders, because they do not adhere to the barbaric creed and refuse its tenets. A broader cross section of non-barbaric males and females of the species is needed to advance gender equity and the type of mutual respect which will enable transformative, non-combative species advance. The root of the matter is barbarism.

Mean Girls

This rise of 'mean girls' and the 'nasty bitch' is further evidence of the infiltration of barbarism into female social realms. 'Mean girls' and the 'Queen Bee' phenomena which emerged in the recent barbaric insurgency involved young females who had some element of power they could wield and the willingness to be barbaric in the use of that power to intimidate and subjugate others. Their power was usually based on a combination of body privilege (physical attractiveness) and other privilege (such as socio-economic status or particular talent) which, when combined with a willingness to be savage and cruel to others, becomes lethal to less privileged or less aggressive teens. Mean girls bought into barbaric philosophy to use their power to bully and intimidate others to establish their own 'realms and kingdoms.' Typically they used the barbaric tactics of being willing to inflict pain, finding satisfaction in the suffering of others and being willing to criticize savagely. The wounds on the hearts and minds of their victims, as well as the very real loss of life for those who suicided as a result of being targeted in this way, are reminders of the real effects of barbaric philosophy when it is enacted in the real world. Queen Bees accurately read the wider culture in which they were being raised and understood that social censure for merciless, heartless, vicious and remorseless behaviours had been removed. They capitalized on a culture still naïve about barbarism knowing that they could not be penalized for behaviours the wider culture was encouraging and deifying.

Referred Female Power

Historically there have always been pockets of dominance within female culture. Even the stereotypically sweet housewife of the 50s was subject to, and sometimes enacted, savagery towards other housewives. It was just that the basis for attack was different – perhaps the cleanliness of one's home or the lightness of one's cake was the target for ridicule when packs of women circled and attacked an unfortunate to humiliate her. With Queen Bees the attacks are more prevalent, brazen, violent and public. There are fewer spaces to which an unfortunate target can retreat because only open public subjugation and obeisance is accepted by the bullying group or Queen.

The dominance of married women over single women and particularly single mothers has long been an established social phenomenon. The female borrows the status of marriage and the financial and other power of their mate to assume superiority over other women or social others of lower status. Many women support barbarism and dominance because they get to share the hierarchical power and status of their dominant mate. Women who buy into hierarchical dominance and privilege are often willing to use the barbaric tactics of cruel, unfeeling, calloused behaviour to maintain their privilege. While sisterhood is the rhetoric of feminism white women are notorious for backstabbing other women. There is little solidarity in the wealthy, white female pack.

Barbaric females often go one step further to exploit women who are nurturing, kind or caregiving, 'to cut such women down', and to enact dominance over them, as in the Queen Bee phenomenon. Women support barbarism, not just by being subservient to men but by also becoming domineering, cruel, and exploitative. The woman who becomes mistress to a married man exploits the (relatively) powerless position of the married female in the triangle. She thereby devalues another woman and supports the barbarian notion that women are easily accessible, disposable and replaceable. Among females there is often much sexual competition for males. The extent of this competition devalues females. Competitive women who seek solidarity with males over sisterhood again reinforce the barbarian stereotype of female as of lesser value and inferior. The woman who has excised her own caring/nurturing spirit as surely as a clitedectomy, is every bit as dangerous to caring women as barbaric males. Ego based women carry no sense of responsibility towards other women. Powerful white women carry responsibility to act on behalf of, and to raise their voices for, less powerful sisters around the globe. Female strengths of care and nurturance are meant to be combined with the dominance of privilege to enact change for voiceless, disempowered sisters. In the west there is much allegiance to dominance and to dominant males and little fealty of women for women. The exceptions are not the dominant rule.

Barbaric culture hurts boys as well, particularly those not prepared to use their gender to abuse or exploit others. Young men who are not prepared to enact warlike insensitivity to others may find themselves mercilessly tormented by barbarian packs (barbarians are generally cowards and rely on numbers to further reinforce their already unfair advantage), physically attacked and socially ostracized. Barbarism can be enacted at any level where there is a power differential. Patriarchal concubines (barbaric white women) will also betray children and enact barbaric behaviour to break children and enforce their subservience to dominants and barbarism. The amount of damage that can be inflicted is determined by the referred and hoarded power of the female and the differential in power between her and the victim.

Around the Globe – Seepage Effects for Women

We live in a world which still does not protect the body integrity of the majority of its girls and women. Recently, we had the Beijing +15 campaign to monitor the 15 year old pledge of governments to change laws that legally sanctioned female inequality. After 15 years many governments have not fulfilled their pledge and nor is there any international mechanism capable of impelling them to do so. In India, it has been 5 years since the rape of married women was criminalized however, this is a paper tiger as the law has not been amended so actually that women can file against partners who rape them. Women's movements are still restricted across the globe: Saudi women can't drive, Iraqi women can't travel without the approval of their husbands and additional laws have been enacted in Afghanistan to restrict women. The female policewoman appointed to head Kandahar city's department of crimes against women, herself a mother of 6, was assassinated by the Taliban in 2008, with no retribution. In an interview about women's rights she stated, 'We are trying to apply the law and the constitution is supposed to protect women's rights. But I fear that we are going backwards. More and more obstacles are being put in our path. Instead of becoming more confident, women are becoming more afraid of the threats.' Urgent international attention should be focussed on loss of women's rights in the slippage accompanying barbarism across the globe.

The rights of children and women are inextricably entwined. There are half a million maternal deaths every year. The Chief of the Gender, Human Rights & Culture Branch of the UN Population Fund, Professor Aminapa identified the dilemma behind high maternal mortality as a lack of will, 'In most societies in the world, motherhood is very valued and celebrated. But there is a deficit of attention and seriousness in terms of addressing the issue.' The fundamental species paradox which we face is that the species needs women to birth, but individual women who do so lose social and economic value power, which keeps the female gender in subordination to men. The women's movement has always been hampered by the reality that, because women carry the load of unpaid child-care and work in the home, they have less free time to commit to activism. This situation of inequity enables ongoing male control of female bodies and unwanted births which is spawning unsustainable population growth. Women and girls need the control of their own bodies, just as men and boys need control over theirs.

In any culture formed on the backbone of female unpaid labour, women must be powerful, honoured, protected and accorded full rights; otherwise, it is unsustainable exploitation which will rot the culture from the innards out. Misogyny is still the password into many enclaves of privilege in western nations and around the globe. This was highlighted in the recent war on terror. When Afghan women began to suffer under the Taliban's increased violent oppression, we did nothing. When Afghan women were forced out of public spaces; had their right to education outlawed, and were experiencing such misery that they laid down to die in their black robes in protest; we did nothing. When women in the Congo and Rwanda were raped and slaughtered en masse, we did almost nothing. When we suffered a fraction of this loss of life we came in with boots on and machine guns blazing. This is not to say we should not have responded but it was only when our trade power bases were challenged and our citizens targeted that we had no problem coming in with bombs. Granted, we must protect our own communities, but we must also respond to human atrocities everywhere, with the same swiftness, and willingness to commit. All struggles are connected and none of us are safe until all of us are safe.

What we are willing to fight for tells us much about our barbarism. Our intervention further disempowered Afghani women because we demonstrated solidarity with their males that they were not worth fighting over and that their lives and freedom didn't matter. Are we willing to fight for the 6000 African girls every day who are at risk of having their genitals cut off? What we fight for is more important than the fight because it demonstrates our values and our commitment. Our current priorities are not human welfare.

Violence against women is the most widespread violation of human rights in the globe. One in three women will suffer violence in her life, and one in five will suffer rape or attempted rape. Women's time, energy and bodies continue to be co-opted. This over privileging of male access to female bodies must be resisted and will require a shift in power across the genders. Women of the world need to be free from the violence of unwanted invasion of their bodies and of unwanted pregnancy which is the ultimate representation of male privilege and power without attendant responsibility. An individual woman having power over her own body is never too much power.

Any religion that does not recognize the inherent dignity of the autonomous female body is flawed. It has melded the barbaric creed to its pure origins. Religions that give males control over female bodies narrowly focus their argument on sexual behaviour when really it is about power and control. This is evident in the way this control is invariably implemented through physical violence. All female activities become controlled to assert male control over female bodies for sexual access when human life is so much more than sex. The obsessive focus on sex reflects the poor maturation of religious leaders who need to preserve male privilege in access to females. Refusing to educate women, see them as equal members of the species, and give them the basic freedom of owning their own bodies, is the greatest terrorist act; in scope and impact, the human species faces.

Women still do the majority of unpaid work across the globe, exhausting them, draining their adrenal systems and keeping them more effectively in bondage. Throughout history women have drained their body systems to ensure the welfare of their children but the vampiric draining of women's bodies has reached its zenith in the 21st century industrialized world. Non-government organisations have proliferated in an environment of barbarism and competition where a great deal of their energy is devoted to aggrandisement of their public image, marketing themselves as the lead organisation and competing with other NGOs. This must stop. Consolidation must occur so that energy used to compete for funding can go to the people and causes that need resources.

International and global ineptitude and mismanagement and barbarism have resulted in countless human deaths and resource wastage and low prioritization of women. If humanity is to survive, we have to decrease our response time and respond to extreme barbarism with immediacy and commitment. In Rwanda of the 250 000-500 000 girls and women who were raped and are still alive, up to 70% are HIV infected. The international community knew that women and girls were being raped en masse and did nothing to halt it. If the trillions of dollars that were sunk into the 'emergency' rescue of the 'economy' were sunk into the real emergency, the decimation of women and girls around the world, we would experience global transformation.

It is unclear what sort of relationships men and women would have if women didn't have to depend on individual men physically or financially for safety. We have no idea what levels of productive, synergistic intimacy could be fostered through fair, equal gender relationships based entirely on notions of care. What is clear is that human systems which depend on the control of women's bodies, and the draining of their adrenal and auto immune systems in order to function, are unsustainable. They are blood fiefdoms, not civilizations.

We need to talk to impoverished black African women, to Brazilian women living in the slums of Recife, to Dalit women, about the fate of the planet so that its not just businessmen and privileged white populations making critical decisions from our limited understanding and consciousness. These women know how to prioritize female safety, education, health, and welfare, and how to foster community life. They know where and how to spend money. Such women can still access both common sense and the deeply ingrained learning of their hard lived experience – they are expert in the issues of survival and the impacts, costs and consequences of privileged insulation at a level and a depth we can only imagine. There is no need for us to stumble blindly onward when experts at recognizing and surviving oppression are at hand.

CHAPTER 8: PRIORITIZING CHILDREN

In the recent 'economic meltdown' power holders were 'suddenly' able to agree to invest trillions of dollars as a matter of urgency. Why? Human rights? Protection of women and children? Halting genocide? No. To pump life back into the archaic body of the market Frankenstein. When this happened it became crystal clear that the standard arguments against funding human welfare and wellbeing are simply regurgitation of barbaric priorities and beliefs. Human transformation will occur when human wellbeing is prioritized over profit and when barbaric mythology ceases to be the foundation of decision making. Currently, barbaric belief systems, like death ghouls, hold humans in their sway mesmerized by the Death instinct. Economics cannot be master; it must be placed in service to the central organizing principle of the Life instinct: Preserving human welfare and advancement. When the 'market' is posed as master it merely means that those with most money will rule, irrespective of their ethic. If their creed is barbaric, people will suffer and humans and the environment will be degraded and destroyed without compunction.

Prioritizing the market destroys the protective systems and relationships which create the social amniotic fluid and emotional oxygen supply for small children. Barbarians peel back the protective layers around a child and leave their sensitive inner world exposed to the harsh elements of the adult world. Early exposure of small children to adult aggression, impatient hostility, and vicious competition; before they have protective barriers around their self systems; causes the inner world to be flooded with toxins. Bathing the brain in stress hormones and chemicals destroys normal brain homeostatic functioning and can cause the brain to be permanently set at a higher RPM, as in the case of children with ADHD. When facing this type of developmental damage in children, learning difficulties, or the social problems of delinquency, barbarians don't consider their contribution to the damage done to children, but 'blame the victim', (Tenet X of the Creed). We need a more complex system than the barbaric creed for integrating our common sense and scientific knowledge in ways that prioritize the health and wellbeing of humans and assure that the needs of children are met. Any society that cannot take care of its children is useless.

What Matters?

1. Infants Matter

As previously discussed, brains require experience to grow. In our infinite wisdom and after billions of dollars spent delving into genetics and genomes, scientists have finally affirmed that the growth of a child's brain is determined much more by the experiences we give them than by their genes. Neuroscience is getting hard data explaining why infancy is so important to human development and lifelong wellbeing – something that we can all know by looking at a newborn child and using common sense.

There are critical periods during which the brain undergoes spurts in development – sort of like an electrical power surge, where specific skills develop rapidly and where irreparable damage can be done if skill development is ruptured. Neuroscientists have now identified that if an infant is deprived of essential experiences and, particularly experiences within the relationship with the mother, then some parts of the child's brain are harmed. In depth brain imaging of infants and mothers has visually demonstrated that the experiences given to infants not only affect their brain capacities but can create psychopathology and affect relational capacity for their whole lives. Basically, neuroscience is now recognizing that mothers and small children matter – something caring people have been saying for millennia.

Studies conducted with institutionalized children, such as the brain scans performed on Romanian orphans, have pictorially demonstrated some of the aspects of the profound damage infants experience when deprived of care. Starving these children of responsive, soothing nurturance, touch and care has caused them to have irreversible physical damage, specifically, underdevelopment of specific limbic and midbrain sections of their brains – the sections which influence abnormal behaviour and thinking capacity. In effect these children's living selves have been mutilated by global adult carelessness. The studies of Romanian orphans have provided tangible, graphic evidence for ignorant adults of the physical brain damage caused by neglect but such scans do not capture the emotional suffering of tiny children as their desperate cries went unheeded and their inner world was painfully maimed. Nor do such studies focus on the role that male control of female bodies played in these births and subsequent painful deformation. In Romania, Ceausescu's ban on abortions was followed by Reagan and Bush's Gag rule. These male power games over the realm of female bodies caused the births of many unwanted children who then suffered unimaginably.

One of the 'new frontiers' for avid neuroscientists is now considered to be the domain of 'maternal love.' Researchers (predominantly male) are clamouring in the race to develop brain theories to explain why the mother-child bond is 'so important.' Compassionate mothers through the ages have not required brain scans to know this. A better research question would be: Why have humans ignored the deep knowing of maternal love for so long? Why have the voices of compassionate mothers, the cries of suffering Indigenous mothers and babies as we callously separated them, and the cries of small children, been ignored until (predominantly) old, white men could take pictures of damaged children's brains? Pardon, but our barbarism is showing.

2. Emotions Matter

Again, after millions of dollars of neuroscientific research, scientists now not only acknowledge that infancy and childhood matter but that how we feel (the emotions generated by our human experience) has the greatest impact on our brain structuring and on our development as people. With complex language, hormonal and blood samples, brain scans and statistics, scientists are trying to say that how people feel matters and specifically, that how we make children feel matters very much.

We do not rationalise and think when we are babies - we feel and sense – and much of our body and emotional regulation is affected by the emotional ponds around us, most particularly by those of our mothers. Humans come into the world as super sensory beings able to pick up non-verbal nuances and communication at subliminal levels. As newborns we are emotional and feeling bundles with only our right hemispheric somatosensory body system having any myelination (super highways). Everything else is still subcortical (cobblestones). How we feel when we are small is strongly linked to whether, and how, we are cared for.

Again trailing behind the wisdom of compassionate humans through the ages, the cutting edge of psychobiological science has now moved from focussing on conscious thoughts and rationality to realizing that emotion is far more critical to the development of the intact, vital human person.

It is how we are made to feel as children — not whether or not we can read — which defines the quality of our inner world and much of our adult capacity.

Our early, primary emotional responses are preserved by our brains to reduce the energy needed to deal with any new experience. Emotions we experience as adults are feedback, based on the interpretation system set up in early childhood, about how we are succeeding in the external world. If early experience programs body memory and right hemisphere with pleasant, relaxed emotions and happiness, then these are the emotions we will feel as we face new or challenging experience. Our left brain is programmed to interpret this emotional feedback as 'success', irrespective of external reality. Thus, much of our adult sense of calm, confidence and capacity, comes directly from childhood programming.

If our childhood was one of care and positive experience this gives us the psychological advantage of confidence and feeling good when we face something new. If we were harmed, threatened, or brutalized in early childhood it gives us enormous disadvantage. If our early experiences programmed fear, anxiety or terror into our brain then we are more likely to perceive ourselves as failing in the social and external world, irrespective of performance. In this case any new learning or the unknown evokes dread, terror, the expectation and the emotional feelings of failure. In an attempt to avoid these negative emotions (emotional pain) we are likely to avoid new experiences. Our capacity to negotiate the external world is damaged which then effectively imprisons us in the damaged environmental conditions with which we are most familiar.

Neuroscience is finding that rational thought has been overvalued in the evaluation of what affects people's behaviour and, instead, that feeling plays the strongest roles in affecting daily actions. Emotion, relationship and care are the core structures for healthy human life and it is these components that foster child growth into strong, capable adults, not the experience of mansions, money, status or dominance. It is how children are treated and made to feel that matters. Again, neuroscientists are clamouring to be the 'first' to identify the physical brain pathways that are activated when we accurately access complex knowledge on the basis of our emotions, or what is known as instinct. It appears in the enlightened 21st-century that instinct is finally going to be scientifically legitimated and validated as a real knowledge access system. We are only 50,000 years behind Aboriginal Australians.

3. New Mothers Matter

The emotional pond comprised by a mother's health, safety, social support, sense of self, capacities and values; strongly influences the feeling system of a baby. Even in the womb the baby is affected by the mother's level of stress.   Studies have found that 40% of the woman's stress cortisol crosses the placenta during the period when the baby's brain amygdala is forming; affecting future well-being. Where mothers are depressed or in situations of danger or hostility, the newborn baby is affected because their early development draws upon the sensory pond of the 'feel' and quality of the mother's world. Calm and soothing creates the sense (feeling based) that the mother, and therefore the 'external world' is safe. Civilized cultures have therefore always respected the vulnerability, primacy and complexity of the bond between mother and baby and, intuitively, protected them.

Newborn babies are bundles of highly amplified, sensitized feelings. Their visual capacities are initially poor but their capacities for smell, touch and sensing are highly tuned. The newborn baby knows the mother's smell and sound of her voice distinct from any other. Because only the brain's somatosensory system is myelinated at birth, babies' bodies are highly sensitive to touch, smell and sound and they are processing information from the outside in an inner world, feeling oriented manner. The subcortical nature of other, more rational systems is reflected in their low impact on a baby. A baby is acutely sensitive to sensory factors of light, warmth, cold, hunger, loud noise or pain which is why keeping them, warm, dry, fed and soothed with regular, consistent response is so much of their early care. The mother's accurate 'reading' of the baby's non-verbal and body communication is essential if she is to select the correct soothing response for the baby. Her gentle, caring response is central to the baby's sense of wellbeing. The central communication between mother and baby is feeling based. Contrary to popular belief, this is not simple but involves complex, nuanced, synergistic reading of each other's nonverbal signals and brain patterns in concurrent and simultaneous feedback loops.

The caring mother is serving as a connective passage for the intense internal world of the infant to the new external world. Her feelings are serving as primary pylons of the bridge for the crossing. To the highly sensitized feeling system that is the new baby, the mother's feelings and reactions become the amniotic fluid of their new world. The familiarity with the mother established within the womb (heartbeat, voice) assists the baby to be calmed in the new environment assaulting their senses. The care formed by the mother for the baby as he or she grows within her, helps motivate her to be able to deal with all of the intensive labour demands of complexly reading, and responding to, the tiny, completely dependent, demanding, non-verbal baby.

Researchers have found that bonded mother and baby communications are accompanied by the strongest feelings and emotions in the child. The baby needs the mother to minimize their negative feelings and experiences, through soothing, and increase their positive feelings through happy, warm and caring interactions. In brain terms, when this happens, the brain is being soaked with oxytocin, the baby's stress hormones are dropping and the immune system is being boosted: all ideal brain development conditions. In other words, the baby feels good.

The more consistently this is done for an infant, the broader the range of the person's wellbeing and positive emotional self that develops. These consistent, ongoing caring and nurturing interactions create actual biological connections between mother and child, mediated through intuitive, synchronous communication in indefinable paths between the inner and outer world. These are powerful enough to regulate the body systems of both mother and baby. In fact, the complexity of the biological and emotional regulation in a healthy mother-baby bond is the greatest depth of human connection in neuroscientific as well as relational terms. The deep relationship between well bonded mother and baby who live, breathe, and reflect one another, occurs synchronously with one side of each of their brain's communicating at a level that seems almost telepathic with the other. The bond occurs at such a deep, complex and sensitive level that this homeostatic connection functions even when we are sleeping. This is at a level of complexity and nuanced sensitivity that is beyond all of our neuroscientific understanding and therefore should be approached with great respect and care.

The Care of New Mothers

The mother keeps the complex internal homeostasis of the baby's system intact by regulating the child's environment and providing the immediate emotional resource of herself to soothe in order to soothe and calm the child's internal world. In protecting and soothing the baby's internal/external world connection through loving care and through closely attending to the baby's signals in order to accurately interpret his or her needs, the mother is fostering the wellbeing and healthy development of the small person. While this is obviously not her primary focus, a mother who is bonded to her baby in a relationship of deep love and care, is also growing connections in the child's brain and nurturing species' possibilities for advanced, creative, complex future cultures. In effect, mother and child become each other's inner world.

We often do not focus on the human, community and environmental factors which can cause profound, lifelong damage in childhood, through harsh, unfeeling responses to mothers. Creating high stress for the mother through work and social practices that devalue women and do not factor in the physical and emotional labour of caring for small children, damages the child's developmental pond. Overwhelming the adrenal and body systems of women through an unfair load of labour drains the child's resource systems of care. This can also happen when the primary carer is forced out of the home with no adequate replacement so that the child is deprived of the buffering from harsh external world provided by the soothing, complexly bonded, caregiver. The reality is that we can create brain damage in children not just through cruelty and neglect and violence but also through depleting their environment of the critical resources they need. These resources are not only physical but are often emotional and psychological and are time, labour and care intensive primarily for mothers.

As it is usually the mother who is providing nurturance in infancy the ongoing cumulative impact of highly stressed home environments, domestic violence, poverty, maternal depression and multiple negative factors on the mother should therefore not be underestimated. Critical psychological learning for a child in the first months of life is: 'When I am under stress someone will respond to me and hence I will manage.' This becomes encoded into body memory and enables future strengths of emotional self-soothing and healthy emotional range. A well loved baby is well on the path to becoming a compassionate, emotionally intelligent adult. The defining characteristic of a well balanced, healthy human is broad emotional range with ability to feel and respond to one's own pain and that of others (compassion). Psychopathology represents narrowing of this emotional range. The entrenched criminality of the antisocial psychopath seems to spring from a shutdown of the homoeostatic system in the face of too much pain where the system is overaroused, not soothed, and goes into overload. The functionality of this shutdown is that the baby, the developing person, is then inured to pain but also to feelings of happiness and comfort. We can't afford to be squeamish about gender on issues affecting children. We need to prioritize healthy infant development by supporting mothers because the mother is the baby's resource. Protection and social, legal and financial support of mothers is critical to preventing social ills.

Uncaring, Unfeeling Responses Afterbirth

In this context we can examine the barbaric processes of shortened hospital stays for mothers after birth; low provision of maternity pay so that mothers are forced back to work before physical recovery; and the increasing barbarism of standard care offered to women around birth in western cultures. Increased male and barbaric cost oriented approaches to birth have meant escalating caesarean rates and practices of discharging mothers 24 hours or a few days the surgery. Women are sent home with a major abdominal wound without nursing aid or healthcare assistance into a context where they often must also care for other small children. This is barbaric practice at an extreme. Lack of care for the mother after the physical trauma of birth is compounded by lack of post-operative surgical care for the large physical wound in the lower body.

Such lack of care after similar surgical wounding would be considered unconscionable for anyone not birthing. It is as though health care professionals believe that the physical size of the wound is irrelevant because the operation also involved a birth. The fact that the woman's healing must occur in the context of primary, labour intensive care for a vulnerable infant makes these early discharges doubly negligent. Cost cutting to discharge someone 24 hours after major bowel or other surgery is similarly reprehensible. Even half a century ago two weeks of bed rest was a social norm. Many 'developing' cultures still provide assistance to mothers for 30 days after the birth. Barbarism can include the tendencies of lacking pity or compassion for others; being prepared to act in a merciless manner; being able and disposed to inflict pain, and being predisposed to inflict hardship on others – all attitudes displayed towards mothers after birth.

Australia is particularly harsh and unfeeling in its treatment of mothers. Public outcry on behalf of mothers in our culture is virtually non-existent. Postnatal depression and ill-treatment of children is rarely linked to wider social positions towards mothers. An economic study, conducted in the UK, found that Australian men do less household labour than men in any other OECD nation and the significance of this norm of unfair distribution of labour and exploitation of women's energy should not be underrated. It affects women critically in the post-birth period of exhaustion and sleep deprivation. After childbirth, the addition of household labour to labour intensive tasks of infant care, affects the overall care available for the baby. This social norm of unjust distribution of unpaid labour is a sign of wider, hard hearted, attitudes towards women and children in Australian culture.

As at the date of this writing Australia and the United States are the only two OECD countries without government-funded paid parental leave, although state based schemes have been providing leave to about half of all American mothers for some time. Canada has 28 weeks, the United Kingdom 39 weeks and Sweden 47 weeks. The decision to provide women 18 weeks at minimum wage beginning in 2011 has had Australian businessmen up in arms and calling for compensation. The negative, outraged response taken by employers demonstrates, not only low compassion for the work required of females to birth a child for the culture, (and its future citizenry) but a sense of hostile aggression about males having to share or bear any of the social costs of this work. Anyone who has completed the physically draining body work of growing a child within their body, the pain of labour and the intensive sleep deprivation and work of caring for a human infant can only be astounded. We need to collectively protest such a petty minded, penny pinching, uneducated approaches to human welfare. Child wellbeing must be prioritized.

The Child's First and Primary Resource

Globally, the low prioritization of the wellbeing of mothers is reflected in appalling maternal death rates. Every minute in the developing world a woman or girl dies of pregnancy related causes, most of them preventable. Pregnancy is a body risk for the human female and labour is a body trauma which requires appropriate care, support and social prioritization. As we have such a calloused attitude to women in our own cultures around the matters of birthing it is no wonder that maternal deaths are rarely on the global agenda.

The mental health and resources of the mother are critical to the healthy development of the child in the early childhood period. At-risk mothers who face multiple disadvantages, stresses and stigma should be the focus of health resourcing. This includes Aboriginal mothers, single mothers, mothers from low SES groups, teenage mothers and women who have addictions, have experienced domestic violence, or other multiple exclusion criteria. Ongoing mental health disorders are precipitated mainly by early childhood experience and in particular by early childhood neglect and trauma caused when mothers in these groups are not given adequate support. The fact that pregnant women and mothers with infants and small children are such a low cultural priority attests not only to our barbarism but also to our stupidity as a culture.

Brain science takes too long...it is too slow. This is the best investment period for the optimal development of our next generation even from a narrow economic perspective. Why such profound wastefulness in a manner that would not be tolerated in the financial world?

4. The Bond between Mother and Child Matters

Incursions of the Intimate

Throughout history, any culture that heartlessly separated mother and baby was considered depraved. Instinctively, healthy cultures have protected the mother child bond by calling it sacred and have acted to prevent unnecessary separation of small children from their mothers. Ancient cultures did not have access to neuroscientific findings but used common sense and basic humane principles of human dignity and compassion for small children as their guide. Any society that has overridden this wisdom has experienced massive social decay and devolution. Even Spartan society, arguably the most disciplined military society that has ever existed, did not separate boys from their mothers until age 7. Irrespective, calloused so-called 'experts' in the 21st century have felt free to blithely disregard the record of human progress to assert that the mother child relationship is unnecessary, easily replaceable and even damaging to the child. They have neither scientific nor cultural evidence to back such an assertion but often have significant political power and the support of powerful barbaric potentates.

Barbarians have no way of understanding, let alone measuring, the invisible and irreplaceable treasure of the deep attachment between a mother and child, where care is present, and where the mother has been the primary caregiver. This was evidenced in Australia in the barbaric decision to remove Aboriginal children from their mothers and the heartlessness and cruelty with which the cries of both mother and child were silenced. The decimation to Aboriginal people should be enough evidence of the shocking social and individual devastation that can be caused by allowing arrogant male potentates to privilege their intellectual theories over the bonds of love. Barbarians cited social Darwinism and genetics to suggest that Aboriginal mothers, as a race, were 'less attached' to their children than whites, and in fact, 'forgot' their children, hence absolving barbarians, and the complicit public, from facing the reality of the atrocity they were perpetuating.

The ongoing evidence that this was a human atrocity continues to be minimised, distorted and ignored in Australian culture. The statistical evidence is overwhelmingly frank in every available research that we conduct. From early death and suicide, to alcoholism and domestic violence, the intergenerational damage caused by the severance of the sacred bonds between Aboriginal mother and child, child and community, is incontrovertible. In our culture, these real consequences of severing mother and baby and deep bonds of connection, are rarely connected to the statistics. The suicide rate of Aboriginal people is seven times higher than the general population; they represent 41% of all children in corrective institutions and, as adults, are jailed at 14 to 20 times the rate of other Australians. They have a life expectancy twenty years less than the rest of the Australian population and their babies are twice as likely to die at birth. What other evidence do we need? As a society can we afford to allow barbarians to continue to dismiss such weighty evidence on no other basis than that of their own harsh, dogmatic belief system?

Besides the obvious barbarian reluctance to have to pay damages (cost-cutting) if the damage be acknowledged, the more disturbing possibility is that barbarians have not progressed at all in their understanding about human relationships, attachments and the value of human bonds. Historically societies have used common sense to understand the centrality of the relationship with the mother to a small child and have protected children's rights to access to the mother. Witnessing the distress of mother and child when separated was enough evidence for most societies to be able to adhere to basic principles that preserve mental health and wellbeing. Cultures wanting to foster healthy, strong adults have always acknowledged the centrality of the early mother-child relationship and protected it. Evidence that gross barbarian ignorance of the needs of children and the value of the bond between mother and child is still as high as ever, is evident in Howard's pro-barbarian legislation which repealed two centuries of legislative process to enforce ruptured attachment for the benefit of adults.

In the 21st century we have, again, allowed the self-interest of opinionated, uneducated barbarians to pillage the precious resource of the deep, care relationship of mother and child in the early years. Unless we regain common sense and gain greater understanding of the depths of human life, including the invisible but powerful bonds that occur when people care and attached to one another, we have no way of dealing with the social ills we now face. In addition, unless we gain greater clarity about the need to protect and defend relationships and other intangible but precious life resources, we have no way of defending our families, our lives, and our world from barbarian incursion.

Beyond Solomon: Carving Up the Child

In humane societies the relationship between mother and child is protected, not on the basis of some barbaric power struggle between adult men and women, but on the basis of the wellbeing of the child. The fact that we now understand the complexity of early bonding which results in connection of the inner world of mother and child with the transfer of an inner world 'map' to each others brains with embedded communication codes and complex, multi-lateral routes; should foster, not detract from, our protection of this intricate, irreplaceable resource.

Our most advanced neurobiological studies have uncovered only a small corner of the deep human and brain connection fostered in the unique relationship between mother and child. We know that compassionate responsivity is focussed at such a level that the mother and infant are responsive to each other, even in sleep, and that the healthy mother's capacity to read the baby's nonverbal signalling is at such a complex level that it appears to be more akin to the mother being able to read the brain waves of the child in the moment. Children must be left in the care of those who care for them and who have the commitment and the developed skills to do this well. This is evident in the committed care evident in the woman who is willing to sacrifice personal career, physical, social, and emotional wellbeing for that of her baby.

During the recent barbaric insurgency, John Howard, in a behind-the-door, handshake move between himself and the politically powerful men's movement, overthrew rights of mother and child in a dismembering of Family Law. The changes were made in spite of, not as a result of, all research and statistical evidence documenting the centrality of the primary caregiver in the early years to the emotional and physical wellbeing of children. In Australia young families are the most likely to break up, with half having a child under 3 and only 7% having children older than 12. Thus, this law targets families with very young children and where the overwhelming majority, more than 95%, of primary caregivers are the mother ie: 95:5. Irrespective, this 'reform' enforced a 50:50 split of children after relational breakdown. This has meant cases where breastfeeding babies are forcibly taken from the mother for the father's access. The courts are held to upholding the demands of males even when this is not in the best interests of the welfare of the child.

In Australia it has been culturally normative for mothers to be the primary caregivers of small children. Howard's change was simply re-imposition of the centuries' old position of male ownership of children, irrespective of mother-child relationship. The notion of ownership is problematic. If we don't own children then how we treat them is our only real link and the bond of relationship becomes the tie. It is important to note that, in the deeply bonded relationship of mother and small child they have become each other's inner world. When this bond is ruptured, what is being damaged is the inner world of mother and small child (where resides future sanity, emotional wellbeing, sense of safety, learning and social capacity). The mother-child bond in the early years is a unique human relationship in its depth, its loyalty, in the deep responsivity and labour required, and in its impact. The loyalty the small child experiences is the foundation of their sense of safety through life. When small children are removed from the emotional responsivity of their primary caregiver their emotional safety is removed and they are traumatised. Such statements are not politically popular but it does not serve the species well to ignore the needs of small children and their need for complex bonded caregiving when they are pre-verbal or only partially articulate. We can learn from the past.

Nineteenth Century Ownership of Children

Any cursory examination of the massive body of psychological evidence in relation to child development makes the possibility of real damage when primary attachment is ruptured abundantly clear. This legislative change set Australian society back two centuries and effectively removed the capacity of the Family Court to act in the best interests of the child, regardless of adult demands. Judges are forced to separate mother and child unless there are extreme, documented cases of abuse, and, even then, judges must demonstrate willingness to privilege the demands of adult males, to avoid being in contravention of the legislation. Most concerning is the enforcement of the 50:50 split when the male has had no previous caregiving responsibility for the child and has enacted violence towards their partner. The vast amount of empirical research on the trauma and damage inflicted on small children when they are forcibly removed from their primary caregiver is ignored.

Small children are the majority of those affected by parental separation in Australia. They are mainly non-verbal or partially verbal and therefore need their caregiver to know them well enough and to have developed the complex skills to accurately read their individual non-verbal communication and to respond consistently to soothe their unique needs. They need a caregiver who, over time, has developed the capacity to withstand the labour intensive demands of using their brain to constantly monitor the feeling state and needs of the child. This constant ongoing monitoring which preserves the child's optimal brain homeostatic state (and wellbeing) is the most draining and demanding work on the planet. It is work which is unpaid, unrecognized and which continues 24 hours a day, 365 days of the year. The deeply bonded mother has her own internal world affected by the child's inner feeling state which provides her with accurate signals as well as motivation for her to care for the child. When the child is cared for, her own world is soothed and if the child is being harmed, the mother suffers as well. The screams of Aboriginal mothers as their babies were torn from them, echo through time. Only an adult who is complexly bonded to, knowing of, and deeply caring for, the unique child is willing or able to do this intense work of constantly monitoring and accurately caring for the child in a way that fosters their development. When the child is removed from the carer who loves them and does this for them, they are damaged. If they are removed from a mother with whom they share an inner world, their inner landscape is ravaged with Hiroshima like consequences.

If, for a moment we can separate from the gender (and therefore emotion laden) biases of this issue and approach it from the analysis of the barbaric code we see that, because the role of carer requires sacrifice of career and other assets, females are unlikely to be dominant financially or legally. Dominants have been able to assert their adult interests remorselessly in over-riding the child's need to have the emotional safety of being with their primary caregiver who has developed the skill to accurately read and compassionately respond to their critical developmental needs. In January of 2010 three reports were released to the government – each reporting that the threat of violence for mothers and children is increasing. One of these was a 1200 page evaluation of the impact of Howard's so-called 'Law reform' on children. The report raised clear concerns and recommended that effective immediately, children under 2 be exempt from the 50:50 split. The Men's Movement swung into high gear with the next days and weeks of the paper inundated with headings such as, 'Fathers Fury on Custody.' As a result of this politically powerful outpouring The Australian reported on January the 13th,

> 'The Australian understands that the report highlights SIGNIFICANT PROBLEMS with the Howard Government's law but, given that it is an ELECTION YEAR, and that any changes would be interpreted as a roll back of the shared parenting law and would certainly ignite the IRE OF MEN'S RIGHTS GROUPS, no changes are likely to go before parliament before first being referred to a committee for ANOTHER LONG EXAMINATION.' [Emphasis added].

The traumatisation of children is being sanctioned by subordinating their wellbeing to the interests of the politically powerful.

Money, Money, Money

Critically, and most significantly, the 50:50 split relieves men of having to pay child support when they leave a partner. For males who have advanced their career during their children's early years on the basis of the unpaid labour of their former partner this represents an economic goldmine. In effect, Australia has legalized the exploitation of unpaid female labour donated in pregnancy and early childhood. Individual women are required to bear all of the financial and career losses of pregnancy, infancy and early childhood, but have no rights as caregivers. Children are not in a position to advocate for themselves and so this primarily political decision was made on the basis of which gender had the most political power during a conservative regime. In Australia, it was unquestionably the males.

Once relationship becomes the basis on which human affairs are weighted and principles of dignity and mutual respect are the scales, then the option of exploiting other humans is removed because individuals are held accountable not to take more than they give. A relational framework marks unpaid labour within a culture as socially problematic. Unpaid labour has to be balanced by respect, protection, social privilege, care and real power if the delicate balance of justice is to be maintained. Without justice there can be no human advancement. If women are to be the unpaid carers of children then the laws and norms of society must privilege that caring relationship in respect, not only of the social contribution of unpaid labour, but also, and more importantly, in protection of the child's sense of safety, wellbeing, and own internalized understanding of justice vis-à-vis caring and gender. Is it any wonder that barbarism continues to be perpetuated when both boys and girls are inculcated that caring and relationship are of no import and that dominance is the ultimate scale?

Legalisation of Violence Against Children and Mothers

In Australia men constitute approximately 90% of all homicide offenders. When children are murdered the mothers are often young and in a hostile relationship with, or separated from, the male. While our child homicide statistics are similar to the UK, Wales or Canada the exception is that Australia has a higher number of fathers than mothers as offenders. 70% of all children murdered are murdered at home. If you google 'Australian fathers murder children' you will get many entries reflecting the reality that the changes to the law mean that the Family Court is now a site where violence against mothers and children has been legalised. You will get an even greater number of posts from economically powerful men's groups advocating for the rights of men and systematically flooding such sites; and all other media, with propaganda. Significantly, mothers caring for children have neither the time nor the energy to put into this type of political marketing. This is part of the reason that their rights and the rights of their children have been overridden. Australian media is virtually silent about mothers.

It is because humans, at this historical time, have a poor understanding of the realms of the sacred and the invisible treasures of human life, that the needs of babies and small children were able to be pillaged and subordinated to the financial and emotional demands of adults. The faddish idea of splitting a child between households doesn't attend to any of the stability, routine, and regularity needs of small children, nor acknowledge how such predictability soothes them and helps them to deal with all their major developmental tasks including schooling.

The Ultimate Revenge: Dismembering the Child

Barbaric, retrogressive changes to Family Law have also given violent males a vehicle to continue bloodying a past partner through the children. Child murders, where clearly disturbed and violent men have been given half time care of a child, without the protective influence of the mother has been a rude shock to Australians. Inability to identify these men and protect the children is a reflection of the courts naivete' about power relations between men and women, and about the dynamics of relationship abuse. Punishing a former partner through murdering the children has become all too common since the imposition of the so-called reform. Males are aware of the power the 50:50 split gives. In one example, a four year old was killed when her estranged father threw her off a bridge on the day she was to begin school. The mother had tried on many occasions to have the father's access limited but was ignored. The family made the following comments after the death reflecting the inability of the hamstrung Family Court to ensure children's welfare: 'For the past two years, the various authorities have been made aware of our fear for the safety of the children and unfortunately no one would listen.... We feel the judicial system has failed our family.'

This is not to say that divorce is a problem as a concept. It is the acceptance of barbarism within intimate relationship, and barbaric merchandising as a substitute for intimate relationship that is the problem. In a barbaric culture it is important that aggressive, exploitative, hostile or abusive relationships be terminated. Given the ignorance we foster in young women it is inevitable that many of them will end up pregnant to exploitative, abusive males. Children need to be protected from being raised in aggressive environments if we are to effect social change. When women take the courage to leave such relationships they should not be forced to send their children back into them. It is the use of the law to enable vicious males to continue violence through removal of, and damage to, children that is the problem. For mothers who deeply care for their children, this is the ultimate punishment.

The use of children to punish former partners must be halted and the best way to do this is to leave children with their primary caregivers when there is a relationship breakdown. The lack of deep, authentic attachment which fosters use of people as objects without reciprocal responsibility for loyalty, care or recompense for received resources is de-evolved behaviour which we cannot afford to enshrine in our cultural framework. The domineering, aggressive or violent partner, and the wealthy octogenarian, shares the same philosophy about the disposability of nonconforming female partners. Unfortunately, the child-support record would suggest that this barbaric perspective on the use of female bodies is alive and well and that the 'reformed' legal system is acting to ensure that it can be done without cost to exploitative males.

Dumbing Down Emotionally

The Family Law Court now enforces barbarian ideology by ignoring the distress of children (cruelty), allocating all of the blame for childrens' suffering on the shoulders of the caretaking parent (blame the victim) and legalizing the exploitation of unpaid female care of children (exploiting the vulnerable and pillaging the resources of the future). Those who adhere to the Barbaric Creed go so far as to suggest that the screams and distress of small children separated from their primary caregiver are not 'real'. The distress, suffering, and subsequent evidence of trauma in small children, is explained away using the faddish notion of 'parental alienation syndrome.' This scientifically unsubstantiated idea has been inappropriately borrowed from family therapy and a systems theory of extramarital affairs. From this mythological notion, children are carelessly described as 'triangulated' between mother and father, (as in the role of a mistress). Under the notion of the syndrome all suffering expressed by the child is just the 'selfish' mother manipulating the child. This unsubstantiated idea overrides all scientific, neurobiological, evidence based data and excludes the only communication non-verbal children can give: their emotions.

This hard hearted adult position silences the child and cruelly ignores real suffering in order to privilege adult males. It does not acknowledge that any work, sacrifice, or real bonds, could be formed in the care of a child day-in and day-out over the child's entire life. It refuses to acknowledge that the child's psychological sense of safety is rooted in their primary caregiver and viciously silences any expressions of distress from mother or child. It ignores the right of the child not to be forcibly deprived of their fundamental sense of safety,

'Parental alienation' mumpsimus places the blame squarely on mothers for refusing to condition the child (preferably through harsh treatment) to submit to the enforced separation without showing distress. When small children are removed from their externalized source of safety and soothing (their primary caregiver) they suffer profound damage. Instead of pathologizing the mother, the child, and the mother-child bond; the courts should identify which parent has been primary caregiver, interpret the child's distress from this perspective, and seek to maintain regularity, routine, soothing and safety for the child. If the adult world will not attend to their need for care or their cries of distress then the external world becomes a very unsafe space for the child. If the adult world violates the attachment bonds which give a child safety then the child has no hope.

Instead, the Family Law court advocates programs such as 'Mums and Dads Forever' which assert equal parenting responsibility (a good thing) without acknowledging any differential in commitment, experience or skill in taking care of the child's needs (a bad thing). Australian women are increasingly subjected to psychological tests ordered by courts and ex-partners with the express aim of demonstrating that they are 'unstable' in order to further silence those who express distress at being separated from a child or children with whom they have formed deep bonds. The 50:50 split therefore not only ignores the cultural norms but rips women from the 95:5 caregiving role once the primary pregnancy and post-birth load of unpaid labour is complete and forces them back into the workforce identity behind their male counterparts due to the career interruption and unpaid work of caring for children. With their unpaid labour ignored and effectively socially exploited and dismissed, women must work at double the pace to try to catch up to peers who have not made this social contribution. In an equitable system, males who have primarily been career oriented could take a year and work as unpaid carers to develop the levels of complex responsivity and skill of their former partners if they wished to be given half time care of the child. Such a system, which would generate mass outrage and aggression from powerful males, would, in fact, be placing the developmental and emotional needs of the child before the demands of adults. The Family Court is not based on care and child wellbeing, but on power, and hence has difficulty distinguishing between caring and uncaring adults. This capacity to assess real care should be a core skill in any system determining the lives of children.

5. People Matter

In barbaric cultures relationships become superficial or impermanent and easily severed. We are encouraged to act as if people didn't matter. Whole communities can be torn apart for financial profit with the same uncaring, cruel heartlessness, and refusal to heed cries of distress, seen when separating mother and small child. Inner worlds can be pillaged by barbarians running amok. Humans do recover from traumatic deep loss, but this may take much time and recovery may never be completed. The calloused barbarian doesn't 'waste' time with grief but grief is a sign that we cared for, and were attached to, someone. Any time we attach, truly love, or care for, another human being we risk loss, and being hurt. The capacity to be hurt by another, seen by barbarians as a weakness, is in fact, a sign of a healthy human heart.

In a barbaric society, loyalty in relationship becomes relative to, and subordinated to, whether or not one can get a 'better deal' elsewhere, regardless of loyalty and resources already committed to the relationship by the other party. This applies as equally to corporations which heartlessly dismiss long term employees simply to increase profit as it does to the divorce of older wives by husbands seeking younger bodies. The issue is the refusal to acknowledge the importance of human relationships of safety and loyalty. We must address the myth of the disposable, replaceable female. As the recent Jesse James-Sandra Bullock example illustrated, even the most wealthy and powerful of women are not safe from the cultural normalization of male use of multiple female bodies which devalues the unique female self. People are unique, not replaceable; and the resources of relationship, kinship, caring, belonging and loyalty matter. These are the connections barbarians sever, in order to more easily access and exploit more resources.

The barbarian focus of moving quickly to the next conquest is one of the signs of a calloused heart, and damaged ability to care. The increased prevalence of barbarism in our cultures has lowered levels of feeling, care and attachment in relationships with accompanying effects on intimacy. People are seen as disposable and replaceable. We cannot afford a society in which any of its members are considered disposable. When we derogate one another in this manner we derogate our own humanity.

The barbarian worldview has no way of understanding love, intimacy, and care. None of these activities generate profit, and therefore they don't exist in the barbarian value system. Barbarians see the intangible resources that give quality to human life as expendable and purchasable. The wealthy octogenarian can purchase a new wife, loyalty and a new family if he so desires. The barbaric overtones of this behaviour are too often ignored in our cultures. The implications such behaviours broadcast about the disposability of humans and the impermanence of human relationship, ravage our sense of what intimate relationship can be. Individual actions of wealthy elites have cultural and social ramifications because they legitimate detached, exploitative behaviour between humans. They denigrate human capacities for deep care and relationship. When this detachment is admired at a social level and envied, the same behaviours are fostered at every level of the culture - to our detriment.

6. Human Relationships and Deep, Loyal Bonds Matter

By 2020 WHO estimates that mental health disorder will account for nearly 15% of disability-adjusted life-years lost to illness and that this suffering is largely preventable through the implementation of low cost, low technology interventions. Ultimately, technology isn't going to save us. In Australia mental health is the leading killer and cause of disability for people under 45. If emotions matter, then human relationships and how humans relate to one another are the new 'technology' that needs exploration and deeper, more penetrative understanding.

In profit oriented cultures, the concept of relationship has been dumbed down to the superficial notion of 'networking', the claim of instantaneous 'depth' in relationship which enables quick and easy utilization of the resources of the other with no long term commitment required. Once 'networked', a participant might feel free to ask for significant access to information or other resources, simply on the basis of having met another at a gathering. On the extreme end, requests by hundreds of even thousands of casual acquaintances or even 'randoms' to be listed as 'friends' in virtual communities attest to diminished understanding of relationship and the irreplaceability of in-depth committed friendship based on knowing and reciprocity over time.

- Work matters some, but not as much as people.
- Industrial production matters much less than we think.
- Money matters only insofar as it facilitates human life and joyous human living.
- Human life matters.

In a humane system (that is, one that responds well to humans and human need) deep bonds of care are able to be forged between people with the expectancy of loyalty, love and respect remaining over time. People adhere to codes of interpersonal loyalty that dignify not only the other person, but the humane concept of caring relationship. Community life becomes a web of caring where individual people are accorded the rank of belonging and where people's lives are noticed. People are nested in webs of care that accord their individual life merit and respect. Human life matters.

Vive La Resistance!

We need radical relationship revolution. We can resist cruel and heartless behaviour and the notion of superficial exploitation as an adequate framework for human societies and systems. We can insist on societies based on deep, authentic relationship bonds which require respect for the inherent dignity of the human person and which honor the reality that loyal, caring bonds formed between humans should not be violated or dismissed lightly. Caring relationship is as essential to human development and survival as potable drinking water and as needful of protection. Where authentic bonds of care exist between people we can refuse to sanction aggression used to rupture those bonds.

We can refuse to participate in movements that exploit bonds of care for financial profiteering. We can resist the notion of cruel, heartless behaviour as an acceptable social standard and insist that family and community relational life be respected. Ultimately, we can have the courage to identify barbaric acts as violent and refuse to accept them as necessary. We can refuse to accept interpersonal aggression from governments, corporations or individuals, and protest when relationships of care (such as communities or effective carers) are being exploited for financial profit. We can refuse to conceptualize this as tolerable.

We can forge deep bonds of authentic care in our own lives and resist the penetration of barbaric norms of cruelty and hard heartedness into our family and personal lives. We can nurture and be deeply caring for all members of our own family and intimate circle and be fiercely loyal to this circle. We can act protectively and non-apologetically when people in authority act barbarically or with aggression towards our children or vulnerable people in our circle of influence. We can increase our circle of influence and advocate, and extend care to, as many other humans as we can. We can actively, verbally and publicly, identify barbarism in its many forms wherever and whenever we see it. We can politely and firmly refuse to accept interpersonal aggression from others. We can form communities of solidarity to resist barbarism in the public domain and refuse to remain silent when barbarians are using aggression to assert dominance in any domain. We can refuse to acknowledge barbarism as a superior philosophy and highlight flaws in the creed.

We can rationally draw attention to instances of barbarism in the public arena and remind others that there are multiple other rational and far more effective options available to us. We can refuse to accept the current status quo as inevitable and challenge media and other propaganda that asserts that it is so. We can act.

We can act every day in tens and hundreds of small ways. In every way, at every opportunity, and in every choice we make we can resist barbaric incursion into our intimate relationships, our family lives, our work lives, our communities, our systems, our culture, and every circle in which we move. Instead of apathetically accepting barbarism as the normative standard for human relationship we can constantly and gently remind all of those around us of the many options and ongoing opportunities for change. In small and big ways, on a constant and sustainable basis, we can refuse to accept barbarism as inevitable. We can support ourselves and all those we come into contact with, to conceptualize and action other futures and to refuse to act barbarically towards other human beings.

We can become resolute, obstinate, educated blocks to barbaric imperialism and refuse to accept the roll-out of the creed in our families, communities and systems.

We can become quietly, effectively, humanely radical.

CHAPTER 9: SOME STEPS FORWARD

WAKING UP

Step One: Re-orient Toward Truth

The barbaric phenomenon, whereby entrenched privilege has enabled a few to increase their own profit aggressively at the expense and detriment of many, has been repeated through history. The most pressing issue of the 21st Century is how to rouse humanity from the inertia that stops us from responding when our environmental, social and human survival is clearly at risk. We need to consider how to rouse our survival instinct within a media and life context where our body systems are already raised to levels of mania or panic on a daily basis.

In the media and on the net we are deluged by a pandemic of real and imagined issues. Simultaneously we are titillated and distracted by the trivial so that the deadly gets lost in the blur of information irrelevancies that bombard us on a daily basis. Issues that are real threats to human survival become indistinguishable from frippery when deodorizers are presented with greater fervency than the need for human safety, family life, intimacy and rest.

Workplaces aggressively impose inhumane workloads which leave people running from task-to-task with no time to think seriously about social issues or about what reaction they should choose. When people come home and collapse exhausted in front of the television their stress is numbed by the onslaught of issues, information and products. Meanwhile, the deadly continues to inflate to demonic size and to slide under the radar of public attention. We have lost the art of discrimination so that serious issues which threaten ecological, species, human, psychic and soul life and freedom; look the same to us as frivolous trifles and products. In an era of media bombardment we need to redevelop our capacity to distinguish between the important and the silly. To reclaim our capacity to discriminate we need to reclaim our time to be able to consciously direct our energy to important tasks.

Many of the aggressive legislative and corporate acts of the twentieth century were cloaked in complex language and enacted covertly so that the vulnerable did not immediately realize that their human rights and resources were to be taken. Barbaric raiders however, immediately recognized these acts for what they were; opportunities for the powerful to garner the resources of vulnerable and unprotected sectors of the population with impunity. They acted swiftly once legislation was passed to gather as many resources as possible for themselves. The resources which became most available included, but were not limited to, those of Indigenous people, the aged, single mothers and children.

At the moment most western people survive from day-to-day with the steady infusion of money as the morphine that dopes them from the wider realities occurring in society around them and in the world at large. Around the globe the morphine is administered by business leaders and bureaucrats who say, 'Just trust me' but whose focus is their own advancement and aggrandizement. We are not in safe hands when this occurs. A calloused person feels nothing and faces no ethical dilemma in carving up someone else's child (through inner world decimation) or amputating someone else's family life if it increases their bank balance. We can't afford to be so doped out on illusion that we do not respond to protect ourselves and our families.

Acknowledge Lived Reality

We have no more time – and for the most oppressed there is no time at all. Ask any suffering Australian Aboriginal person how much time there is left for their culture as yet another generation of Aboriginal children is destroyed and they will tell you, 'No time at all.' Even white conservatives admit that we have 50-70 years before we lose unique Australian Aboriginal culture forever. We will have destroyed the connection to land and to life itself which keeps Aboriginal dreaming and way of life alive. We need to be able to separate out truth from fiction, have the courage to examine truth and to be afraid, very afraid if necessary, so that we can be motivated to DO something. It is no good wailing about it. The work that has to be done has to be done. Facing it and beginning immediately means that we are on the road to recovery instead of ruin. The words of William James can be of service to us, 'To change...life: Start immediately. Do it flamboyantly. No exceptions.' Real care means being willing to do something, otherwise it is simply a rhetorical, fanciful notion. We don't need to worry about the whole journey, just the next step. Barbaric incursion can be halted now.

We are living in an era of war. A war which may not threaten the existence of every human alive but which threatens the possibility of future generations and drains and saps most people of the joy in living which is their birthright. There are pockets of resistance in this war. While some privileged individuals, particularly in developed countries, may be able to wage a fight and reclaim their own personal sanity and peace of mind; usually through the investment of significant amounts of money in therapy, meditation or other spiritual practices; there are millions on earth who do not have this privilege. The few people who are reclaiming their lives are doing so in the face of an assault on human life which threatens all individuals. The question must be raised...why should individuals be continually fighting to reclaim their lives? Why aren't we questioning the systems and practices which humans have put in place which are taking people's lives from them? Why isn't anyone protesting the system which is destroying the capacity for individuals to live full and peaceful lives in the first place? Why have we come to accept this as the 'best there is' – when we know for a fact that it is not?

We are flooded with 'reality TV' that distracts us from the reality of our daily lives. We need a global alarm buzzer that wakes us from the delusion of 'greed and money as life,' to ask ourselves, what is really happening? What is 21st Century reality?

Step Two: Acknowledge the Lies

When we found isolated indigenous cultures: in Australia, America, New Guinea, Samoa, Hawaii, Africa, Tibet and across the globe we said, 'Primitive' and set about destroying them. Now when we find their remnants, we comment on the extraordinary joy and peacefulness in these people's lives and the 'idyllic' childhood in their culture. Their children have their senses fostered by freedom and nature and their hearts strengthened by a community who sees, knows and loves them. We then turn around and decree this is not possible for our children. Not possible in an 'advanced' society. Not possible in a society where there are technological 'advantages.' We are so sure of this. We have so certainly swallowed the story that there is an either/or scenario where either we have technology, inequity and vast human misery or we have a primitive existence without technological advantage but with a happy, peaceful life. Who is advantaged by this story? Why have we accepted the story that we can't have technological advancement and material progress while maintaining humane standards for existence in societies where human potential is nurtured, protected and valued?

We have been told lies about the work involved in non-industrialized and less barbaric societies. The reality that, in hunter gatherer societies work only consumed 1-4 hours of the day is rarely touted. 'Work' was not coerced, monitored, or forced by controlling others; the individual was not placed in an alien environment; and 'work' was conducted within communal life and the joy and meaning of daily living. In such societies each person was deeply valued, cared for, and assisted throughout their life journey. They were known, not just for their individual life, but for the lineage from which they had come and for the contribution they were to make to the future. Human development was seen as an ongoing task where each individual belonged to the group and had great value and an irreplaceable contribution to make to that task. In such a society, the individual's life was deeply honoured and held with great care in times of vulnerability, while also being seen as part of a collective whole of human life that mattered and had a purposeful trajectory. The work of the individual and the culture had meaning and was taken seriously. Relationship was central. The truth is that such frameworks for community life, societies, systems and relationships are not only possible but are eminently sustainable for millennia unless barbarism is allowed to invade, pillage and destroy them.

Even in agrarian societies people were known, and, with daylight and 'holy day' boundaries on work, there were evenings, feasts, celebrations and days of rest spent together in kinship, belonging and relationship. We have been trained to fear nature and to see our homes and palaces as 'protecting us' from the 'ravages of nature.' So much so that we have become imprisoned in huge grey concrete blocks where we cannot see the sky and where we must pay to have the very air that we need to breathe cycled to us. We have so swallowed the story that industrialized, technologically driven societies save us work that we are working ourselves to death every day of the year to prove it is so. Arbeit Macht Frei.

It is not a choice between progress/technology/advance and agrarian or backward/hard labour as barbarians would have us believe. This is a false dichotomy. There are many alternatives that can utilize a better balance of conscious thought and choice; prioritize people over profit; and create nurturing, visionary, exciting and enjoyable options.

Social Responsibility

There are a number of myths that confuse people and discourage them from seeking transformative global change. The first is rooted in the generalised confusion that people have been trained to utilise when thinking about the future. We have been conditioned to think of a fairer future with fear and trepidation, not with curiosity. We have been trained to focus on short-term losses, usually of expendable items that do not actually contribute to our quality of life, or our happiness. Anyone who thinks that halting over-production and over-consumption would mean lack of employment opportunities has not looked hard enough at the massive urban decay in slums from India to Mexico, from Recife to Detroit; the need for re-forestation and ecological reclamation around the globe; the vast work involved in building lasting products and recycling responsibly; or the endless, diverse, expanding employment options which could be generated through human advancement and transformative process. We have been so conditioned to accepting the negative by-products of over mechanisation, that we don't realise we are operating under the flawed assumption that a prosperous planet, where all human beings are safe and have their needs met, would not be better for us all.

Secondly, we are constantly exposed to propaganda, which tells us that opening our doors to consider any other options except the industrialised, mechanised, bureaucratised status quo, will end badly. Specifically, we are threatened with visions of having all of our resources looted and pillaged so that we become the deprived ones and as, individuals or individual nations, are left with nothing. The fear that any change in the status quo would simply result in a redistribution of which dominants hold the wealth is a conditioned fear that comes from experience during barbarian rule. It is only a reality under barbaric imperium. Under barbarism, altruism and willingness to open up access to one's own resources may not be safe. When safe parameters are established for humanitarian behaviour, supportive community life, and cultural and global safety, then laying down our weapons and opening up our grain houses, will actually be our safest alternative.

When we stop to think about it, it is patently obvious that creating a global context, where all members of the human species experience basic safety and quality of life in humane communities would be idyllic for us all. Emerson observed of the aggression based system, 'Each man takes care that this neighbor shall not cheat him. But a day comes when he begins to care that he does not cheat his neighbour. Then all goes well. He has changed his market-cart into a chariot of the sun.' It is craziness to continue to feed people fear about the outcomes of a humane global context. It is antiquated, outdated rhetoric which does not contain nutrients for species progress.

It is hugely incongruous that societies which pride themselves on 'progress' in the technological realm should be unable to transfer the optimism with which they face enormous technological challenges to the simple issue of creating systems, cultures and norms to foster the dignity, happiness and belonging of individuals. If the focus, money and resources we put into issues such as how to keep satellites orbiting in space, how to reach Mars and gather data, or how to dissect the human cell to isolate genes, were transferred to issues such as how to create relational societies that were pleasurable for humans and that could foster human capacity and potential, the results would blow our minds. The truth is that it is eminently possible for us to transfer the working aspects of our current cultures to other models IF there is willingness to learn and IF the power-brokers in the old culture don't block this happening. And therein lays the problem of barbarism. Aggression is not necessary for species advancement but protection from aggression is essential. Therefore, we need to learn how to address and deal with barbarism.

Identify and Change the Game

Essential knowledge points:
1. What is true and what is a game?
2. What is the cost of the game?
3. Who is being hurt?
4. Who is being advantaged?
5. How does the game need to change?

Barbarism is a game based on aggression, power, domination and exploitation. Our aim is to change the game, not to destroy individual players. In a world where dominance is blocked and abuse of power is penalized the barbaric Pterodactyl loses his strategic advantage. A new world order does not require victims, it requires only champions. There are countless alternative game plans that can be pursued once we challenge the mythology that barbarism is the only way the game can be played. To do this we have to be willing, in solidarity, to challenge aggressive dominance. This requires networks of protective, caring

196

relationships, committed to the wellbeing of other carers and to passive and active resistance. We need Gandhi's solidarity of non-violent resisters at the global level. What is required is a critical mass of people willing to change the game, not just the players.

Step Three: Acknowledge Injustice

Injustice

Injustice means that what is fair, right and just, does not occur and instead, that there is some form of inequity, slight of hand, or undue favour which sways an outcome away from that which should, justly, have occurred. Injustice includes the notion that an educated white man in the industrialized world can work hard for a decade or two, and, in that time, accumulate enough wealth and assets to never have to work again. Then, through no other attributes than material fortune, can hold considerable sway over the decisions and choices of other, less fortunate people for the rest of his lifetime – perhaps as a landlord, employer or investor. Injustice includes the notion that a black woman could also work hard through her teens, twenties and thirties and then have to continue that work pace for the rest of her physical life while never accumulating more than the clothes on her back and the daily food in her belly. We have two humans, each of equal human value, giving equal effort but having unequal opportunity and reward. One of these is in a form of modern slavery facilitated by barbarism. Of these two, who benefits from the concept that we exist in a world of perfect justice where the concept of injustice is no longer 'necessary'?

Without the notion of injustice we lose the capacity to live our lives with due regard for the reality that all humans who live require dignity. The problematic of believing that universal justice has been achieved is that this delusion excludes the realities of greed, exploitation, rape and corruption. Under such a delusion, victims have no voice for their experience and can be blamed for their own suffering. Predators then have a captive field and an open license to exploit those with less power without any individual consequence and with no social expectation to provide recompense. At a wider level, without understanding of the reality of injustice we lose, in human societies, any sense of urgency in relation to systemic and social change. We also lose any rationale for the human quality of compassion and our understanding of its centrality to human advancement. Importantly, and strategically, without keen understanding of justice and injustice, we lose any motivation to challenge barbarism.

Without clear understanding of the reality of inequity and injustice our perspective becomes narrowed down to the nitty gritty of our individual, and often just our daily, lives. We can then become lost in the psychotic belief that we, as individuals, live external to the social system and to our fellow man. The concept of a just world allows us to focus on our own prosperity with no need to have to do the messy and hard work of considering what social structures we need to develop to safeguard, and foster, wider human life and human dignity. The idea that all of the privilege which accrues to us is the result of our individual effort and merit seduces us into the fallacy that we hold no responsibility for any other human besides ourselves. We also lose the larger notion of individual lives having some contribution to humanity as a whole. In contrast, in Indigenous cultures, individual wellbeing was inextricably embedded within cultural systems and customs which were founded on a collective perspective capable of including, not only the individual and social system, but also the natural ecology and cosmos of the globe.

Self-Made What?

It is ironic that the story of the self-made individual has arisen at a time where we live in proximity and interdependence with more human beings, within more social systems, than at any other time in history. A society structured on the 'rugged individual and self-made man' delusion forces people to focus increasingly on their own welfare. We are fed the myth that we can survive on our own and that social support for those who have less is not only unnecessary, but detrimental to them personally, and to society as a whole. This is a psychotic delusion with the capacity to destroy human life. The mythology that our social systems have already ensured that the world is just and that there is equal access to wealth and opportunity focuses the average person on devoting all of his or her energy on ensuring that they personally accrue as many resources as possible. The individual in such a society must become a walled castle with his own stores and resources to defend against calamity. In addition, greed must become socially acceptable and de-stigmatised. The individual becomes caught up in, and servile to, the species' Lemming rush to ecological and social destruction.

Multiple Co-existing Realities and Rotating Focus

Human systems must be embedded in a collective perspective of wellbeing and individual humans must be trained in the skills of rotating focus so they can manage this reality. Multiple realities co-exist at the same time. This means that the raped and prostituted Tibetan child co-exists in time alongside the nurtured, socially and individually supported Danish one. The co-existence of all levels of reality means that the happy family picnicking together on a beautiful day in unspoiled nature co-exists with the global deforestation destroying that individual forest's ecological sustainability. For individuals to enjoy life, without using heavy functional delusion and destruction, they must exist in systems which are developed to maintain and develop life at the level of the globe and the cosmos. Indigenous societies give us one model of the many possibilities where human justice for individuals is linked to fostering health at global and cosmos levels in an ongoing and advancing manner. Such systems foster individual safety, mental health and wellbeing, and the capacity to sustain both social and individual responsibilities.

In the barbaric system, individual lives are exploited and diminished to feed elite storehouses, and then they are burdened with the myth that they must individually 'fix' global problems. This inappropriate burden is given without also promoting the need for systemic frameworks for social justice. An individual cannot 'fix' collective damage without a collective framework which halts the ongoing destruction being perpetuated on a daily basis by barbarism. Unless the global dominance of the barbaric creed is challenged and overturned the cumulative damage it causes will always outweigh the good actions of non-violent but naive individuals. In non-barbaric systems individual wellbeing contributes to, and is symbiotic with, rather than in opposition to, the health of the macrocosm. Without this framework individuals face compassion burnout. Compassion burnout advantages barbarism by suggesting that anything other than calloused cynicism is unsustainable. Nothing could be further from the truth.

In societies where the care of humans and justice are the central foci, and organizing forces, for all systems and decision making, individuals do not need to feel guilt when they care for their own self system (inner world, physical body), intimate relationships (family, children) or community life. Nor do they feel that they have to sponsor all of the starving children in Africa before they can feed their own children. When a global system of justice is operating each individual contribution is made within a collective framework which feeds their individual contribution into the greater whole, so that it can't be funneled into the storehouse of an elite. Just systems ensure that the individual contribution does not facilitate the ongoing barbarism and exploitation which causes the starving children in the first place.

Conservatives insist that only the status quo is sustainable in order to maintain the delusions that earth's health is being maintained, her resources are limitless and that we are not faced with overpopulation or difficult choices. At this historical point we need to develop the skill to be able to take care of the self (first resource) and then, with resolute will, to focus on the difficult task of acknowledging wider aspects of reality and begin to address them. This will ensure that our responses are sufficient to address the full reality and not just a fragmented slice. If, as a species, we don't respond realistically to the full chronosystem (historical) realities of our time we, like the ancient Greeks, Romans and Persians, will be unable to design a system of sustainable continuance.

In a healthy, functioning, responsive, social system all levels of reality are included for consideration in appraisals and planning responses. In healthy human systems, multiple co-existing levels of reality can be acknowledged rather than denied. This means that large portions of the population don't have to be silenced, punished or excluded, in order to make the designated social system appear functional. (For example, homeless people, Indigenous people, children, refugees, the elderly, the poor and so on). We exclude and silence such groups to our peril. The world will not transform on the words of the wealthy and the privileged but on the basis of the words of the poor and the oppressed. We would do well to listen.

Step Four: Refuse to Trivialize Human Life

We live in the era of iconization of the mediocre. Those humans who are shallow, empty, plastic and false, are aped and idolized by the masses. As a direct result of this reification of the shallow, the greedy and the inhumane, the progress of human development has stalled. Environmental and human ecology are now at stake. We live in an era where barbaric acts against the poor and the defenceless, even conducted by the wealthiest and the most powerful, are condoned or ignored by the majority. This sense of apathy in regards to injustice must be addressed. Luckily we have a catalogue of human history demonstrating that mediocre and shallow people have not always been adulated and that humans are capable of far greater aspirations. While humans have some willingness to pay attention to the abuses of the environment – global warming has attracted much attention even if little action – we seem less willing to pay attention to the destruction of human ecology and human sense of possibility - core resources for joyful and dignified human existence. Creativity and human capacity are not fostered by living in high pressure environments motivated primarily by aggression, anxiety and dread. Barbarism is based primarily on the use of fear and coercion. It is fundamentally opposed to the processes of human empowerment.

In the 21st century the concept of injustice is no considered longer fashionable and has been replaced with plastic, shallow phrases such as profitability, economic gain, viability and individual responsibility. These concepts are marketed as 'new' modes of social organization which, we are assured, will take us further, farther and faster, than concepts such as justice, fairness, equity and care. We are told that such concepts are quaint relics of a past age and no longer 'necessary' in the modern world. Such rhetoric leaves us with an emasculated human dignity and erases the lived reality of any person who suffers from exploitation or aggression. It takes away the voice of the oppressed and the possibilities for different response. 21st century humans have no need to swallow such nutrient deficient swill.

The marketing and reification of greed in itself is not surprising, nor really is the ploy. It is one which has been long utilized by aristocrats and those in possession of unearned privilege to convince the have nots that their 'not having' is a function of their own undeserving. What is perhaps surprising is the depth and breadth with which we, collectively, have imbibed the advertising spiel that universal justice and equity are meted out at birth and therefore that all gain made in the material world is a function of individual effort conducted on an equal playing field through a fair game.

We can challenge the pre-historic code of barbarism and begin, once again to become conscious of what is in our communities, our systems and our families. Any person who does not understand the basic concepts of prejudice and discrimination cannot be allowed to rule a country – let alone to have sway at a global level. Feeding ourselves on illusion and delusion has been to the detriment of all. We can face reality without the opium haze of marketing that tells us we are consumers first and humans second. Only in facing what is in human life and societies in the times in which we live, particularly in the industrialized world, can we respond effectively to the reality of the human species in the 21st century and do what must be done.

Barbarism restricts and blocks the majority of humankind from experiencing full, passion-filled life. Much of the energy of the majority goes into feeding the insatiable greed of barbaric elites and into anxiety about gaining enough personal power to be able to fend off barbaric attack. Because barbarism only offers immunity to its own elite aristocracy, and limited immunity at that, those with little power often believe that 'pleasing the oppressor' will grant them some protection. A fear based culture cannot be truly productive.

Step Five: Learn to Discriminate

Where there is too much power even the whining tones of the smallest man sound impressive. Power, the amplification of voice, must not be confused with the quality of the voice. In the West these two are confounded so that, as in the Wizard of Oz, the most noxious fool may be thought right if the speaker system is loud enough. We must once again regain our capacity for discernment. Unwillingness to acknowledge the impact of abuse of power at higher levels may be part of why we don't put energy into discerning the difference but ignorance does not protect us from the impacts of different types of leaders and their use of power. Westerners seem unable to discern the difference between those with power who care and those who do not. This is a dangerous lack of judgement, because the leader who exploits, and the leader who enables, have vastly different impacts on life at every level.

Our target is not anti-American or anti-capitalism or anti-communism or anti-Islamic, black or white, male or female. Our target is an attitude of brutality and aggression towards humanity. It is this that must be addressed. We can have the discrimination to know when barbaric behaviour is occurring and when someone is acting or living by the barbaric creed, regardless of their professed value category. We then need to be able to block their ploy. We have not effectively resisted barbarism in our own culture to date, but nor have we clearly separated it as a creed from the founding intentions of democracy. Other cultures haven't known how to resist barbarism either. From the Indigenous cultures we decimated centuries ago, to the thousands of diverse national and local cultures homogenized in recent multi-national 'market penetration' strategies; people have usually been surprised by barbaric incursion, unprepared for its forceful violence, and unable to defend and keep their own resources, personhood, customs and cultures.

Anti-barbarism is a non-violent stance which opposes the dominance of an ideology that enslaves, feeds off, and destroys, the best of human life. Such a strategy is for people, not against them, as barbarism serves no human well. We need to be able to oppose the old barbaric Pterodactyls who cling to power with rigidified claws and whose ongoing involvement in decision making retards human progress. The last two decades demonstrated how old white men can not only stall human progress but cause massive backward steps. As China and India develop as economic super-powers there will be Chinese and Indian males to join the ranks of barbaric potentates who oppose any moves away from fossilized barbarism.

Within economics based systems of values there is no way to discriminate between the wise elderly, who are a public resource of community wisdom, and those elderly who have spent their entire lives feeding off the misfortune of others. Unless we can discriminate we don't know whose influence should be enhanced and whose should be dismantled. Our inability to discriminate between the caring and the cruel human being is problematic in many areas, but particularly in this area of entrenched, rigidified, socially and economically legitimized, power. Old barbarians need to be removed from decision making processes, all honorary and fellow positions, and all positions of influence. Concurrently, as we learn to identify and include older people who have held to caring principles throughout their lives and who are living archives of caring, we will gain tools and processes of great value to an anti-barbaric movement.

ACTING

Step One: Resist

In the 21st century the poor have had their human rights eroded and been 'acted upon,' drained, exhausted and pillaged, with few avenues of resistance. Elite barbarians see the poor (the homeless, the ill, the marginalized, single mothers, the uneducated, refugees, Hispanics, Aboriginals, whoever....) as a formless, faceless mass to be induced or forced into compliance with economic ideas of profit. In other words, their sole life purpose is seen as supplying energy for other life forms (in this case the wealthy). The compliant soul is depicted as the good soul. The poor man who endures his lot, with aspiration, is lauded. The wealthy man, who by aspiration, increases his lot and engorges himself on the profits gained at the expense of life quality for others, is also lauded. Hope for the poor is thereby subverted to prosper the rich.

We are told that the best path is for the average person to remain inert in the face of market forces; to comply; and not to resist losses in their home, family and community life. What happened to the concept of acknowledging a force as negative (as the Allied forces did resisting fascism), and, where that force could not be immediately overcome, organizing effective resistance? In the 21st century, the overworked poor have most of their life energy as well as their family lives, enslaved to pulling the cart of the privileged towards the constantly moving target of increased profit. We need to be teaching strategic resistance instead of compliance. Significantly, conservatives focussed their Industrial Regulations Legislation on 'workforce compliance.' What is needed is resistance. Martin Luther King's astute observation would serve us well: 'Cowardice asks the question, 'Is it safe?' Expediency asks the question, 'Is it politic?' But conscience asks the question, 'Is it right?' And there comes a time when one must take a position that is neither safe, nor politic, nor popular but because conscience tells one it is right.'

Australian Universities used to be sites of resistance until they became the new bastions of medieval profiteering. Students were traditionally the vanguard of resistance but were suppressed by the enforcement of production line approaches which require enormous amounts of rote learning to regurgitate; and simultaneous withdrawal of financial assistance so they have had to cope with workforce exploitation. They have joined the ranks of the muzzled poor. The threats and intimidation meted out to those who spoke out publicly against the pillaging being effected under global profiteering effectively silenced and muzzled many. In just one example, in 2003, when the Dixie Chicks lead singer spoke out against Bush these young women had their lives threatened, their career savaged and their music boycotted. After surviving this onslaught the lead singer commented, 'It hasn't taken courage to stand strong, just first-grade education' however, in reality, the willingness of barbarians to react with vehement force when they are angered, silences many. Many of us have been so intimidated by witnessing the violent, frenzied fury of powerful barbarians when challenged that we are not even speaking privately anymore. We are going along meekly and mildly. We can remember Wiesel's words, 'Silence encourages the tormentor, never the tormented.' To pathologize healthy resistance is to pathologize life itself. In your own life, refuse to mutilate or cauterize your own children through harsh, unfeeling behaviour or to be cruel to your partner. In so doing you are refusing to damage your own circle of care, the first skin of your world.

Step Two: Foster Solidarity

A first step for sustainable resistance is to build solid, sustainable relationship links with others who value social transformation and who are willing to remove barbarism as the primary global philosophy. The solidarity of the links and the authenticity of the relational loyalty and ties must be at a level that is prepared for, and understands the violence of, the committed barbarian and particularly the barbaric high Priests. Barbarians value dominance and control and are not at rest unless dominance is established and the creed is being fully enacted. Calm for barbarians therefore means suffering for others. This will have to be resisted. This may not be a peaceful process and needs to be firm, but it doesn't need to be violent. We do, however, need to be prepared to face barbaric attack and this requires solidarity. The French Resistance was not conducted by a lone individual. Initial resources for resistance will consist of completing our own inner world challenges in areas where we believe the creed, withdrawing from external complicity to economic vampirism and reclaiming our own creativity, care, labour, relationship and rest, currently wasted on profiteering. Our energy can then be focussed and reallocated to fostering relationships of supportive care and transformative change.

Shared Understanding One: How we let Barbarians in the Gate.

Soldidarity can be fostered by clear understanding and agreement about basic areas including: How we are complicit to, and how we foster, and advance, barbarism. This should be an expanding knowledge domain which is added to in ongoing, iterative fashion. Developing a library of cumulative understanding alongside a library of alternatives can be helpful. Here are just a few rudimentary ways we allow barbarism to invade our lives, systems and families:

1. We select our leaders, primarily on the basis of economics instead of on the basis of their humanitarianism, commitment to social well-being, capacity for complex, educated thought and their capacity for loyalty, trustworthiness and moral courage.
2. We become seduced by the delusion economic growth is the primary vehicle for social advance.
3. We choose manic people as our CEOs and leaders.
4. We focus exclusively on our personal self-advancement without concurrently maintaining awareness of the need for protection of the vulnerable, for social change and for assistance to the most needy. We forget, the African American feminist mantra, 'Lift as you climb.'
5. We begin to be harsh and dismissive instead of gentle and attentive to the needs of children.
6. We forget the moral, social and economic responsibility of present-day adults to children.
7. We become careless and lazy about our responsibility to discriminate between the greedy and the cruel. We allow and facilitate the advancement of uncaring people into positions of influence as leaders, teachers, lawyers, doctors and other powerbrokers. 'All that it takes for evil to win is for good, kind people to do..... Nothing.'
8. We forget our responsibility to other, less fortunate nations and peoples in the human family. Wiesel, 'We must take sides. Neutrality helps the oppressor, never the victim.'

This knowledge is not new. The 10 Indian commandments clearly articulated an equally applicable standard for human behaviour.

Shared Understanding Two: Common Values

There are some areas where general agreement should be quickly claimed to avoid contentious nitpicking in irrelevant lesser domains. We can begin simply and build complexity as we go. One group forming some basic agreement for anti-barbaric solidarity used the following:
Codes for Anti-Barbaric Behaviour
Our aims and values are:

1. The provision of respectful, mutual support for colleagues.
2. Process before outcome: working cooperatively not competitively. Relationship before power.
3. We willingly take on the responsibility to notice, nurture and encourage each other's work and progress. 'Lift as we climb.' We actively advance each other and work and publicize/highlight each other's achievements, insights and strengths.

4.   We value non-aggressive, non-coercive interactions and together maintain this in meetings.
5.   We block aggression when it occurs.
6.   We aim to provide a safe environment of resources and inspiration for activists.
7.   We value egalitarian interactions, equal involvement and equal responsibility for outcomes.

Common areas of agreement need to be defined to build a base from which the group can coalesce and expand. Again, this list of agreements should be done non-exhaustively or conclusively:

1. Pregnant women and women with small children must be tended, nurtured and protected so that children can be cared for appropriately.

2. People who make decisions about the built environment and the natural environment must have the care of the human species as their core decision making criteria, not profit for the self or a few others.

3. A global priority must be to educate women and give female access to choice, power, ownership of their own bodies, education and contraceptives.

4. Decision makers who actively exploit or harm human persons for the purpose of profit must be prosecuted and held to account for the human impact of their actions – irrespective of the economic gain made from their ventures.

5. All leaders must be held accountable not only to the Human Rights standards but for duty to advance human rights within their nation with gender and racial equality as foundational givens. The wellbeing of children must be a primary outcome measure of their governance, particularly those in the 0-4 age group.

6. Persons who exploit other people's lives or vulnerabilities for the sake of profit, particularly harming those who are less powerful, must be held in the lowest regard and have the lowest social status in the social order. It must become shameful to be a profiteer who profits from others' powerlessness and vulnerability without giving equal recompense and reward; without attending to the responsibility for the impacts on the social system or the social conditions created, or without empowering and assisting others.

7. Greed needs to have low social status and need to be a source of shame, not pride. Not the small idea of greed which is associated with food but the greater manifestations of greed in profligacy without considering human equity and without due regard for the limited resources greed leaves for others.

Shared Understanding Three: Conserve and Reallocate Personal Resources

We cannot afford to commit too much energy to complying with barbaric market advancement; needless consumption and wastefulness. Such compliance strengthens the very system of exploitation which empowers positions of aggression and violence. We need to rationalize the amount of time and energy we focus on money-making and the economy in order to be able to expand other areas of concern. An anti-barbaric movement will need to be large enough, and united enough, to insist upon kind, firm containment of current profiteering; prevention of future human aggression; and to be implemented across national boundaries. Movements united in the desire for humane relationships, societies and cultures founded upon, and supportive of, human dignity can overthrow the current domination of barbaric imperium. Nothing less than a complete overthrow of barbarism will suffice.

Those of us living in the relative comfort of Western nations must find ways to decrease the sense of distance we feel from the suffering of our brothers and sisters in other countries. We must actively work against the insulation effects of privilege and the illusion of boundaried moral community to mobilise ourselves to help the rest of the human family. Barbarism relies on the intimidation of the many to garner the mass support and cooperation that enables mass scale profiteering and the exploitation and aggression which currently dominate the global stage. A mass movement of individuals – equally committed to a humane creed, and clearly understanding the limitations of the barbaric creed and its self serving basis – will not have to use violence to overthrow barbarism. The clear, absolute refusal to cooperate with the creed and the willingness to stand up for the things that matter with humane but dogmatic clarity will make the difference. Once a clear and strong position is taken there will be some fun to be had. The kind but firm intransigence of the mass of human beings, who clearly identify, and refuse to cooperate with, tenets of the creed will have ample power. If the mass of individuals refuse to collude with barbarism or to donate the resources of their own personal, home, family and community lives to profiteering, then the current system will be transformed.

Shared Understanding Four: Be Astute but Not Rattled by Barbaric Threat

Humane movements must be astute, they cannot be naïve. They cannot afford to underestimate the huge stores of power and resources barbarian magnates have accumulated in the last 50 years and the viciousness with which they will defend their dominance. We should not use our own humane value system to create a trajectory of expected barbaric response. We should expect the forceful, aggressive viciousness that is barbarism – merciless rage and attack; not fair, kind, just behaviour. We must not underestimate the barbarian and should expect a fight.

Loyal and supportive relationships between carers are critical to any anti-barbaric movement. Such movements must be able to actively support and restore the wellbeing of those who are at the coal face of spearheading change in an anti-barbaric movement. These people are at highest risk of being targeted for attack and having their own life resources pillaged. The group must be prepared for this outcome and take mutual responsibility for the care and support of all members in ways that ensure restorative process. We must be prepared to be strong enough, and resolute enough, to stand and to get up again when the inevitable barbaric counter-attack begins. Not just for ourselves but for children and for those who don't have the power or means for defence. Kind people need to be prepared for flak and to have a strong enough support system around them that they can cope with, and recover from, violent interpersonal attack without either being overwhelmed or having to become calloused themselves.

Thus, it is critically important that we build deep, committed, loyal relationship with other anti-barbarians. It is such solid bonds, woven between people, which individuals refuse to break even when under attack, which will provide a resistance impenetrable to barbaric propaganda. We need to be able to honor rebellion when it is in the service of life itself. In the final analysis, Oppositional Defiance Disorder may save humanity from itself. Stubbornness is also strength of will.

Step Three: Clear Your Brain Wiring

Resistance involves thoroughly routing barbaric beliefs and habits from our inner and outer worlds: our own 'flesh and blood.' For self transformation we must be willing to de-barbarize our own ideology, psyche, intimate relationships, family life, community, culture, country and globe. In the words of Monty Python, 'No-one expects the Spanish Inquisition!' yet, as surely as the external world has been colonized, so has our internal world. We can examine our own belief systems for evidence of adherence to barbarism. Resisting this first and primary incursion of our own beliefs means being willing to step past our own conditioned cynicism, apathy and fear. Each of us must also reject elements of own personal faith and religious dogma that are barbaric. Individuals can keep their faith and root out barbaric precepts with total assurance that such precepts (racism, sexism, classism, cruelty) have no connection to pure religion. Solidarity needs to be based on anti-barbarism, not on religious creed.

Besides being an act of will, compassion is a product of proximity and personal experience. If you are physically close to a suffering human it invariably affects your own life, unless you harden yourself against the other person's experience. Hardening your heart in calloused, uncaring response will damage your own capacity for feeling. This is why homelessness is not just harmful to the homeless person, but also affects the quality of life of everybody in the culture. Being forced to step over and ignore fellow human beings, damages us as well as them. Proximity to the issue and bearing a visual witness to a social problem reduces denial, ignorance, and the tendency towards complicity.

Step Four: Protect Children

Our imperative must be ensuring that all humans born on this planet can live with dignity. All children need to be well loved in respect of the inherent dignity of the human being. The healthy humans raised in such a manner will be productive and will not need to be enslaved to force their productivity. When developed nations allow barbarians and elite citizens to exploit the poor and unfortunate in their societies what hope do the poor in developing nations have? What help do they have to resist the pillaging not only from multinationals but from the rising powerholders in their own 'developing' system?

Parents need to take an active stance towards the protection of their own children. This includes challenging authorities, teachers and adults who ridicule, shame and target your children. Parents also need to collectively challenge school and social systems that are aggressive and harmful. This is the second step in de-barbarizing our own 'flesh and blood.' We need to insist on dignity for all children and acknowledge the power differential; and therefore the primary adult responsibility; within and for, all interactions with children.

We need to ensure that our legacy to our children is an unpillaged inner world, protected from the barbaric incursion of harsh, cruel and controlling adult behaviours. We can work on providing them with an unpillaged outer world as well. One step in this is changing global priorities so that human atrocities such as genocide are identified and halted immediately. A UN system which is not given the power, or the resources, to intervene effectively and to halt human atrocities is inadequate as a representation of the might of all combined nations. Once we will, determine, commit, and act, together we will actually begin to be able to enjoy life without the spectre of neglected species' responsibility hanging over our shoulders.

Step Five: Address Corrupt Systems

Caring adults have to take greater interest in, and responsibility for, the systems in which our children and families are embedded and not allow uncaring bureaucrats and greedy entrepreneurs to dictate their design. We can insist that systems be based on notions of care and mutual responsibility and refuse to accept policies, legislation and practices that are barbaric. We can protest, agitate, defy, resist and transform. We all need to take mature responsibility for the living world which extends beyond our families and in which our lives are embedded. We need to be prepared to be elders.

De-powering Barbarism

'Negotiating' respect in a respectful way is difficult at any time, because it means that the other already is not taking full responsibility to monitor their own behaviour and ensure it adheres to codes of human dignity. Ideally, in cultures of low aggression and high interpersonal intelligence, mutual respect would be the basic standard for interaction and hence never have to be negotiated. With barbarians, one cannot 'negotiate' respect because of the intrinsic violence of their beliefs and their valuation of competitive dominance. Such an approach obviates respect for other humans. Therefore, we must consider the conundrum of how we can de-power barbarians without becoming barbaric.

The current system, not only does not protect, but actively exploits defenceless care. Vulnerability is seen as something to pillage, not something towards which we have responsibility. Barbarians are basically opportunists, they show their colours when they have power; not when public opinion moves against them; but when the poor are undefended. They lack self-discipline in caring and cannot self monitor, therefore, they need strong legislative, socially normative, interpersonal boundaries, to contain them. Without these, the current system is adversarial to, and exploitative of, defenceless care. When dealing with barbarians, communication is enhanced by clear, enforceable boundaries; preparedness to respond effectively when boundaries are invaded; commitment and capacity to strongly contain violence; and refusal to discuss or 'negotiate' human welfare or humane standards for interpersonal behaviour.

In the words of Indigenous people, we need to be able to once more tend the 'web' in which all life is suspended. Instead of making our ultimate

211

aim idle retirement we need to see life as productive and use our lives all the way through to take care of systems and life worlds. Merton's words, 'Do not look for rest in any pleasure, because you were not created for pleasure: you were created for joy. And if you do not know the difference between pleasure and joy you have not yet begun to live.' All systemic structures must protect the ecology of sustainable human life.

Step Six: Recalcitrant Focus on the Future Possibilities

A primary tactic of a successful movement is to focus past the decay of present barbaric structures onto the pleasurable, creative and exhilarating future possibilities of non-aggressive human cultures and cooperative human developments. If we do this and invest our energy in such alternatives we can simply allow barbarism to die the natural death of a spent cadmium battery. We can dispose of it carefully but be clear that there are far more suitable, enervating, effective, productive alternatives available to power human development with renewable, long term, utility. Calm acknowledgment of this fact will provide a major psychological defence against the barbaric dogma that promotes unsustainable productivity, corruption, profiteering and cruelty. We can foster relation based capitalism where money is made within nested relationships of mutual responsibility for care, profit and public good.

Communism's error was its primary focus on economy and on material goods. Dignifying, fair, empowering relationships between humans need to be the essential focus of a society. Such a focus will bring the material into line. A focus on only the material, while denigrating the bonds of love and the unseen qualities which enable human life, such as compassion, care, belonging, fairness, gentleness, and kindness, to name a few; means that communistic systems have the potential and propensity to be as barbaric and inhumane as capitalistic systems. We can only imagine societies and systems where the most noble are the most caring. Aboriginal peoples in Australia are on the right track when they say, 'Feed the elders and take care of the children.' We have an example of difference when we observe their welcoming of a child into the world with ceremonies that acknowledge that child's uniqueness and that thank them in advance for what they will bring to the tribe.

All great creations begin first in the mind's eye and then become manifested in the outer world...ask Dali, Michelangelo, Van Gogh or Hundterwasser. There were no Hunderwasser buildings in the world when he began. All thermal power plants were ugly, grey, square, industrial blocks. Now there exists in the material world physical evidence that they can be different. Peter Gabriel, Musician and Activist states this process succinctly, 'From the pain comes the dream. From the dream comes the vision. From the vision come the people. From the people comes the power. From this power comes the change.' Just as we currently accept design in the service of bland, species enslavement and the violation of environments, we can just as easily promote and accept designs which innovate humane alternatives. Again, all actions and decisions must be based on the ecology of sustainable, advancing human life, not on an outdated creed or belief system.

The Value of Mass Intransigence, Resistance & Recalcitrance

Industrialisation and mechanistic technological production, gave us running water, electricity and a range of modern conveniences that increased some aspects of quality of life, however, these should have been some sort of graph constructed to remind us that technology could only increase our prosperity and quality of life to a point and then it would decline in usefulness. Arguably, we passed this zenith some time ago, and our befouled and cluttered societies with high rates of human stress, anxiety, fear, suffering and crime, attest to this truth. Harder and faster won't necessarily get us to the peak quickest. This rule applies equally to production, sex, and transformative human existence.

The barbaric creed is an explanatory system filled with limited and flawed suppositions. Barbarism is a mindset and a way of life which can be changed. Individuals, groups and cultures can change beliefs and adherence to the code. Just as it has become faddish and socially normative to be barbaric, it can also become unfashionable to adhere to a passé, outdated, antiquated code. It is of no benefit to the human family. How barbarism is overthrown can be a multi-faceted jewel of human experience. We can explore new ways, 'It will cost us nothing to dream and everything not to.' We have the power to valorize a good future for humans with new explanatory bases. We can remember that when we deny vast numbers of the human family the right to hope, we deny the entire human race the possibility of transformative revolution.

Generally we underestimate the vast utility of mass intransigence, resistance and recalcitrance. While rebellion can be fun, mass

213

intransigence is a kinder, firmer, more permanent position. Removing barbarism requires setting things right. This task can be a cleansing activity and work for all. Engaging in this work en masse will give all of us essential clarity about barbaric incursion and how to prevent it in the future. During Nazism, only those who did something while barbarism was the totalitarian rule had to use courage and are remembered. It is easy to be humane once a barbaric regime has been overthrown or dismantled. Gandhi reminded us that the effort to create change is well within our reach, 'The difference between what we do and what we are capable of doing would suffice to solve most of the world's problems.'

HUMAN TRANSFORMATION - EVERYONE'S LIFE MATTERS

Once we halt the unnecessary damage being done to human beings, particularly early in life, and begin to nurture their capacity, which previously we have constricted, drained, or mutilated, we will be astounded by the depth of as yet untapped human capabilities. If we do no more than simply get out of the way of the amazing, creative capacity of undamaged human beings, and actively prevent systems and individuals from perpetuating damage, more than two thirds of our problems will already be resolved. It is not astounding that we have social problems under barbarism, but that caring human beings manage to sustain human life in spite of barbarism. Once everyone's life is rich, stimulating, fascinating, and evolving, each person will be contributing because of the pleasure usefulness affords to undamaged human beings. Each will be absorbed with their own capacity to act upon the world transformatively and the pleasure of making their own unique and valued contribution. Once people fully grasp their power for transformational capacity vis-a-vis relationships within their own circle the energy this will generate will be nuclear in possibility. Nuclear fission, and the atomic bomb, will pale in comparison.

Wistful obsession with the lives of the privileged famous few will fade as people begin to experience their own power and possibility. Once the massive, creative capacity of valued and nurtured human life is experienced the human race will be much more difficult to enslave and indenture. An actualized, creative population who have experienced their own capacity will not be so easy to fool; control and exploit, and barbarians will suddenly find the Barbarian creed far less profitable.

Barbarians are shrewd, and they are constantly calculating the economic and power return on their behaviours. A human transformation revolution with mass solidarity against barbarism would provide the necessary impenetrable wall to protect human life from the ongoing colonisation, damage and subjugation that we currently experience. It is only an impenetrable and unmovable wall of human intent and solidarity that can halt ongoing barbaric penetration and pillaging of human life. It is the firmness in the parent's voice as they stand against brutality in their child's school system; communities demanding their right to prevent damage in the domain in which they must live; and a thousand other acts of resolute will enacted by the many, not the few, which will give victory and simultaneously transform our cultures.

The stance against barbarism can become a new cultural revolution in which the general public, neighbours, communities, parents, children, legislators, policy workers, rich and poor stand in solidarity. When people stand together in non-violent refusal of barbarism miracles can occur. This resolute commitment, coupled with the empowerment of mass creative capacity will make the difference. As people discuss and resist barbarism in their relationships with one another, in how they raise their children, and how they resist neoliberalism, a new basis for solidarity will form. It is this solidarity which will make the movement absolutely safe. If people will band together to help those individuals who barbarians attack, then barbarians will find it more difficult to rule through the gestalt of fear and terror. When one voice stands up and says, 'That is aggressive and must stop now' and then millions of others stand and say, 'I agree', then barbarism will stop. When many voices say, 'These are people we are talking about, and human lives here. This matters and these people must be cared for,' then barbarism can no longer exploit with impunity. When kind, quiet voices are heard over those that are violent; when the voices of the voiceless are sought out and honoured for the precious truths they can provide; then barbarism will be fading to a mere memory.

When we all stand together to identify, name, resist and refuse barbarism at every level that we encounter it, speaking about it consciously and clearly with our families and friends, we will make it harder for barbarism to manipulate, confuse and exploit. When we know that this can be done and that humans are powerful beings who can make a difference then barbarism will be broken. We will finally get on with the important and far more enjoyable work of human transformation and bringing human evolution to the next level.   Barbarism is boring, predictable and damaging – let's try something else for a change.

E' Ala E'!

[With honour to the great Kamakawiwo'ole]

Vive' La Transformacion!

THINGS EASILY DONE

CHILDREN:

Demand child centred global policies and planning. Ask, what will the world developed from this plan or policy be like for a child?

- Be protective towards all children everywhere.
    - Love children.
    - Develop your own gentleness to be trustworthy to children.
        - Gain control over your ego self and aggression so that you are a safe space for a child.
        - Meditate on adult responsibility for all children.
        - Adopt a child, internationally through a sponsorship scheme but also locally where time spent together and your care will nurture their developing self.
    - Activate against the social acceptability of ridiculing, shaming, harsh punishment and standards for children.
        - Promote gentleness towards children as the social norm.
        - Don't ignore adults verbally abusing children. Help if you can.
        - If you are aware of a child being abused, act.
        - Agitate for the removal of cruel, seductive or overly bureaucratic and uncaring individuals from roles where they have great power over the developing person: teachers, childcare workers, any adults who spend significant time in control of small children.
    - Insist on the prioritization of children's needs in all family, social and community interactions.
        - Activate for higher pay for those individuals who have well developed, complex nurturing skills to care and be compassionately responsive to small children.
        - Insist on greater public respect and honour for those who nurture children.
    - Honour mothering and insist on higher social status for mothers.
        - Remove discriminatory laws that penalize women for their social contribution of the unpaid labour of mothering.

- Protect mother-child relationship where the mother is the primary caregiver in the early years.
- Insist on the reinstatement of the human rights of women to have mothering work recognized as a contribution to the economic wellbeing of a culture.
  - Publicly highlight children's vulnerability and the social responsibility of all adults for the protection of their individual safety and wellbeing.
  - Prioritize children in any planning or questioning of public officials about future planning.
    - Insist on child friendly communities with public spaces and built environments which can sensorily soothe and nurture children (low noise and pollution).
  - If you are female, refuse to bear more than one or two children. If you are male, refuse to spawn more than this number.
    - Provide well for their emotional and social wellbeing and give them sure knowledge that they matter and their lives matter.
    - Make the development of conscious, caring people your parenting aim.
    - Protect them from barbaric attack in every domain where they are outside of your care: including daycare and the classroom.
    - Actively defend your children against cruel, overly punitive barbaric bureaucracy.
    - Make loving and tending to the needs of your children your highest relational and parenting priority.
    - Seek the support of others to create a village of anti-barbaric adults who can assist in the nurturing of the child.
  - Care about what happens to children.

THE ENVIRONMENT:

- The Basics : Reduce, reuse, recycle.
  - Begin to view water as more valuable than diamonds. Consume it with thrift and respect. Act to protect any body of water that is under threat of pollution or disrespectful consumption.
  - Resist the concept of 'disposable' man-made materials. Whatever we make, we are responsible for within our ecological system. Insist on long life for all products where materials are not biodegradable. 'If you won't care for it, you can't have it.'

- o   Insist on legacy and heritage product standards on all goods which can be passed from generation to generation.
  - o   Protest forced product obsolescence. Insist on product usability for the full period of time that the product's parts work. Agitate against arbitrary product upgrades which force new purchases ie: computer chips which curtail the print number of a cartridge and the life of a printer, irrespective of its condition.
  - o   If it ain't broke…keep it or pass it on, and ensure it gets used by someone who needs it.
  - o   Take personal responsibility for all of your purchases.
  - o   When a new non-biodegradable gadget is proposed for the marketplace insist on specifics about where it will go when it is discarded.
  - o   Refuse packaging. Ask for unpackaged items in the grocery store and resist obsessive paranoia about germs when purchasing food stuffs from barrels.
- Guerilla gardening: Be a renegade tree planter and practice random garden beautification of ugly urban spaces.
- Join the mailing list of human rights and environmental activism sites so you can be swiftly contacted and, with a minimum of time investment, can add your signature and voice to global petitions to prevent and halt barbaric acts.
- Choose a territory: Air, land, sea. Commit to agitating for its protection and the wellbeing of all species in its domain.
- Tackle industrialization and production pollution as a bigger issue than your weight or the effectiveness of your tooth whitener.
- Live simply. IF strong of body and mind consider a vegan or vegetarian diet.
- Resist barbaric incursions of your community, blocking of your skyline and uglification of the environment where you live.
- INSIST that multiplex type structures be built underground and that the visual domain be pleasant.
- Laugh when told it is not possible or too expensive and remind barbarians of the high cost of human extinction and that it is ok if they don't always get their own way.
- Identify and publicly resist the dissemination of lies in the public arena. Challenge industrial assumptions and visions based on inaccurate environment facts.
- Defend activists coming under barbaric onslaught. Provide solidarity and safety for those brave enough to lead the charge.

PEOPLE:

- Refuse to behave barbarically.
- Challenge the barbaric code and barbaric behaviour being enacted toward any group, community or individual.
- Care:
    - Identify anti-barbarians and invest time and energy in building real relationships of care and connection to one another.
    - Use these deep bonds for gentle solidarity where you can stand shoulder to shoulder with kind, resolute, non-violent people who care about other human beings.
    - Provide mutual respect.
    - Remind caring people that they are the many, not the few. Encourage each other of the worthiness of the struggle.
    - Know that it can be different and refuse to be dissuaded from this solid truth.
    - Notice and laud each others courage. Be prepared to give real, material and loyal emotional support to each other.
    - Care. Care. Care.
- Global species' problems will require solidarity amongst people across nations and global implementation driven by mass insistence. INSIST.

COMMUNITIES OF CARE:

- Insist on safety and fairness for each member.
- Address gendered oppression, sexual predation or interpersonal aggression immediately.
- With the violent, be strong; with the non-violent, be fair; with the vulnerable, be kind.
- By yourself and with others:
    - Understand that the mass solidarity of good, kind people opposed to violence and aggression can be a community. Promote this knowledge.
    - Constantly treat each other with the utmost dignity and respect.
    - Address barbaric breaches of interpersonal respect and care with swift, effective action which prevents recurrence and protects those who are non-violent.
    - Actively block all dominance and power posturing: verbal, physical and interpersonal.

- In safe and caring circles generate ideas, solutions and alternatives. Constantly talk about and discuss alternative visions, flesh out the details, begin to implement them on a small scale. Use every success to feed confidence in the global capacity of caring alternatives.
- Enjoy your own generative capacity and use it as evidence of wider, as yet untapped species generative capacity.
- Encourage others in their alternative visions. Use mature, considered, pragmatic adult discussion together to see in which ways and which aspects can be implemented. Test and develop those which address the needs of many generations to come.
- Put workable ideas into the public realm. Share with other transformative circles.
- Expect barbaric attack. Stand back-to-back in such a scenario and don't leave individual members undefended. Sidestep when possible but be prepared to kindly and firmly prevail.
- Care.

QUICK CODES

- **Global Consciousness:**
  - Neither foolish, denying, and optimistic,
  - Nor aware, depressed and pessimistic,
  - but cognisant, informed and optimistic.

- **Discriminate:**
  - With the violent, be strong;
  - With the non-violent, be fair;
  - With the vulnerable, be kind.

- **Act:**
  - Protest oppressive inhumane or exploitative behaviours.
  - Refuse to oppress the poor, the elderly, the young, the marginalised.
  - Demand humane sustainable systems.

- **Being:**
  - Inner world – maintain knowing and conviction.
  - Outer world - refusal to comply
  - Use creative rebellion. "If you don't care for it, you can't have it."
  - Cheerful, clever non-compliance.
  - Be an actively developing, living, non-barbaric, alternative self.

'Start doing the things you think should be done, and start being what you think society should become. Do you believe in free speech? Then speak freely. Do you love the truth? Then tell it. Do you believe in an open society? Then act in the open. Do you believe in a decent and humane society? Then behave decently and humanely.' Adam Michnik

DEFY   RESIST   TRANSFORM   CREATE

VIVE' LA TRANSFORMACION!

AUTHOR NOTE

The statistics cited in this text were selected on the basis of their accessibility in the public domain by Googling the statistic or going directly to UN or National Department Databases. Academic references were deliberately eschewed because of their inaccessibility to the general public who need to challenge and validate knowledge in order to utilize its power. The aim of using accessible statistics was to allow the validation process to be conducted openly in the public domain and not as a hedged bet behind closed doors. Unusable elite knowledge may be as wasteful of vital resources as environmental degradation.

AUTHOR BIO

Dr. Katie Thomas is a Senior Research Fellow with the Centre for Development Health and Honorary Associate with the Telethon Institute for Child Health Research. Her research interests centre on issues of social justice and the nurturance of children. At the macro-social level this includes public policy and the feminization of poverty. At the meso-level it includes the psycho-social effects of exclusion, trauma recovery and the development of social support for marginalized people. Her work gives her a base of applied knowledge and she is committed to research that provides immediate practical benefits for participants and that promotes positive social change. Dr. Thomas has conducted industry and social profiling for government and NGOs at national, state and local levels. Her clinical experience includes group and individual psychotherapy across a range of presenting issues, with particular clinical interest in Postnatal Depression. She is involved in, or supporting, research documenting the leadership and resilience of migrant and refugee women; the health status of women in Papua New Guinea; Australian Indigenous leadership, governance and trauma recovery and development impacts on Indigenous communities in Latin America. She has conducted community research with rural and remote communities and conducted multiple social research projects with marginalised groups in the State. She is a member of ACP, APS, AWID, FOMEX, SCRA, WASS and UCP-SAR. For further information go to http:katiethomas.elementfx.com.

6212158R0

Made in the USA
Charleston, SC
27 September 2010